IF YOU SEE ME

IF YOU SEE ME

MY SIX-DECADE JOURNEY
IN ROCK AND ROLL

Pepé Willie

——— *with* ———

Tony Kiene

Foreword *by* Clarence Collins

MINNESOTA
HISTORICAL
SOCIETY PRESS

Title page: On a promotional tour with Prince in North Carolina, 1978

mnhspress.org

The Minnesota Historical Society Press is a member of the Association of University Presses.

Manufactured in the United States of America

10 9 8 7 6 5 4 3 2 1

∞ The paper used in this publication meets the minimum requirements of the American National Standard for Information Sciences—Permanence for Printed Library Materials, ANSI Z39.48–1984.

International Standard Book Number
ISBN: 978-1-68134-176-7 (paper)
ISBN: 978-1-68134-181-1 (e-book)

Library of Congress Cataloging-in-Publication Data
Names: Willie, Pepé, 1948– author. | Kiene, Tony, author. | Collins, Clarence, writer of foreword.
Title: If you see me : my six-decade journey in rock and roll / Pepé Willie with Tony Kiene ; foreword by Clarence Collins.
Description: Saint Paul : Minnesota Historical Society Press, 2020. | Includes index. | Summary: "The story of Pepé Willie, the 'Godfather of the Minneapolis Sound,' who helped to groom and mentor the likes of Prince, Morris Day, André Cymone, and more"— Provided by publisher.
Identifiers: LCCN 2020022204 | ISBN 9781681341767 (paperback) | ISBN 9781681341811 (ebook)
Subjects: LCSH: Willie, Pepé, 1948– author. | Sound recording executives and producers—Minnesota—Minneapolis—Biography. | Rock musicians—Minnesota—Minneapolis—Biography. | Prince. | LCGFT: Autobiographies.
Classification: LCC ML429.W553 A3 2020 | DDC 781.66092 [B]—dc23
LC record available at https://lccn.loc.gov/2020022204

This and other Minnesota Historical Society Press books are available from popular e-book vendors.

To my mother, the late Agnes Collins Leake.

—*—

To my first musical inspiration, Uncle Clarence.

—*—

To the legendary Rock and Roll Hall of Famers
and my brothers for life,
Little Anthony and the Imperials.

—*—

To the late Teddy Randazzo.

—*—

To the greatest of all time, Prince.

—*—

To Kristie and Marcy.

—*—

And to my daughter, Danielle.

Let me tell you a story
From a long time ago.
Let me tell you, man,
I was there.
Livin' in Brooklyn
Round the start of rock and roll.
There are things to remember
And stories to be told.
Let me tell you how I used to
Run up and down the stairs,
Playin' gopher to all the stars,
Performing there.
Man, I can tell you about
Murray the K,
How he and Clay Cole
Could put on a show.
They had acts from all over.
Man, let me tell you.
The Shirelles, the Chantels,
The Chiffons and Ray Charles,
Little Anthony and the Imperials,
Johnny Mathis, the Coasters,
Chuck Jackson and Chubby Checker.
Man, I can tell you
I could go on forever.
The Paramount Theatre closed
That's when it all broke loose
And things really got hot.
The shows moved to the Brooklyn Fox.
These groups did five, maybe
Six shows a day.
Back to back, Saturdays,

Sundays and Holidays.
The Temptations, the Vibrations,
The Marvelettes, were all there.
Ruby and the Romantics, the Four Tops,
Smokey Robinson and the Miracles,
Timi Yuro and Wayne Newton,
The Ronettes, Dionne Warwick,
And of course the Five Satins,
Dion and the Belmonts,
And a young Stevie Wonder.
Man let me tell you,
I could go on forever.

PEPÉ WILLIE, 1987

CONTENTS

FOREWORD

MY SISTER AGNES gave birth to Pepé Willie on July 22, 1948. Though Pepé was my nephew, he was, in actuality, more like a younger brother.

We were both raised in Brooklyn. In my early teens, I founded a musical group that eventually became known as Little Anthony and the Imperials. My mid- to late-teen years were very exciting as our group became world famous, had several Top 10 hits, and toured the United States and overseas performing in a multitude of venues.

I first took Pepé under my wing when he was a young teenager. Given the conditions in Brooklyn at the time, Pepé was exposed to street crime and other undesirable things. However, he always had an abiding interest in music and in Little Anthony and the Imperials and our success.

Pepé became our young assistant, so to speak. We would have him run errands and do our individual bidding. While working with us, he absorbed anything and everything he could regarding show business in general, and the music industry in particular. As it turned out, this early education contributed significantly to Pepé's own future successes.

Pepé was always a kind, caring human being. He had a gentle, artistic side that bloomed when he was involved with Little Anthony and the Imperials and our music. He took that teaching, and his own significant talents, to Minneapolis, Minnesota, when he relocated there in 1974. Upon arriving in Minneapolis, he quickly established himself as a driving force in the music industry of that city, where he produced, composed, performed, arranged, and recorded music.

While pursuing his own career with his group, 94 East, Pepé began to tutor Prince Rogers Nelson. He would squire Prince, only sixteen years old at the time, and his fellow musicians around Minneapolis to gigs and recording sessions. Pepé became a trusted mentor to Prince and helped him greatly during the early years of his career.

In 1975, Pepé brought Prince into the recording studio for the first time, making him lead guitarist of 94 East. While they planned Prince's musical career, Pepé opened up his home to Prince and was instrumental in preparing him for his first record deal with Warner Bros.

Pepé went on to help Prince establish his first publishing company, act as Prince's interim manager, promote Prince's first concert, and accompany him on early promotional tours. Through the years, Prince continued to treat Pepé as a mentor and would often call him for advice and assistance.

Prince's untimely death in 2016 affected Pepé deeply. Pepé often wonders if there was something, anything, he could have done that may have changed the course of events so that Prince would still be alive today. Knowing Pepé, I have no doubt that he did everything he possibly could do to help Prince at any phase of his life and career.

I feel like I am an older brother to Pepé. I have mentored him in the music business just as he mentored Prince. I have observed firsthand his tremendous artistic talent as a writer, producer, arranger, recording artist, and performer. In my view, Pepé Willie is one of the most talented people remaining today in the music business. I am thankful for our long association and for knowing Pepé as I have all these years.

This book recounts Pepé's life in the music industry. It is an excellent read, and I believe anyone will find the stories within this book most entertaining and illuminating. So read on and enjoy this creative, and historic, project.

Clarence Collins
LAS VEGAS, NEVADA

INTRODUCTION

IN HIS BEST-SELLING BOOK *Outliers: The Story of Success*, author and social theorist Malcolm Gladwell writes, "No one—not rock stars, not professional athletes, not software billionaires, and not even geniuses—ever makes it alone."

I am not friends with any software billionaires, but I know some professional athletes. Plus, I have spent my life around rock stars as well as a few geniuses, including Prince, who was unequivocally both. So these words resonate with me.

As I process this quote, it brings to mind another recent best seller, *The Other Wes Moore*, which chronicles the lives of two young men born months apart, growing up in the same city under analogous conditions, and sharing the same name.

The author Wes Moore, after rising above a troubled adolescence, went to graduate Phi Beta Kappa, earn a Rhodes Scholarship, distinguish himself as a member of the US Army's 82nd Airborne Division, be selected as a White House Fellow, and ascend to CEO of a venture philanthropy company, all before the age of forty. The "other" Wes Moore is now nearly twenty years into a life sentence at a maximum-security prison.

Now, I am profoundly aware that my own résumé doesn't quite measure up to author Wes Moore's. That said, I could have just as easily suffered the fate of the "other" Wes Moore.

It was my uncle Clarence, and his bandmates in Little Anthony and the Imperials, who more than anyone helped steer me away from a life without hope, meaning, and purpose. Rock and roll became all those things to me and more.

Although I straddled the world of music and the gang life for the better part of my teenage years, the fact that I had something promising to hold onto saved my life. Not only did I get to study at the feet of the Imperials and their songwriting partner, Teddy Randazzo, while I sought to hone my own craft, I had the good fortune to occupy the same world as some of the biggest names in the history of popular music. I carefully absorbed everything that I saw and heard. Through these experiences I learned—among other things—discipline, perseverance, dedication, self-confidence, and what it means to be a professional.

One of the most important lessons Uncle Clarence ever taught me was to "share this knowledge with the right people." And that brings me back to the quote from Malcolm Gladwell.

Although no one makes it on their own, Prince might have come as close as anyone, or at least anyone in the history of rock and roll. I've said time and again that Prince's singular talent, coupled with his superhuman drive, was undeniable, and that if, for some reason, he didn't make it in this business, it would have been through no fault of his own.

That said, I made it a point to share everything I knew about music and the business of music with Prince and those who came up with him in Minneapolis. To his eternal credit, Prince imparted that knowledge along with everything that he learned afterward to his fellow musicians all over the world. And, without question, he shared with me as well.

I like to believe, as many have conveyed to me over the years, that I was able to help Prince as he plotted his course toward rock and roll supremacy. And that the knowledge I shared with him made it a little bit easier for him to pilot through the tumultuous and oftentimes cruel nature of this industry.

Yet, it's not lost on me that I would not be where I am today were it not for Prince. And that is what it is all about: sharing your knowledge, sharing your life, sharing your love. There are so many of us who loved him when he had nothing. If only we could have been there for him in the end.

PROLOGUE

DREAMS
SUMMER 1984
Minneapolis

IT WAS A WARM SUMMER AFTERNOON in Minneapolis when I returned home from a leisurely stroll around nearby Lake Calhoun. I was in a reflective mood that day as I was approaching my thirty-sixth birthday and pondering what the rest of my life might have in store.

I couldn't have anticipated what was waiting just around the corner. Shortly after I walked inside my house on Upton Avenue South, the phone rang. On the other end of the line was a distraught, almost tearful voice.

The voice belonged to Morris Day. "Pepé," he said, "Prince is trying to ruin me."

It had been six or seven months since filming for *Purple Rain* wrapped in December 1983. To say that Morris left Minneapolis on bad terms with Prince would be an understatement, as the two of them had nearly come to blows on the film set at First Avenue.

Now living in Los Angeles and attempting to establish a

solo career, Morris found himself without a ticket to what would be his own Hollywood coming-out party: the world premiere of Prince's first major motion picture, *Purple Rain*. Not only was Prince trying to keep him from the premiere, now just days away, to Morris's mind he was trying to make sure Morris was broke. For all intents and purposes, Morris was still under Prince's financial umbrella, as they shared the same accountant. Morris told me that Prince was going out of his way to keep him from getting paid.

It took me a few minutes to calm him down and convince him that it would all work out. "Morris," I said, "let me make some calls, and I'll be in LA tomorrow."

The first thing that came to my mind was to put together a management team for Morris. And it couldn't be just any team. He was on the verge of stardom, and he needed the best representation we could find. I started working the phones, and the next day I was on a plane to Los Angeles.

SANTA MONICA

I started to settle in as soon as I arrived at Morris's condo in Santa Monica, knowing there was a lot of work that needed to be done and fast. I was committed to staying in California for as long as necessary to help Morris get what he deserved.

That first night in Santa Monica, the phone rang sometime after midnight, not long after I had gone to sleep. As I awoke, I could hear Morris whispering to someone on the other end of the line. My instinct told me it was Prince. I got up and asked Morris to hand me the phone. He refused. I insisted, noting that Prince respected me and always listened to me.

Nonetheless, Morris wouldn't give up the phone. "Damn it, let me talk to that motherfucker!" I yelled. But Morris resisted my plea.

This was something Prince liked to do: call late at night and remind Morris of the power he had over him. The psychological grip that Prince held over so many musicians and associates in his camp never ceased to amaze me. Without question, Prince lifted a lot of people up, and a multitude of folks owe their careers to him; that much can never be overstated. Still, some of those artists ultimately sought the freedom to chart their own course in this business. And it was hard to say no to Prince.

So I chose not to push it and I let Morris finish his conversation with Prince. I didn't bring it up again. After all, we had a lot of work ahead of us.

I had been in touch with Warner Bros. and arranged a meeting at the company's Burbank headquarters. When Warner Bros. president Mo Ostin found out what was going on between Morris and Prince, he offered us his full support. As the president of Frank Sinatra's Reprise Records, Mo had famously signed Jimi Hendrix in 1967. He was also influential in the careers of Ella Fitzgerald and Sammy Davis Jr. Not long after signing Hendrix, Mo became the president of Reprise's parent company, Warner Bros. Records. At Warner Bros. he signed a string of iconic artists, including the Beach Boys, Neil Young, Paul Simon, Frank Zappa, Eric Clapton, and Van Halen, among others.

Prior to this visit, I had never met Mo in person, but I had a lot of respect for him. Ever since Prince signed with Warner Bros. in 1977, my impression of Mo was that he was a fair man who treated his artists and others well. It appeared to me that he took good care of Prince as his career developed from a little-known wunderkind to an artist on the verge of superstardom. Mo was certainly good to us that day, and we left Warner Bros. with tickets to the *Purple Rain* premiere, as well as passes to the official party to be held afterward at the Palace. Mo even gave us money to buy clothes for the premiere and secured two limousines to ensure that we arrived in style.

Having cleared that hurdle, it was now time to put Morris's team together. Within a few days, we were in Century City to hire renowned music lawyer David Braun, who among other achievements was instrumental in the founding of the Rock and Roll Hall of Fame. A mentor to some of the most prominent industry attorneys today, Braun counted among his clients Bob Dylan, Neil Diamond, George Harrison, and Michael Jackson.

Next we were able to secure the booking services of Triad Artists, Inc. A smaller but extremely influential agency, Triad represented several A-list clients in the worlds of film and music.

Shortly thereafter, we hired the accounting firm of Gelfand, Rennert & Feldman. With offices in Los Angeles, Nashville, and New York, GR&F, as it was called, was a major player with a notable roster of clients in the literary world, performing arts, and professional sports.

Last, but certainly not least, we needed to find suitable management for Morris. Fortunately, that search began and ended with Sandy Gallin. Gallin, who helped to book the Beatles on *The Ed Sullivan Show* in early 1964, managed a who's who of entertainment legends. Like Braun, Gallin represented both Neil Diamond and Michael Jackson, as well as Richard Pryor, Barbra Streisand, Cher, Dolly Parton,

Whoopi Goldberg, Patti LaBelle, and the Pointer Sisters, among other prominent artists.

Things were beginning to come together for Morris. Still, I had no idea how brightly his star, and of course Prince's star, would shine once America witnessed them onscreen in *Purple Rain*.

HOLLYWOOD

To the casual observer, Thursday, July 26, 1984, was like any normal sunny summer day in Southern California. Along Hollywood Boulevard, however, there was a buzz in the air that ascended beyond what typically accompanied a red-carpet event in Tinseltown.

It was on this night that Prince would be launched into a new level of fame and glory, one that I don't believe any of us around him could have envisioned, perhaps even Prince himself. The star-studded world premiere of *Purple Rain* was set to take place at the world-famous Mann's Chinese Theatre. Originally known as Grauman's Chinese Theatre, this historic venue at 6925 Hollywood Boulevard had hosted the world premieres of such renowned films as Cecil B. DeMille's *King of Kings*, *The Wizard of Oz*, and the original *Star Wars*. While no one expected *Purple Rain* to achieve a comparable level of cinematic success, there was genuine anticipation that this night could be a groundbreaking event, particularly in the age of MTV.

As the hype intensified hours before the premiere, I took stock of the phenomenon I was witnessing and how amazing it seemed that I had played a role in all this. And yet, I was no stranger to the company of celebrity or the world of rock and roll. In fact, I had been front and center during the early years of rock as the teenage valet for Little Anthony and the Imperials. Originally known as the Chesters, this legendary R&B group was founded in Brooklyn by my uncle Clarence Collins. Clarence, along with Anthony Gourdine and the rest of the original members, were inducted into the Rock and Roll Hall of Fame in 2009.

While working for the Imperials, I had the tremendous fortune to witness firsthand impresarios Alan Freed, Clay Cole, and Murray "The K" Kaufman. These three visionary concert promoters and influential deejays audaciously and successfully integrated concert audiences well before the Civil Rights Act of 1964.

During my teen years and into my early twenties, I was blessed to come across, and in some cases work for, the likes of Ray Charles, Marvin Gaye, Ronnie Spector, Wayne Newton, Jackie Wilson, Ike and Tina Turner, Chubby Checker, the Supremes, and Stevie Wonder. I'd even had the occasion to meet the two men whose fame, at least to me, was out of this world: Jimi Hendrix and Elvis Presley.

And yet, with everything and everyone I had seen before, I could sense that I was experiencing something extraordinary that summer night in 1984. There was no hotter ticket in town, not just for that night but the entire year as well.

Morris and I arrived at the theater, along with his mother, LaVonne Daugherty, in two separate limousines. As much as Morris loved his mother, he didn't think it was cool to ride in the same car as her. I guess I can understand that. I mean, it didn't really mesh with Morris's image. Still, I was thrilled that LaVonne was able to share in this extraordinary moment with her son, and I'm sure he was too. Years earlier, LaVonne had briefly served as the manager of Grand Central, the Minneapolis-based band that featured a teenage Prince,

André Cymone, and Morris. She had contributed a lot to their individual and collective development, and it was only fitting that she was there to see her son make his big-screen debut.

As we walked the red carpet—Morris and I dressed in our new, dapper white suits, courtesy of Mo Ostin's generosity—the electricity in the air was palpable. There were celebrities everywhere representing the worlds of film, music, and media. MTV had set up camp to broadcast the pre-film red-carpet event as well as the after-party.

MTV's Mark Goodman, who had just finished speaking with Eddie Murphy, recognized Morris as we approached, and he pulled Morris in front of the cameras for a quick interview. Goodman asked Morris if his band the Time had a new tour in the works. Morris sidestepped the question, as unbeknownst to Goodman or the fans watching at home, the Time was no longer together.

We entered Mann's Chinese Theatre, with Sheila E. just behind us, and I noticed Jon Bream among the throng of music journalists and reporters. Jon, who began writing for the *Minneapolis Star Tribune* in 1974, was a close friend and had covered Prince's career since the beginning. Upon seeing him, my mind was transported back to those early days in Minneapolis, and I was trying to process the last decade or so and how it all led to this moment.

While others made their way inside, including members of the Revolution, Dez Dickerson, and cast members such as Jill Jones, Apollonia Kotero, and Clarence Williams III, thousands of fans gathered up and down Hollywood Boulevard, anxiously awaiting the arrival of the night's main attraction. Prince, accompanied by his faithful bodyguard "Big Chick" Huntsberry, finally made his way to the red carpet, and the crowd's reaction was beyond enthusiastic. Even from inside the confines of the theater, Morris and I could hear the screams and thunderous ovation.

Not long after entering the building, Prince noticed Morris and me. He didn't say anything, which didn't surprise me, but I will always remember the look of disbelief on his face upon seeing the two of us. Notwithstanding his efforts to keep Morris from attending, Prince should have known that he couldn't control me as he did others in his circle. After all, I was family. I was the first person to take Prince into the recording studio. I was the first one to cut him a check, affirming that he was, in fact, a professional musician. As important as this night was to Prince, it was just as important to many others who had made this journey with him, including Morris and myself.

Sitting there in Mann's Chinese Theatre as the curtains opened and the first chords from "Let's Go Crazy" reverberated from the screen, I knew this movie was going to be big. I sensed that everyone in the theater was feeling the same way. It was mesmerizing.

During the opening montage of the film, Prince poses in front of his dressing room mirror, strums his guitar, sweeps his hair back, and delivers that signature wry smile. I felt like we were back at rehearsals in my house on Upton Avenue in south Minneapolis. There was a studio mirror along one of the basement walls, and on more than one occasion we'd catch Prince preening in front of it. What can I say; the kid knew before anyone else that he was a star. And the ensuing reviews of *Purple Rain* confirmed that.

Renowned film critic Roger Ebert called the film "one of the best combinations of music and drama I've ever seen." Writing for Brooklyn's *City Sun*, noted film and music critic Armond White stated that "Prince is as incendiary an icon as has ever existed on film" with "the genuine musicianship, singing and performance style to match all the musical legends."

While it was clear that Prince was destined to become an absolute megastar, I recognized that Morris's performance in the film would surely position him for a shot at stardom as well. Several critics even asserted that Morris's blend of charisma and comedy ultimately stole the film from Prince. At the after-party, Morris was again interviewed by Mark Goodman, who impishly noted that he thought Morris's performance was great.

The night was overwhelming. Lionel Richie, Lindsey Buckingham, Jeffrey Osborne, John Mellencamp, and other top musicians wandered among the crowd, stopping to tell MTV, *Rolling Stone*, *Entertainment Tonight*, and other media outlets how great the film was. Little Richard, who brought a personally engraved Bible as a gift for Prince, told Goodman that he believed "Prince is me of this generation."

Prince and the Revolution played a short set, and as the party began to wind down, I again paused to take it all in and reflect on how we got here. I was absolutely thrilled for Prince. I was equally happy for Morris and pleased that I was able to help him participate in his big night. I also thought about André, Dez, Bobby, Matt, Mark, Jill, Gayle, Lisa, and Wendy, as well as others who shared in this incredible journey. That included the original members of Grand Central, the original members of 94 East, plus Bernadette Anderson, Charles "Chazz" Smith, Linda Anderson, Sylvia Anderson, Chris Moon, Owen Husney, and my former wife and Prince's cousin, Shauntel Manderville.

My mind went back to that Minneapolis party in December 1974 where I first encountered this otherworldly talent. Not long after arriving from Brooklyn and landing at the Minneapolis–St. Paul airport, I found myself face to face with Prince and the other members of Grand Central. I knew from the first moment I saw him that Prince had not only exceptional talent but also certain intangibles that couldn't be taught—the "it factor," if you will.

Nearly a full ten years later, standing in a legendary Hollywood theater, I thought back on all the ups and downs along the way, remembered the many trials and tribulations. And here was Prince, emerging as one of the most iconic figures in popular culture. My heart swelled with pride that I was able to be a part of all that. I had shared with Prince and the younger cats from Minneapolis who came up with him my expertise and experience in the music business. I've been told that this helped Prince sidestep a lot of the land mines that many young artists trip over.

I smiled and reminded myself that I had been a part of the music business for well over twenty years at that point, including nearly ten years with Prince. I was still only thirty-six years old. My career was not over. It was just getting started.

1

BROOKLYN BORN, BED-STUY BRED

I WAS BORN ON Thursday, July 22, 1948, at Brooklyn Jewish Hospital in the borough of Brooklyn, the largest of New York City's five boroughs.

As seems to be the case for a lot of Brooklynites, the borough shaped my identity and my worldview in many ways. There was just something cool about being from Brooklyn. Brooklyn native and comedy legend Mel Brooks perhaps put it best, in Marc Eliot's *Song of Brooklyn: An Oral History of America's Favorite Borough*, when he said: "I'm a Brooklyn guy, it's in my bones and it's there in Brooklyn. There's a certain rhythm you get growing up there. Every Brooklyn kid has it. Always on the right beat. The Bronx, no; Queens, you were out of it; but Brooklyn, that was it."

I was named after my father, Linster Herbert Willie Sr. Linster was a name that had been passed down in my father's family. It is also a name that I have hated my entire life. Fortunately, when I was still in the hospital as a newborn, I was christened with a nickname. One of the nurses, who was originally from France, told my mother I looked like a "Pepé." My parents must have liked it, as the name stuck, and I have answered to Pepé ever since.

I don't know much about my father's youth aside from the

fact that he was born in North Carolina. During his child-hood, the family moved to Brooklyn, where my grandfather, Herbert "Guy" Willie, started his own moving company on Lexington Avenue. My grandmother's name was Anna.

My father was tall, about six-foot-one, with a slender build. He had been a track star in high school and was quite fit and much stronger than he looked. He had a smooth, dark complexion and was considered handsome. He was a true ladies' man and almost always the center of attention. People just wanted to be around him. However, as charming as he could be, he was never more than a split second from unleashing his temper.

My mother, Agnes Collins, was born in Pasquotank County, North Carolina, to an African American father and full-blooded Algonquian mother. Prior to European settlement, the Algonquians dominated this region where the Pasquotank River flows into the Albemarle Sound and is separated from the Atlantic Ocean by the Outer Banks. As was common among African Americans during the first half of the twentieth century, my mother's family followed the Great Migration north to New York City. Her mother, Mary, gave birth to eleven children but died giving birth to the last of them, a son. My Grandpa Collins later married his second wife, Dolly.

My parents eventually met in elementary school in Brooklyn. In fact, they became childhood sweethearts and attended school together all the way through high school graduation.

My mother stood about five-foot-six and had pretty brown skin. I've been told that during the time they were married, my parents were viewed by family, friends, and just about everyone else as an attractive couple. I don't remember my parents as a married couple, however. They divorced when I was very young, and I grew up living with my father, while my sisters stayed with our mother. I didn't really get to know my mother in a meaningful way until I was about ten years old. To this day, I don't know why our family was divided in this way.

I was the fourth of five children and the only boy of the bunch. Pearl, who was born in 1942, was the oldest. Growing up, her dream was to become a nurse. She attended the Clara Barton High School for Health Professions in Brooklyn, which offered a licensed practical nursing program. Pearl got pregnant, however, and instead became a stay-at-home mom.

Born a couple of years later was Delores, whom everyone knew as Dodie. Dodie was a fighter and wasn't afraid of anybody. She could kick just about anybody's ass—boy or girl. Then came Carol, my "Irish twin," who was born eleven months before me. What I remember most about Carol is that she was always a tomboy. A little more than a year after I was born came Tina, the baby of the family. She was everybody's little sweetheart.

After my parents divorced, my father and I lived in a five-bedroom apartment at 291 Grand Avenue between Greene Avenue and Clifton Place, in the heart of the Bedford-Stuyvesant section of Brooklyn. For a brief time, Pearl and Delores lived with us while Carol and Tina remained with my mother in another area of Bedford-Stuyvesant. When Pearl was caught with a boy in our apartment, however, our father smacked her, and she and Delores immediately moved back in with our mother.

At the time of my birth, Bedford-Stuyvesant—or Bed-Stuy, as it is more familiarly known—had the second-largest concentration of African American residents in the United States. Only the South Side of Chicago had more black people living within its boundaries. And much like Chicago's South Side and many other urban centers, Bed-Stuy had more than its fair share of societal ills that disproportionately affected African Americans and other people of color. Poverty, unemployment, and homelessness, along with educational and health disparities, were rampant dating back to the Great Depression, when large numbers of African Americans began moving to Bed-Stuy. The neighborhood also became an epicenter of street-gang activity as well as the site of one of the earliest urban uprisings by African Americans during the volatile decade of the 1960s.

Despite its mean streets, Bed-Stuy was, and still is, bursting with community pride. It was instilled in me from a young age that Bed-Stuy was the cultural mecca of Brooklyn. The neighborhood produced luminaries in the fields of music, politics, drama, journalism, education, and sports. Among the noteworthy artists nurtured in the streets of Bed-Stuy were Lena Horne, Richie Havens, Carl Gordon, and Stephanie Mills. Civic and political leaders such as Shirley Chisholm, June Jordan, and journalist Juan Williams also called Bed-Stuy home. And Bed-Stuy has produced more than its share of celebrated athletes, including heavyweight champion Floyd Patterson and Basketball Hall of Fame inductees Lenny Wilkens and my cousin Connie "The Hawk" Hawkins. In more recent decades, Bed-Stuy has held a central place in hip-hop culture, and Brooklyn native Spike Lee helped bring the neighborhood to cultural prominence in his critically acclaimed film from 1989, *Do the Right Thing*. The early childhood home of Mike Tyson, Bed-Stuy also features in the work of comedians Chris Rock and Dave Chappelle.

During my youth, Bed-Stuy was a hub of music and culture, and the Collins side of my family represented a slice of that life. They were so hip. Although I never lived with my mother, the time I spent visiting her home and that of my Grandpa and Grandma Collins are some of my fondest memories of growing up. My mom's family was artistic, adventurous, loving, and fun. They loved to throw parties, play cards, tell stories, and crack jokes. There was never a dull moment with the Collins family.

Music was the defining feature in the Collins home, as numerous family members were musicians or involved in the industry. My mother was an accomplished singer, and I can recall visiting her home just hoping to hear her sing. She especially liked to sing while she was cooking. I was mesmerized by her amazing voice. My mother could effortlessly sing anything, from standards by Dinah Washington to Lena Horne and countless others. Unfortunately, her musical aspirations were pushed aside when she became a homemaker.

My mother was one of eleven children, and her five brothers and five sisters shared her musical dreams and talent. From a very young age, I was close to all my aunts on my mother's side. Muriel, Dottie, Annette, Gussie, and Lorraine treated me as if I was their own son. Aunt Muriel sang with blues icon Etta James as a member of the Peaches, who were originally known as the Creolettes before being discovered by Johnny Otis and signed to Modern Records. My aunt Annette went on to sing with the Impacts.

Aunt Dorothy, known by everyone as Dottie, honed her musical skills at Brooklyn's famed Erasmus Hall High School, which boasts as alumni musical giants such as Beverly Sills, Neil Diamond, Barbra Streisand, Gilbert Price, and Stephanie Mills. After high school, she made quick friends with a young Miles Davis, who had come to New York from East St. Louis, Illinois, to attend Juilliard School of Music. Dottie and Miles would hang out with up-and-coming jazz men Thelonious Monk and Wynton Kelly. The four friends would often gather at my grandfather's house on Carlton Avenue in Brooklyn. My grandfather, George Collins Sr., had a piano in his living room that they all loved to play.

Now, Grandpa Collins was not a man to be messed with. He expected to be addressed at all times as "sir" or "Mr. Collins." He also believed that a song should be played exactly as it was written. He didn't think much of improvisation, which of course is a basic element of jazz. One family story that was passed down to me from Uncle Clarence was about the time Monk sat down at Grandpa Collins's piano and began to play the 1941 classic "I Don't Want to Set the World on Fire" by the Ink Spots. My grandfather always liked Theo (as he called him), as he was a respectful young man and a fellow North Carolinian.

However, when he overheard Monk playing on this particular day, my grandfather came storming into the room shouting, "Theo, what's the matter with you? You're playing that all wrong!" To which Monk politely responded, "But Mr. Collins, I'm just playing what I feel." Fortunately, Monk remained true to his instincts and would develop one of the most distinctive improvisational styles as he rose from house pianist at Harlem's Minton's Playhouse to a world-renowned jazz composer and musician.

As gifted as they were, the Collins sisters didn't have the family market cornered on musical talent. My mom's brothers Clarence, Charlie, Clinton, Curtis, and George also exhibited a range of musicianship. My uncle Charlie was a master on the saxophone and played with the great jazz composer and drummer Max Roach, who was born in Pasquotank County, North Carolina, like my mother and several of her siblings.

Though I loved all my uncles dearly, Clarence was always the coolest, most charismatic guy in the world to me. He was handsome and tall, and always dapper. He looked exactly like my mother and possessed what everyone used to call the "Collins smile." Moreover, he had a great personality and a positive attitude. Clarence is one of a kind, and his musical journey would ultimately lead to the Rock and Roll Hall of Fame.

Although music was a fundamental component of life in the Collins family, I didn't embrace it during my early childhood. Sure, future music legends regularly wandered in and out of family members' homes, but I was unaffected by it. I was too young to understand what was going on. These were just people who came around my mother's house or my grandfather's house from time to time.

In sharp contrast to the musically inclined and high-spirited Collins family, the Willies were more reserved, much less affectionate, and generally seemed to be discontent. That said, they were a proud family, and my grandpa Guy Willie was respected in Bed-Stuy as an honest, hard-working businessman. As for my father, I never actually knew what he did for a living. I always assumed that he worked in a factory somewhere in New York City. He would leave in the morning and come back in the evening—at least most of the time he would. Where he went during the day never came up in our conversations. My father also had an entrepreneurial side to him, although his primary venture in this realm was as a bootlegger. He would sell seventy-five-cent bottles of wine out of our apartment to many of Bed-Stuy's winos.

Regrettably, my father was an alcoholic himself, and he was exceedingly abusive. You could not call him simply a "strict disciplinarian." No, make no mistake about it: my father was an abuser, plain and simple. He didn't tolerate anything that he construed as nonsense.

My father hit me so often I didn't even know that it was wrong. I assumed this was normal behavior. There were times when my father would come home drunk, sometimes as late as two or three o'clock in the morning, and for no good reason, he would wake me up and start beating me, or he would say something unintelligible, and when I stared back, not knowing how to respond, he would beat me. One of the things he hated most was for me to look him directly in the eyes.

Sometimes I simply took the beatings, and other times I would try to escape to my Grandma Anna and Grandpa Guy. Their house, which was the equivalent of about four New York City blocks away, was the only safe haven I knew. It didn't matter what time of night it was or what the weather was like, I just wanted to get to safety. Of course, my father would chase me down the street to his parents' house. He was in pretty good shape, but I was always able to beat him to the front door because he was drunk, plus I was determined to avoid his fists. My grandma would always open the door and let me in, knowing that my father was right behind me. After I was safely inside, my father would reach the front door and pound loudly. He would yell, "Let me in, Mama." To which she would defiantly reply, "No. You gotta stop beatin' on this baby." This exchange would go on for a while until my father finally made his way home to go to sleep.

Although it was never any fun to sprint through the

Bed-Stuy streets at night, I felt lucky that I had a place to go and that my grandma would keep me safe, if only for the night. I have a lot of memories, both good and bad, from the times I spent at the Willies' house on 445 Lafayette Avenue in Brooklyn. Unfortunately, those times didn't last long. The New York City Department of Education bought up several homes, including my grandparents', on that block of Lafayette Avenue to build what would become Public School 270. This was the school where I would ultimately start sixth grade. But that didn't mean much to me at the time. I was only concerned about where my Grandpa and Grandma Willie would live. There weren't many occasions as a child in Bed-Stuy when I felt powerful, but when I considered that my grandparents were being forced out of their home, I understood what it felt like to be powerless. I don't think I had ever been more worried about anything up to that point in my life. Would my grandparents be able to find a decent house nearby? Would I get to see them as much? Would I have a safe haven to run to when my father tried to beat on me?

I am certain I got beatings from my father more than anybody, but I wasn't the only one to face his wrath. He was always ready for a fight. I remember watching him beat another man, nearly to death, in the hallway outside our apartment. I had no clue why he did it, and I never asked.

My father and his brother Edmund fought all the time as children, and they fought as adults too, even though I believe they loved and cared for each other. One time, when I was six or seven, I awoke to hear my father and Uncle Edmund fighting in our living room. As they rolled around on the floor, change fell out of their pockets. I didn't hesitate and sort of pirouetted around them, collecting the change. I imagine they were too drunk to notice.

In my father's house, it was understood that I had to carry my own weight. From a young age, I was doing everything for myself. I was making my own food and cleaning my room and other rooms in the apartment. When I started school, I would get myself up, dress, and head to school on my own. I was responsible for my own clothes, including washing, ironing, steam pressing, starching, and mending. I'd even spit shine and polish my shoes. I always looked sharp, even as a youngster.

I know my father believed it was important to be self-sufficient, but I had to learn all these tasks for myself, as he was seldom around to help. These skills and the independent attitude that came with them would serve me well throughout my life.

It was hard for me to understand why my father was the way he was. Although they weren't overly warm or affectionate, my father's parents had not been abusive toward him. I always wondered how his experience in the military affected his outlook. My father served in the US Army during World War II. More than 125,000 African Americans served valiantly for this country during that war, and still they were subjected to segregation, discrimination, and severe mistreatment. While millions of veterans benefited from GI Bill provisions that provided such assistance as inexpensive mortgage loans, low-interest business loans, college tuition, and other financial support, African American veterans, by and large, were systematically denied such assistance. I don't know if this caused resentment in my father or if it had anything to do with how he was as a man and as a father. I think about how it must have been to grow up in the Jim Crow South, move to the segregated North, and then risk your life for your country only to still be treated as less than a man. It must have had some effect on him.

Regardless of what may have caused my father to be who he was, even the most pleasant moments of my youth were tempered by the constant threat and fear of being beaten. Still, even though he may not have openly shown it, I felt like he always loved me.

Whenever my father came home from work, or from wherever he might have been, he would announce his arrival by yelling out "Yoooo!" as he opened the door. I would respond with the same call, regardless of where I was in the apartment, to let him know that I heard him and that I was all right. I also had to make sure that any mischief I had gotten into while he was gone was well covered up by the time he got home.

When I was young, the world I discovered in that big five-bedroom apartment became my own fantasy land. I would rummage through my father's closets when he was away, and I came across some pretty interesting stuff. I once found two rather nice bugles in his closet, even though I never sensed that my father had a musical bone in his body. Years later, when I was sixteen or so, I joined Brooklyn's famed Blue Jackets Guard Drum and Bugle Corps for a short time, and I used one of the bugles that had belonged to my father.

During my preschool years, I found many ways to entertain myself during the day, but what I looked forward to the most was going to school. I could not wait to start kindergarten. As I reached school age, however, my enthusiasm was replaced by disappointment. Much to my chagrin, my father did not believe in sending his children to kindergarten. I remember him saying, "All they do is give you milk and cookies. You don't learn anything there." To which I responded, "But I love milk and cookies." Kindergarten sounded great to me.

But it wasn't to be, and in the fall after my fifth birthday, my father held me out of kindergarten and began teaching me himself. He schooled me on my ABCs, basic arithmetic, and even some science and history. I remember that he had one of those old-fashioned rolltop desks in our apartment. I would sit there and write the numbers from zero to one hundred on white paper pads.

Being taught by my father wasn't much fun, but he made sure I was learning. When I entered first grade the next year at PS 45 in Brooklyn, I was prepared. Everything that we were taught in first grade, I had already learned from my father.

I was a good student, but I was also mischievous. It wasn't long before I became disinterested in school, and I compensated for my boredom by being the class cutup. I was frequently scolded by my teachers, and getting into trouble at school became a routine fact of life for me.

The trouble I got into at school was inconsequential compared to the trouble I got myself into at home. And my father wasn't the only one who liked to beat up on me, as my three older sisters made a habit of it as well. It seemed like every time they came over to visit, they would gang up on me and hit me as hard as they could. I was always hesitant to retaliate. For one, these were my sisters, and I knew that it was not right to hit a girl. Furthermore, hitting them back would no doubt earn a beating from my father. Finally, though, there came a day when I couldn't take it anymore.

My father used to keep some brass knuckles hidden in his room. One day after absorbing another round of fists from Pearl, Delores, and Carol, I retreated to my father's room. Returning with the brass knuckles on my hand, I yelled out, "Hit me now!" After that, the beatings from my sisters stopped for good.

Having successfully fended off my sisters, I gained a little confidence. I felt more prepared to protect myself in the neighborhood, as fighting in the streets of Bed-Stuy was becoming more commonplace, particularly for me. Even by third grade, kids were still making fun of my Christian name, Linster. The schoolyard taunts were becoming a little more threatening than they had been in first or second grade. I would declare, "My name is Pepé, not Linster." But it didn't make any difference, and dudes constantly wanted to fight me anyway. I decided that they must be jealous of me since I had such a cool name like Pepé.

I took my share of lumps, but more often than not, I was victorious and distributed some serious bumps and bruises among many of Bed-Stuy's preadolescent boys. I also maintained my status as the class clown. I always had a new joke to crack or was cooking up some stunt to draw laughs. Sometimes, when one of my classmates would make a joke, I would yell something like "Hoooooooo!" Everyone would crack up, except for our teacher, Miss Eleven. Nothing I ever did seemed to impress Miss Eleven, and the only thing she seemed to enjoy was hitting me. One of the more vindictive punishments she dispensed was to make me stand at the front of the class, facing the students. I was not allowed to move or speak. Periodically, she would walk up and smack me across the face.

One day my Grandpa Willie came to my school because he couldn't find my father, and he thought I might know where he was. When Grandpa Willie arrived in Miss Eleven's class, he found me standing in my customary position in front of the classroom. I could see the indignation in his eyes as he asked what I was doing there. I explained the situation, and he told me to take my seat. Then my grandpa turned to Miss Eleven and calmly said, "If you ever do this again, I'm going to come back here, and I am going to choke you." I am sure it made Miss Eleven hate me even more, but I never had to stand in front of the class again.

There were also some changes around the apartment during this period of my childhood, as my father started dating a woman named Maddie. Maddie had a daughter, Gloria, who was a few years younger than I was. Not long after my father began seeing Maddie, she and Gloria moved in with us on Grand Avenue.

Maddie was kind and motherly. She was also sophisticated, much more so than my father ever was. When I look back on their relationship, I don't know how they got along as well as they did for as long as they did.

Maddie introduced me to the world of the theater and Broadway plays. I already loved the movies, and going to the movies was one of my favorite things to do as a kid. The old State Theater on Dekalb and Franklin Avenues was a few blocks from where we lived. You could see a double feature for just thirty-five cents, and the popcorn was free. They would first show a B movie, followed by about ten different cartoon shorts, and then the feature film. After that, if you were lucky, the Three Stooges came on. No, not the short films that appeared on movie screens or television, but the actual Three Stooges would come onstage and perform for fifteen or twenty minutes. These appearances were often to promote an upcoming film or stage show. The Howard Brothers, Moe, Larry, and Curly, were born and raised in the Bensonhurst section of Brooklyn, so these appearances were something of a homecoming for them.

How I loved the movies and the performances of the Three Stooges. But a Broadway musical was something different. When Maddie began taking me to shows, I didn't know the first thing about what a play was. I remember her taking us to see Rodgers and Hammerstein's *The King and I* and *Carousel* and Gilbert and Sullivan's *The Mikado*. Even if I didn't quite understand what I was looking at, there was something about the splendor of the performance, the power of the music, and the mounting anticipation of the audience that deeply intrigued me.

The world of Broadway was far outside my own limited view of the world, and these experiences exposed me to art, music, and culture on a new level. In retrospect, I am sure it helped to pique my interest in popular music as well. I learned a lot from Maddie about life and the world outside of Bed-Stuy. I will always appreciate that. The experiences gave me confidence and made me feel like I was a pretty smart kid, more worldly than many of my peers.

Even with this new-found confidence, however, I remained disinterested in school. I just didn't care, and I blamed my father for that. I began to resent my father, not only for the beatings, but for not being there in the way I imagined a father should. Sure, he kept a roof over my head and food on the table, but it often seemed like he was a million miles away even when he was right next to me. I think I used my growing sense of despair and rebellious attitude as a way to get back at him.

Fortunately, music, as well as girls, began to fill some of the void I was experiencing at home.

2

ROCK AND ROLL FOREVER

THROUGHOUT MY CHILDHOOD, I was exposed, primarily by my mother's family, to blues, jazz, and R&B. Out of these traditions came a new era of soul music and what pioneering disc jockey Alan Freed would christen "rock and roll." This new music quickly captured the imagination of American teenagers, adolescents, and preadolescents such as me, regardless of race, class, or geography.

Among the most exciting artists that emerged during the early years of rock and roll were Little Richard, Elvis Presley, Chuck Berry, Bill Haley, and Bo Diddley. Fats Domino was probably my favorite at the time. I was fond of the string of number-one hits he put together: "Ain't That a Shame," "All By Myself," "I'm in Love Again," and "Blueberry Hill." Soon, the leading rock and roll artists were appearing frequently on the popular television variety shows of the era. Between September 1956 and January 1957, Elvis Presley performed three times on *The Ed Sullivan Show*, singing such hits as "Don't Be Cruel," "Hound Dog," "Love Me Tender," "Heartbreak Hotel," and the Little Richard smash "Ready Teddy." Although his guest slots on Sullivan's show were as exciting as they were controversial, it was his performances of the Carl Perkins–penned "Blue Suede Shoes" that knocked me out. Elvis performed the song several times on national television in 1956, including twice on Tommy and Jimmy Dorsey's *Stage Show* and on *The Milton Berle Show.*

Everything about the way Elvis performed that song—from his vocals to his guitar, from his choreography to his entire look—fascinated me. I was so enamored with it that I began to imitate his performance of "Blue Suede Shoes" in front of my bedroom mirror. Before long, I was pretty good at it, and I even got up the courage to show my father. He was quite impressed, so much so that he would call me into the living room to perform it for company. People loved it, and many of them gave me money, quarters usually, to show their appreciation.

Even though I was just miming the performance, the reaction I got from my father's friends gave me a rush I had never felt before. I was only nine years old, and I didn't have an instrument to play at the time, nor an outlet, other than my bedroom, to express my emerging musical sensibilities. But I was bitten by the performance bug. I was hooked. Rock and roll brought a passion and excitement unlike anything that had been witnessed before in American popular culture. I knew that I liked it, but I didn't know how I could truly be a part of it, aside from being a fan like millions of other kids.

I didn't realize it then, but the path to my own rock and roll destiny began to take shape in 1957. It was around that time that my uncle Clarence Collins founded an R&B group known as the Chesters. In addition to my uncle, the original group consisted of Tracy Lord, Nathaniel Rogers, and Ronald Ross. Not long after they formed, the Chesters realized they needed a genuine lead singer. They found that singer in Anthony Gourdine, who left his gig with the Duponts in order to front the Chesters. Around the same time, Ronald Ross exited the group and was replaced by Ernest Wright.

With the new lineup intact, the Chesters began recording for Apollo Records and soon produced their first hit single, "The Fires Burn No More." I was aware that my uncle was in a singing group, but it really made an impression on me when I heard "The Fires Burn No More" on the radio. I first heard it at my Grandpa and Grandma Willie's house. The Willies were not the musical side of my family, yet hearing that song remains one of my cherished childhood memories from my grandparents' home.

By the fall of 1958, as I was adjusting to life as a fifth grader and my final year at PS 45, Uncle Clarence's group, now known as the Imperials, rode the success of their first single to sign with George Goldner's End Records. The Brooklyn-based label had signed such early doo-wop acts as the Teenagers (post Frankie Lymon), the Flamingos, and the Chantels; it had even worked with Marilyn Monroe and Wilt Chamberlain. (Chamberlain, who was influenced by the Kansas City jazz scene during his time as a campus disc jockey at the University of Kansas, would later perform his End Records' single, "By the River," on *American Bandstand*.)

But no other artist on the End Records label ever matched the success that the Imperials enjoyed during the late 1950s and early 1960s. By November 1958, the Imperials' first End Records' single, "Tears on My Pillow," raced to number four on the pop chart and number two on the R&B chart. I will never forget the excitement and pride that swept over our family. I remember Clarence came by our apartment for some reason, perhaps to pick up my sisters, and I asked him, "Are you really in the Imperials?" He was only seventeen at the time and thought he was so cool. And, of course, to me he was. He just played it off like it was no big deal: "Yeah, I am in the Imperials." But to me and the rest of the Collins family, it was a big deal, and I was not afraid to let the rest of the world know, at least at first.

Often after school, a bunch of us kids would go to the candy store. One day when we were there, "Tears on My Pillow" came on the store's radio. With great delight, I shouted, "Hey, that's my uncle on the radio!" Of course, no one believed me. One girl began to call me names and even started hitting me and chased me through the streets all the way home. Hurt and embarrassed, I decided to never mention my uncle or his group in their presence again.

Nevertheless, I was proud of my uncle and his success. When Alan Freed, who was with WINS Radio in New York City at the time, first played "Tears on My Pillow," he referred to the group as "Little Anthony and the Imperials," in reference to Gourdine's diminutive stature. Of course, the name stuck. Freed later said of the hit song, "Wherever a jukebox was played, this song was sung and hummed by millions."

"Tears on My Pillow" has indeed become a pop standard and has been covered by many artists across musical genres. Next to the original, some notable versions of the song have been performed by New Edition, Chuck Jackson, Bobby Vee, Neil Sedaka, Reba McEntire, Kylie Minogue, and Minneapolis's first family of freestyle, the Jets. Sha Na Na's Frederick "Dennis" Greene also performed the song in the 1978 film *Grease*.

Not only did "Tears on My Pillow" go on to sell a million records, but the single's B side, "Two People in the World," also became a hit, which was rare in popular music in 1958 and still today. Little Anthony and the Imperials followed up their breakout success with a handful of charting singles, including "Shimmy Shimmy Ko-Ko-Bop" in 1959.

Having so enjoyed the world of Broadway musicals that my father's girlfriend, Maddie, had exposed me to a few years earlier, I really wanted to see my uncle's group perform live onstage. I would get that chance sooner than later.

In the spring of 1961, Little Anthony and the Imperials would be performing at the famous Brooklyn Paramount Theatre on Flatbush Avenue. A distinguished movie house in the heart of downtown Brooklyn, the Paramount was also known for its live performances, including several vaudeville acts and concerts by jazz icons such as Duke Ellington, Cab Calloway, Count Basie, Charlie Parker, Ella Fitzgerald, Sarah Vaughan, Dinah Washington, John Coltrane, and Miles Davis, among dozens more.

In April 1955, Freed had produced the first of many rock shows to be held at the Brooklyn Paramount. Three years before that, he had organized what is considered the first-ever rock and roll show, the "Moondog Coronation Ball" at Cleveland Arena. Nearly twenty thousand fans showed up to the ten-thousand-seat arena, many of them African Americans. An innovative, socially conscious radio and television personality, Freed believed in producing live shows that featured not only both black and white artists, but integrated audiences as well.

The shows he produced at the Brooklyn Paramount were often weeklong or even longer extravaganzas, with several shows each day. To make sure that younger audiences could attend, the concerts generally took place around holidays, namely Easter, Labor Day, and Christmas. Through his bold vision, support of extraordinary artists, and groundbreaking live shows designed to break racial barriers, Freed helped to provide the critical foundation for rock and roll's ascendancy in American culture. Among the big names who graced the stage at his Brooklyn Paramount concerts were Little Richard, Chuck Berry, Buddy Holly and the Crickets, Tony Bennett, LaVern Baker, Jerry Lee Lewis, Fats Domino, Bill Haley and His Comets, Jackie Wilson, Ruth McFadden, Bo Diddley, and the Everly Brothers.

Freed's popularity and influence among rock artists and concertgoers increased for a few more years, but a riot that broke out at a Freed-produced concert in Boston in May 1958, followed by a payola scandal, effectively ended his career. Freed produced the Christmas jubilee concerts that were scheduled to be held at the Brooklyn Paramount in December 1960, but having already exiled himself to Los Angeles, he would not be around for the shows.

Instead, Clay Cole, with help from Murray "the K" Kaufman, stepped in to host. Cole was best known for hosting a popular television dance show similar to *American Bandstand*. In addition to showcasing top-notch musical acts such as the Rolling Stones, the Doors, Richie Havens, and Simon & Garfunkel, the *Clay Cole Show* also featured pioneering comics like Richard Pryor and George Carlin.

Murray the K, who worked with Freed at WINS, eventually took over Freed's primetime slot. Designated "the fifth Beatle" by George Harrison, Murray the K became a close friend of the band and was among the first American deejays to actively promote the Beatles. He also was one of the few people to defend Bob Dylan following Dylan's controversial decision to "plug in" at the 1965 Newport Folk Festival.

Cole and Murray the K, like Freed, were dedicated to the integration of rock and roll and continued the tradition of promoting diverse acts performing for racially mixed audiences. The December 1960 shows marked the first time that Little Anthony and the Imperials graced the stage at the Paramount, where they appeared alongside the likes of Ray Charles, Neil Sedaka, Dion, the Drifters, the Shirelles, and a fifteen-year-old Kathy Young.

I wasn't able to attend those shows, but I was determined not to miss the upcoming Easter Parade of Stars, also hosted by Murray the K and Clay Cole. After getting permission from my father to go to one of the shows, I asked my good friend Bubba to come with me. I hadn't told Uncle Clarence or anyone else in the family that I was coming. As Bubba and I waited in line, we marveled at how many kids had come to see the show. Of course, most of them were older than Bubba and me, which suited us fine. There were so many pretty girls to look at.

As we stood in line with rapt anticipation, I saw Uncle Clarence and the rest of the Imperials heading to the backstage door. He noticed me too and shouted out, "Pepé!" as he motioned for us to come over. Bubba and I quickly walked over. Clarence was excited to see me and said, "You guys come in with us." I didn't know what to think; I was so excited I thought my sides would burst.

We watched the performances from backstage. Not only did we get to see Little Anthony and the Imperials bring the house down, but folks like Chubby Checker, Ben E. King, Dion, the Shirelles, Carla Thomas, Del Shannon, Johnny Mathis, and the Isley Brothers were also on the bill. I know Bubba had a good time, but for me, it was an otherworldly experience. There was something about the atmosphere that spoke to me. I couldn't wait to go again.

Fortunately, Clarence asked me to come back the next

day. There was one catch, which turned out to be a blessing. At the request of the group, I was to serve as the valet for Little Anthony and the Imperials. In this role, I would run and get whatever the members of the group needed in between shows, be it food or anything else. I was pretty much given the run of the place, and as I got to know some of the other artists, I began running errands for them as well.

My first experience outside of helping my uncle's group was making a store run for Chubby Checker. When I got back from the store, I approached the backstage door. Some older kids in line for the next show asked the security guard, "Why does he get to go in while we have to wait out here?" Before the guard could respond, I blurted out that I was on an errand for Chubby Checker and I had to get to him right away. When they heard that I was with Chubby Checker, several of the girls waiting in line blew past security and surrounded me, pulling and grabbing at my clothes. The guards had to pull me into the theater for my own protection. When I was safely inside—minus my shirt, which had been torn to shreds—I asked myself, *What the hell just happened?* It was my first experience with "groupies." I learned a valuable lesson that day.

Having survived the groupies, I continued to watch most of the shows from backstage. I couldn't see the crowd, but I sure could hear them, particularly the girls. Even though I was fully absorbed by the power of rock and roll myself, I didn't understand the bloodcurdling screams. I thought, *These motherfuckers are crazy.* I decided to watch the next show from the audience, to see what all the fuss was about. That's when I started to get it. As cool as it was to watch these artists from behind the scenes, being in the crowd provided me with a whole new perspective. When

Little Anthony and the Imperials took the stage, my adrenaline spiked, and I got caught up in the madness. I started jumping up and down yelling, "Clarence! Clarence! It's me, Pepé." I continued to scream and yell, but they never acknowledged me.

After their set, I ran backstage and asked if they saw me. Clarence looked at me and said, "What are you talking about?" I told him that I had been trying to get his attention from the audience. He explained that when they are onstage, in spite of all the screaming fans and beautiful girls calling their names, they still have a job to do. That was when I came to understand the professionalism that goes into all this. Being a professional musician requires focus, discipline, and dedication. As attractive as the rock and roll lifestyle can be, to truly be successful you must pay your dues, continue to put in the work, and never take anything for granted. I was already hooked on rock and roll, and this new knowledge made it even more impressive to me.

It took me a good week to come down from the high I was on after seeing those shows. All I could think about was the next round of concerts at the Brooklyn Paramount, which were slated for September 1961. However, those shows were not to be, at least not for me.

Not long after the Easter shows, Little Anthony left the group to pursue a solo career. Then Nathaniel Rogers was drafted into the army, and Tracy Lord left the group as well. My uncle hustled to put together a new lineup, but the future of the Imperials seemed uncertain at best. As such, they were not part of Murray the K's "Labor Day Show of Stars" that September.

Even sadder for me, those September shows would be the last rock and roll concerts ever held at the Brooklyn

Paramount Theatre. Long Island University–Brooklyn, which was located right next door on Flatbush Avenue, had purchased the theater a few years earlier, and by 1962 they turned it into a gymnasium.

It felt as though my rock and roll journey was over before it even started. I was crushed. I thought I had found an escape, a path to bigger and better things. Now I didn't know what to think. I was starting to come of age, and my future seemed uncertain again, as uncertain as the winds of change that were sweeping through the nation in the early 1960s. What proved to be America's most turbulent decade of the twentieth century would also be the most formative years of my life, for better and for worse. While I hoped against hope that new and exciting opportunities would present themselves, there were times when I wasn't sure if I'd even live to see my sixteenth birthday.

3

THE STONEKILLERS

IN MAY 1961, an article in the *New York Times* discussed the mounting street gang problem afflicting Brooklyn's Bed-Stuy neighborhoods. In the article, titled "Gang Wars Upset Area in Brooklyn; Bedford-Stuyvesant Tense Following Two Slayings," reporter Alfred E. Clark referred to Bed-Stuy as "Brooklyn's Little Harlem."

There were several gangs in Bed-Stuy at the time, including the Marcy Avenue Chaplains, Buccaneers, Count Bishops, Imperial Lords, Jonquils, and Mau Mau. One of the most notorious gangs was the Stonekillers, who dominated my neighborhood. My father always told me, "If you ever join a gang, I will beat your ass." A lot of folks were scared of the Stonekillers, including a lot of young dudes who eventually became members. However, there was no one I was more afraid of than my father. And for that reason, I had no intention of becoming a Stonekiller.

One of my favorite activities as an adolescent was a trip to the candy store. It was only a couple of blocks from my house, and I would go and load up on sweets whenever I could. Yet, every time I left the house, my first concern was who might attack me as I made my way down Grand Avenue. Anytime I stepped out the front door of our house, I looked left and then right to make sure the coast was clear.

And then I ran as fast as I could. It was always a great relief when I made it to the store and felt safe again.

Going home, it was the same routine: look left, look right, run! One time when I was twelve years old, as I was leaving the candy store, I was confronted by three or four of the younger Stonekillers. We used to call them the "little people." The gang was structured as two units. The "little people" were the younger division of the gang, dudes who were maybe twelve to fifteen years old. The bigger guys generally ranged in age from sixteen into their twenties.

As these "little" Stonekillers cornered me on the street, one of them called out for Preston. Preston was one of the vice presidents of the younger Stonekillers. He was a short, stocky guy, and he scared me to death. I remember how he slowly meandered over and then proceeded to beat the hell out of me on the street. He didn't take my money or my candy; he just beat me up.

Such encounters with Preston became commonplace, but I continued my trips to the candy store anyway, always hoping that I could avoid him and his fellow gang members. If I did run into the Stonekillers, they always called for Preston, and I was always in tears by the time he arrived. And as always, he would beat me up but never rob me.

One summer day, I went to the candy store with my cousin to buy some ice cream bars. We were both in a pretty good mood when we came out of the store, but our happiness quickly turned to dread. The moment we hit the sidewalk, the Stonekillers were there waiting for us. I looked at them and said, "Not today, guys. Please!" Of course, that didn't mean much to them, and as usual, one of them called out for Preston. I looked at my cousin and said, "run home," which he did.

I, on the other hand, stood there waiting for Preston. As he approached, I repeated my plea, "Not today." He looked at me with his evil smile and punched me right in the chest. Although it hurt, for some reason I felt emboldened, and I told him not to hit me again. He did anyway. At this point, I'd had enough and told him one more time, "Don't hit me again." He flashed his arrogant smirk and began to laugh at me. That really pissed me off. As he stood there smiling, I delivered a roundhouse right directly to his stomach.

I saw that he was startled, and I hit him again in the stomach, this time with a left. I followed that with another right-left combination, and he started to fall. Before he even hit the ground, I took off like a shot toward my apartment. As Preston lay on the ground, the other Stonekillers chased me down Grand Avenue. Sprinting toward home, I was surprised to see my mother ahead of me. She happened to be in the area for some reason, and as soon as I saw her, I ran up to her and held on. When the Stonekillers arrived, she stepped toward them and shouted, "You aren't going to gang up on my son. He will fight you all one at a time."

I could see the fear in their eyes as they looked at her. Then she calmly asked them, "Who's first?" To which I enthusiastically interjected, "Yeah, who's first?" Looking sullen and defeated, the Stonekillers turned around and walked away.

I think that was the first time I truly felt that this woman, whom I barely knew, was my mother, and that she loved me. I also believe it was the first time in my life I ever felt powerful. That night when I went to sleep, it seemed as though my world had somehow changed, although I wasn't sure exactly what that meant. I did know I was no longer afraid of Preston or the younger members of the Stonekillers.

That next day, I went to the candy store, where I saw Preston. I looked directly in his eyes and said, "You want some more?" He gave me his usual nasty smirk, but this time it was missing some of its edge. He had a dejected look in his eyes as he turned and headed in the other direction. Watching him stroll away, I yelled, "Yeah, you better keep walking."

After that, I didn't have any more run-ins with the Stonekillers. Then one day at school, some of the younger members approached me on the playground. One of them stepped forward and said, "Pepé, we want you to be our war counselor."

My first thought was, *Cool. They know my reputation. They respect me now.* A tremendous sense came over me. I felt important. I felt valued. And then I heard my father's voice in my head, threatening to kick my ass if I ever joined a gang. But my excitement at being asked to join the gang proved too strong. That day I became a Stonekiller. I was ready to represent my neighborhood.

To my mind, gang life in the 1960s was quite different than it is today. To be certain, I loved my brothers in the gang, both young and old, and I was proud to be a Stonekiller. But today it seems that many young men join a gang because, at least in their own minds, it is the only real family they have. Their whole identity is rooted in the gang. For me, and I think for most of my fellow Stonekillers, being in the gang was simply the "thing to do" in our Bed-Stuy of the time. It made us feel respected and recognized in the neighborhood. The gang life provided me with some sense of self-worth, and perhaps it did help to fill a void that came from living alone with my father all those years. But I never viewed it as the defining feature of my life. I always wanted and expected more for myself, even if the options were limited.

As the war counselor for the younger Stonekillers, I was expected to start fights with individual members from other gangs and, in some cases, instigate all-out fights between the Stonekillers and rival gangs. I helped to start a lot of fights. And although I took my share of whacks, I generally delivered more blows than I received. For the most part, we fought with only sticks and knives, and our fists.

I experienced members of rival gangs flashing their knives at me in the school cafeteria and on the playground. I didn't think much of it at the time, as it just reinforced my loyalty to my own gang and neighborhood. But I was becoming increasingly aware that the gang life was more dangerous than I thought or at least wanted to believe. I was seeing too many young brothers get killed. Some of them were my friends. I just wanted to run from this existence.

Of course, once you join a gang, it's not so easy to quit. I knew that as long as I was living in Bed-Stuy, leaving the Stonekillers wasn't really an option. I also knew that I needed to find something else to occupy my time and interests, ideally something that could ultimately lead me out of the neighborhood. I wanted to experience everything that the world had to offer and to do so on my own terms. The time I spent with Maddie when she was with my father had opened my eyes to the fact that another world, full of opportunity, existed out there. I would have to scratch and claw to find those opportunities for myself.

Although it wasn't exactly glamorous, I was able to divert some of my attention away from gang activities by helping my Grandpa Willie at his moving company. My father also was sometimes called upon to help, but more often than not, he was in no condition to work. Grandpa Willie would tell him that if he was going to mess around on the job instead of working, "at least you could down some real liquor instead of that cheap wine you're always drinking."

I never asked him about it, but I wondered if my grandpa was disappointed in my father. To some degree, he must have been. I was certainly embarrassed by my father's behavior. I just came to accept it as part of my life at the time.

In addition to helping my grandpa, and running with the Stonekillers, I embraced another kind of running and found some solace in athletics. I excelled in track and field at Francis Scott Key Junior High School. The school was on Willoughby Avenue, between Kent and Franklin Avenues where Bed-Stuy and the Clinton Hill neighborhood meet. It did not have a track facility, so our coach had to draw chalk lines on the pavement in order to make something that resembled a track. Of course, I did get to run on real tracks when we had meets at other schools.

I also ran cross-country, which I really loved. Something about running through different parts of the city resonated with me. As much as I loved running on an asphalt track, running along a grass-covered trail gave me a sense of freedom. Even if it was fleeting, I felt as if I was running free of all the things that confined me in Bed-Stuy.

I even joined the gymnastics squad at Francis Scott Key. It was not a competitive program; it was simply for show. We often performed at school assemblies or on the playground. I would sometimes ask the other members on the squad to come by my apartment so we could impress the girls in the neighborhood. We would choreograph a whole routine complete with flips, tumbles, and handstands.

Me and the guys in the neighborhood, and sometimes the girls too, would also keep busy playing games like kings, skelly, and stickball. Kings and skelly were two of my favorites, both of which originated on the streets of New York City in the early twentieth century. These games were part of the culture of New York City kids, regardless of what borough you came from or your racial, ethnic, or religious background.

Another one of my favorite pastimes was the yo-yo. Bubba was my partner, and we practiced all the time. The Royal Yo-Yo Company, based in Long Island City in Queens, used to hold contests in Brooklyn and the other boroughs. Bubba and I were repeat champions and were awarded numerous prizes. That usually meant a bunch of candy or perhaps a brand-new yo-yo, but I also remember winning bicycles at one of Royal's contests. The two of us cleaned up on the yo-yo circuit. Those were some of the better memories of my adolescence.

Of course, not everything that we did was for fun or recreational purposes. It was a rite of passage for teenage boys in Bed-Stuy to start their own hustle. I had learned that from my father and his bootlegging scheme. Bootlegging was not something we could get away with at our age, so we made our own shoeshine kits. Whenever we encountered well-dressed men on the street, we would approach them and ask if they needed a "shine." Our prices were pretty reasonable, and we got a lot of men to agree. It was a way to put money in our pockets.

I think my father seeing me involved in these exploits—whether it was the shoeshine business or running track or playing games around the neighborhood—kept him from getting suspicious about what else I may have been up to. I was still quite active in the Stonekillers; I just had so many other things going on, he had no idea about my gang affiliation. My father also didn't spend a lot of time around the apartment, and when he did, he was most likely drinking if not already drunk. What I didn't realize at the time is that my father was quite ill. In the spring of 1963, toward the end of my last year at Francis Scott Key, he was hospitalized.

While he was in the hospital, I stayed with my Grandpa and Grandma Willie, who were now living in South Brooklyn, on St. Mark's Place. I remember thinking it wasn't a big deal and that my father would come home soon. Then one morning I woke up and my grandparents told me that my father was dead. I yelled back, "No, he's not either!" I ran back into the bedroom and slammed the door behind me. I lay on the bed, unable to move. I couldn't believe it. I didn't shed a tear, but I was devastated. It was April 16, 1963. Linster Herbert Willie died of lobar pneumonia, which is often fatal, particularly for African Americans. He was only forty-one years old. At his funeral three days later, I approached his casket, and the first thought that came to my mind was how young he looked. Sure, he was only forty-one, but he looked to me like he was in his twenties. He looked like he was at peace. I certainly hope he was.

As I tried to process his death, I didn't think much about the beatings or other bad times. I didn't harbor resentment toward him or feel mad at him at all, except maybe for the fact that he'd died. I spent a lot of time thinking about the occasions when I felt his love, even if he didn't express it outwardly. Now that he was gone, I realized something that had escaped me up to that point: my father never hugged me. I wasn't sure what to think of that, so I didn't let myself think about it at all.

After my father died, I moved in permanently with my Grandpa and Grandma Willie. It wasn't terribly far from Bed-Stuy, but it felt like it was. I missed my neighborhood and I missed my friends. And even though my heart was no longer in the gang life, I missed my brothers from the Stonekillers too.

In my new neighborhood, the Comanche Chaplains and Warren Street gangs ruled, and I intended to avoid those guys as best I could. Another difference with South Brooklyn compared to Bed-Stuy was the presence of a lot of Italian and Puerto Rican families. In addition to the Chaplains and Warren Street, there was an Italian street gang known as the South Brooklyn Boys and a Puerto Rican gang called the Renegades.

Initially, it seemed as though most of the kids in the neighborhood got along pretty well. Of course, that didn't last long. I often invited my friends Bubba and Chester from the old neighborhood to make the trip south of Atlantic Avenue to hang out with me at my grandparents' house. One summer day, we were playing stickball in the street when a few dudes from the Warren Street Gang started harassing us. Chester, who was a bit of a troublemaker, walked right up to one of them and threw his hands up as if to say, *Let's go.* Chester laid the guy out, and the rest of the gang retreated, indicating that they would be back. Bubba and I weren't afraid to fight, and we made sure we had what we thought were the proper weapons, which happened to be sticks in this case.

When the Warren Street Gang returned, one of them pulled a knife. Undeterred, I squared off with this one dude, ready to throw blows. Suddenly, something hit me hard in the side of the head. Dazed and confused, I was able to stay on my feet, and I looked up and saw my father's brother Edmund standing there. I don't know how I missed him sneaking up on me, but I realized that he hit me because he didn't want me fighting or being involved in gangs any more than my father had.

As the Warren Street Gang ran off, Uncle Edmund looked at me, said nothing, and walked into my grandparents' house. I generally got along pretty well with Uncle Edmund before and after that incident. It happened, and it was over. We never talked about it.

Circumstances beyond my control, however, soon dragged me into the gang life of South Brooklyn. One late summer night in 1963, I was at my grandparents' house minding my own business. Members of the Renegades, the local Puerto Rican gang, showed up looking for a fight with the Warren Street Gang. Since this was now my neighborhood, I was naturally a target and ended up fighting the Renegades. Thus, by default, I was now a member of the Warren Street Gang. This had never been my intention, but the decision was made for me.

I had been living in South Brooklyn for only a few months when I noticed an upswing in racial tension among area youth, especially in my age group. My impression was that younger kids in the neighborhood tended to play together regardless of race. However, as high school drew near, the attitudes about race started to mirror the ominous mood that was enveloping the rest of the country. Even with the civil rights movement in full swing, in places like Brooklyn and other urban centers, a dark cloud seemed to be hanging overhead. Growing up in Brooklyn was always tough, but this felt different. Things were definitely changing, and not for the better.

My personal anguish about a world that seemed to be crumbling around me only grew when I got word that one of my former Stonekiller brothers had been killed in a gang fight back in Bed-Stuy. Sammy, who was very close friends with my sister Delores, was a really good dude. Now he was gone forever. And here I was still running with a gang. I was fifteen years old, and I was afraid for my life.

In the fall of 1963, I entered the tenth grade at George Westinghouse Vocational and Technical High School. Located in downtown Brooklyn, Westinghouse was an all-boys high school a few blocks from the entrance to the Brooklyn Bridge. Today, the high school is known for a number of famous alumni, including hip-hop legends Shawn Carter (Jay-Z), Christopher Wallace (The Notorious B.I.G.), Trevor Smith (Busta Rhymes), and Earl Simmons (DMX).

I was enrolled in the Vocational Education Program, but initially I didn't think much about what that might mean for my future employment or career prospects. Then one day a teacher in the program, Mr. McCreary, asked a group of students if any of us had ever thought about becoming electricians. I thought about it for a second and said to myself, *That sounds like something I might want to try.* Mr. McCreary said that anyone interested should come to the front of the classroom. My curiosity was further piqued when I saw that only white students were responding to his request. Not wanting to squander the opportunity, I headed to the front of the class.

When I got there, Mr. McCreary said, "Hey, Willie. Do you have any family members that belong to the electricians' union?" I told him that I did not. He then said, in light of that fact, I was not eligible to participate in the electrician training project. Dejected, I walked away.

I was telling this story at the dinner table one night and sharing how disappointed I was to have been left out of the project. My aunt Sarah, the younger of my father's two siblings, was dining with us that evening, and when she heard what happened, she flipped out. She knew what Mr. McCreary told me was a lie, and she went on about all the "racist bullshit" in the schools. I had never seen her so pissed off.

Even though it made me angry to learn that I was lied to, I had already moved on. I was acclimating to life in high school, and I was also looking forward to the upcoming Thanksgiving break and the prospect of a long and relaxing weekend. The Friday before Thanksgiving started like any normal day. Not long after lunch ended, whispers started around school that President John F. Kennedy had been shot while campaigning in Dallas, Texas. I didn't believe it. I couldn't even conceive of the possibility. Shortly thereafter, just before the school day ended, the word was out: President Kennedy was dead.

Heading home from school, I couldn't believe it was true. When I arrived at my grandparents' house, I turned on the television, and I went numb. As I watched the images of grown folks, including professional journalists, crying, I was unable to turn away from the television. I asked myself, *What the fuck is going on? How can this even happen?* It was so unbelievable to me. After coming to grips with the reality, I genuinely started to feel scared. If somebody could kill the president, what does that mean for the rest of us? I thought, *If they can kill JFK, then I ain't shit.*

I woke up the next morning hoping that it had all been a bad dream. Realizing it wasn't, I was overcome with fear and sadness. Since it was Saturday morning, there wasn't much to do other than watch the continuing coverage of the assassination on TV. Lyndon Johnson, who had been president for less than twenty-four hours, declared it a National Day of Mourning. To say that day was somber would be an understatement. It was surreal in the worst sense of the word. The question that I couldn't get out of my mind was, *Now what?*

People on the streets were crying and consoling one another. I thought about how much it would have meant to me to have had my father there to give me a hug, to tell me, "It's okay son. Things are going to be all right." But alas, he was gone himself. And in the nearly fifteen years we spent together, I never got a hug from my father.

As difficult as it was to do much of anything after this national tragedy, life went on. Even with the sense of dread that seemed to follow me everywhere, what else was there to do but try to move forward? I didn't have much direction at that moment in my life. My continued involvement in gangs and the apprehension and chaos that was sweeping not only over New York City but across America made me feel as though any day could be my last on earth. However, fate was about to step in and restore my hope for the future.

4

LIVE AT THE BROOKLYN FOX

FOLLOWING HIS BRIEF ATTEMPT at a solo career, Anthony Gourdine rejoined the Imperials in 1963. When I heard the group would be appearing at Murray the K's 1963 Christmas Show at the Brooklyn Fox, I knew that I had to be there.

After the Paramount had closed in 1961, Murray the K staged a rock and roll show at the New York Academy of Music before finding a permanent home for his holiday concerts at the Brooklyn Fox Theatre. The Fox, another iconic movie house in downtown Brooklyn, opened in 1928, the same year as the Paramount. Also located on Flatbush Avenue, just off of Fulton Street, the Fox had a slightly larger capacity than the Paramount and proved to be a more than suitable replacement.

By this time, Murray the K had put on three separate revues at the Fox, all of which sold out to rave reviews. However, the return of Little Anthony and the Imperials would inject the December 1963 shows with an extra dose of excitement.

I asked Clarence if I could reprise my role as valet. He said that he wouldn't have it any other way, adding that he was sure the other acts would welcome me with open arms as well. As soon as I entered the backstage door for that first show, I knew I was home again. I was so excited I couldn't sit still. As I had before at the Paramount, I went around knocking on dressing room doors asking the artists if they needed anything.

Occasionally, even Murray the K would send me out for food. I didn't realize it at the time, but in later years I learned that a lot of people really disliked Murray. They hated his massive ego and didn't like his style or his penchant for always getting his way. I always assumed the artists loved him because he was so supportive of their careers. Personally, I found him to be a nice guy, although he didn't speak to me very much. In my view, he had a huge job to do and he did it exceedingly well. I was thrilled to be a part of this world, and as Alan Freed and Clay Cole had before, Murray the K helped to make it possible.

One of my biggest responsibilities at the Fox was making sure that artists knew when it was time for them to go onstage. With so many acts, usually a dozen or more per show, this assignment kept me on my feet. When it was nearing showtime for a particular act, I would let them know that "the half was in." That was backstage jargon meaning a half-hour until they were to go on.

If time allowed, I would run to my grandparents' house and bring back huge plates of home-cooked food for all the acts. My grandma made comfort foods, such as her famous macaroni and cheese, fried chicken, collard greens, and various pies. Needless to say, the homemade food was a big hit with the artists, and it helped me to get in good with them.

In addition to Little Anthony and the Imperials, the 1963 Christmas shows featured big-time acts like the Miracles, Mary Wells, Martha and the Vandellas, Jay and the

Americans, the Duprees, and Ruby & the Romantics. I instantly fell in love with Mary Wells. Known by many as "The First Lady of Motown," Mary already had several Top 40 hits and would soon achieve her first number-one single with 1964's "My Guy." As talented as she was, I couldn't think too far past her beauty. She was a knockout. I was shy around her and found it difficult to talk to her. Yet, whenever she was standing in the wings about to take the stage, I casually made my way over and stood by her. I sensed that she knew I was gawking at her. I couldn't hide it; I was always trying to sneak a peek at her shapely figure.

The rest of the acts were fabulous too, and of course Little Anthony and the Imperials left the audience awestruck every time they took the stage. These first shows as the re-formed Little Anthony and the Imperials proved noteworthy for another reason too. One night a young man came backstage looking to speak to my uncle's group. He had some sheet music and said he had written a song specially for them. His name was Teddy Randazzo.

A native of Brooklyn, Teddy had begun his career in the music business nearly ten years earlier as a member of the Three Chuckles. A top twenty hit and an appearance on *The Ed Sullivan Show* caught the attention of Alan Freed, who decided to feature Teddy in the 1956 film *Rock, Rock, Rock!* Appearing alongside Connie Francis, Chuck Berry, and Frankie Lymon and the Teenagers, Teddy performed four songs in the movie, including one with the Three Chuckles. He was barely twenty years old at the time. Teddy went on to record several hits as a solo artist, and he starred in more rock and roll films, including *Hey, Let's Twist!*, *Mister Rock and Roll*, and *The Girl Can't Help It*, starring Jayne Mansfield and featuring Little Richard, Eddie Cochran, Gene Vincent, and Fats Domino. Teddy also penned hits for other artists with his writing partner Bobby Weinstein.

Although he was already quite accomplished, Teddy was slightly before the Imperials' time, and when he showed up at the Fox to speak to them, I don't think they knew who he was. To them, he was just this Italian guy who said he had a song. Nevertheless, they agreed to listen. They pulled in the house guitarist, Eric Gale, who was pretty well known and would go on to become one of the most accomplished session guitarists in music history. In addition to a dozen solo albums, Gale played blues, jazz, rock, and soul on several hundred records, including by Dizzy Gillespie, Quincy Jones, Lena Horne, David Ruffin, Grover Washington Jr., George Benson, Van Morrison, Paul Butterfield, Diana Ross, Paul Simon, Ashford & Simpson, Joe Cocker, Roberta Flack, Billy Joel, and Al Jarreau.

Teddy and Eric began to play the opening measures of "I'm On the Outside (Looking In)." The Imperials joined in to sing, and almost instantly it was like magic. This was my first experience seeing a song come together. I would later learn that it doesn't always happen so easily. But that moment, with the Imperials, Teddy, and Eric, was otherworldly.

"I'm On the Outside (Looking In)" would be the Imperials' comeback hit when it was released on the Don Costa Productions (DCP) label in 1964. The song was later covered by Johnny Mathis and by Smokey Robinson and the Miracles, among others. It was also the beginning of a long and fruitful partnership between the Imperials and Teddy Randazzo, who helped secure the group a new recording deal with DCP.

Although the December 1963 shows at the Fox were over, the triumphant return of Little Anthony and the Imperials was just beginning. They started to play gigs all around the city, and I wanted nothing more than to continue as their valet. Unfortunately, I was still a few months from my sixteenth birthday, and these gigs were often at clubs, bars, or other venues where I was too young to attend. Had I been sixteen, I could have applied for a New York City Cabaret Identification Card, which would have allowed me access to these venues as long as I was working for the group. Established during Prohibition, Cabaret Cards were a requirement for all nightclub employees, including the artists who performed there.

I was close to turning sixteen, however, and I was determined to get a Cabaret Card. Knowing how much it meant to me, my mother and her boyfriend Jesse drove me all over New York City, from one government office to another, trying to make a case for why I should have a Cabaret Card. At every stop, we were told the same thing: "No." My mother insisted to every city employee we saw that I would be with my uncle and he would look after me. Still, no one made an exception. I was heartbroken.

My heartbreak didn't last long. I soon found out that Little Anthony and the Imperials would be performing at the Brooklyn Fox during Murray the K's Easter shows in April 1964. I might not be able get into a New York City nightclub, but nothing was going to keep me from the Fox Theatre. That year's Easter shows showcased an almost entirely different lineup than the Christmas concerts just three months earlier, with only Little Anthony and the Imperials on the bill again. Among the acts performing at the April shows were Ben E. King, Chuck Jackson, the Kingsmen, the Shirelles, Dionne Warwick, the Righteous Brothers, the Tymes, and the Chiffons.

The shows sold out fast. The demand was so great that hundreds of kids slept outside overnight to get tickets. There was a lot of negative media attention over this fact, but hey, this was rock and roll, and the kids loved it.

These showcases typically had four shows per day, but when the demand was high, they would add a fifth. This meant little rest for the artists, and in order to accommodate a fifth performance, the producers would cut the stage time for some of the acts, who might get to perform only one song instead of two. Tough decisions like this were made whenever a show might run long. Most of the time, when artists were asked to cut their set, they obliged and it was no big deal.

On the other hand, Dionne Warwick let it be known that she did not appreciate being asked to sacrifice one second of her stage time. I could understand her position, as she had a couple of high-charting Billboard hits in "Don't Make Me Over" and "Anyone Who Had a Heart." The producers had made their decision, however, and their decisions usually stood regardless of whose feelings might be hurt.

By this time, I felt like I was sort of a veteran at the Brooklyn Fox and knew everyone pretty well. As such, there were a few artists and staff who would allow me to walk right into their dressing room without knocking when I was announcing that the "half was in" or checking to see who needed what. That included a guy named Rick, who was one of the producers.

Making my rounds between shows one night, I went to Rick's dressing room and walked in without knocking, just as he'd always told me to. I yelled out, "Hey, Rick!" before I even saw him. When I looked across the room, there he was with Dionne. The only thing I can say about it is that they were engaged in what I would call a "very private conversation." I quickly exited without saying another word, shut the door behind me, and moved on to the next dressing room. Needless, to say, Dionne's set was fully restored for the next show.

Another memorable moment from those Easter shows came from an encounter between members of the Tymes and Patricia Bennett of the Chiffons. Known at the time for their number-one hit "So Much in Love," the Tymes seemed like pretty cool guys to me. As I was talking to them outside their dressing room, Patricia Bennett, better known as Stellie, walked by. The Chiffons, who already hit number one with their first single, "He's So Fine," were tough, young girls from the Bronx. Barely older than I was, they definitely came with some attitude, which I thought was cool.

When the guys from the Tymes noticed Stellie, they started catcalling her. She didn't appreciate that and proceeded to slam their dressing room door in their faces. Regrettably for me, my hand was still near the door and my index finger was caught in the door jamb. I was taken to the emergency room, where they had to stich up my finger. It was extremely painful, but unforgettable. I guess you could say it was my first battle scar in the world of rock and roll.

I have so many distinct memories and lessons from the shows I worked over the years at the Brooklyn Fox. Most of the memories were pleasant, some were a bit scary, and a few were just downright strange. But that's rock and roll, I guess. Many of the lessons have stayed with me my entire life.

One thing I learned early is that producing something as big as a rock and roll show requires reflection, vision, and innovation. For example, the order of the show is extremely important. Each night, Little Anthony and the Imperials would put on a deft, dynamic, and inspirational performance. As a result, nobody wanted to follow them onstage, and they were usually called upon to close each show.

Sometimes you couldn't predict how the crowd would react, and this could create challenges for artists and the producers. Perhaps the most striking example I ever saw of this was when Wayne Newton was scheduled to follow the Ronettes. The Ronettes came out one night in these little miniskirts to perform "Be My Baby." Ronnie, Estelle, and Nedra were already sensational, but the miniskirts took them over the top that night. The guys in the crowd went absolutely nuts. As the Ronettes left the stage to a thunderous ovation, Newton was introduced and started to sing his big hit, "Danke Schoen." He was booed off the stage. I felt so bad for him. Nonetheless, I guess he did okay for himself in the end.

Another moment that sticks out was one night when I returned to Little Anthony and the Imperials' dressing room after running an errand, and they were all there dying of laughter. I asked them what was so funny. Clarence said that Stevie Wonder, or Little Stevie Wonder, as he was known at the time, fell off the stage and into the orchestra pit while playing "Fingertips." That didn't seem funny to me, and fortunately he was unhurt. However, the Imperials and others thought it was hilarious. I am sure they wouldn't have thought so if he had been injured.

For a brief period, Stevie dated my sister Tina. It was just puppy love, as they were only teenagers at the time. Tina is my only younger sibling, however, and I remember feeling somewhat protective of her and a little suspicious of Stevie's intentions. But he truly is a good guy and one of the all-time geniuses of pop music.

I would run into Stevie decades later at the Twenty-Fifth Anniversary Rock and Roll Hall of Fame Concert in 2009. Little Anthony and the Imperials had been inducted into the hall of fame earlier that year, and they were invited to perform "Two People in the World" at the anniversary concert at Madison Square Garden. The two-night event at the world's most famous arena featured a who's who of modern music history legends, including two of Motown's all-time greats: Smokey Robinson and Stevie Wonder. I went up to Smokey to talk about the old days at the Brooklyn Fox. I had run quite a few errands for him back then. He didn't remember me or anything about that time. It was a long time ago, and I suppose that's understandable when you are such a big star and have crossed paths with tens of thousands of people during your career. Stevie, on the other hand, seemed to recollect all of it, and he was pleasantly surprised that I recalled our encounters too. He said, "You remember that? Really?" It was a special moment, and it made me appreciate even more all I have seen and done in this world.

After Stevie and I parted company, my mind went back to those first shows at the Brooklyn Fox. I was just fifteen years old at the time, and I didn't really understand that I had a backstage pass to history in the making. The artists I was able to witness were phenomenal, and many of them were just starting out. No one knew what the future would hold for them or for rock and roll fans everywhere.

What I did know, at least for myself, was that rock and roll was my best chance for a life outside the one I had been living. The more I thought about it, the more I realized that I didn't have to relegate myself solely to the role of a valet. As important as that role was, and I cherished every minute of it, I told myself, *I can write, play, and perform too.* That is when I decided that I would take all the knowledge, skills, lessons, and insight I was learning as a valet and put them to use as I charted a course in pursuit of my own musical career.

5

TEDDY

FINISHING MY SOPHOMORE YEAR at George Westinghouse High School provided me the respite I needed to dedicate my time to becoming a musician. It was June 1964, and Freedom Summer was just beginning, as various civil rights organizations and volunteers from all over the country descended on Mississippi to help African Americans register to vote.

Just a few weeks into the voting rights campaign, three activists, all in their twenties, went missing. James Chaney was a native of Mississippi, while Andrew Goodman and Michael Schwerner were both natives of New York City. By August, the bodies of Chaney, Goodman, and Schwerner were found in Neshoba County, Mississippi. They had been murdered by members of the Ku Klux Klan and local law enforcement.

Now a decade into the civil rights movement, violence was becoming increasingly common. The summer before, civil rights leader Medgar Evers was assassinated in his own driveway in Jackson, Mississippi. Just months after that, Addie Mae Collins, Carole Robertson, Cynthia Wesley, and Carol McNair were killed in the Sixteenth Street Baptist Church bombing in Birmingham, Alabama. In considering the barbarity and cowardice of that crime, it was not lost on me that three of the four girls were basically the same age as me. Then, of course, President Kennedy was assassinated in November. As the violence continued into the summer of 1964, I wondered, *Can things get any worse?*

In early July, President Johnson signed the Civil Rights Act into law. The photo of the president signing the bill at the White House, with Dr. Martin Luther King Jr. standing behind him, gave me hope that things might get better. Then, just a few weeks later, James Powell, an African American teenager, was shot and killed by New York City police officer Thomas Gilligan in front of multiple witnesses on Manhattan's Upper East Side. As you might expect, accounts of the shooting and the events leading up to it differed. That night, a few hundred teenagers confronted members of the police department, and the Harlem Riot of 1964 began.

Before long, rioting spilled into the streets of Bed-Stuy. Since I was living with my grandparents in South Brooklyn, I was somewhat insulated from the violence. Nonetheless, I worried about my family and my friends from the old neighborhood and so wanted to be in Bed-Stuy. My grandparents weren't having any part of that, and I was forced to stay inside.

After six nights of violence, the uprising led to hundreds of injuries and arrests, and one death. The Harlem Riots of 1964 ended on July 22, 1964. It was my sixteenth birthday.

James Powell was only fifteen when he was killed by the police. It just as easily could have been me or one of my friends. Having been a gang member now for nearly four years, I'd had more than one encounter with the New York City police. None of those encounters had gone sideways, so to speak, but who's to say the next one wouldn't? I had already seen friends and gang mates die. Whether at the hands of the police or another gang member, what was the difference? Dead is dead.

Of course, things weren't always like this in Bed-Stuy. Even though poverty was the norm and you might have to look over your shoulder from time to time, it hadn't felt like this before. There had been a time, not long before the 1964 uprising, when New York City police officers regularly walked their beat, getting to know people in the community, including us kids. In my neighborhood, most everyone knew and loved "Pete the Cop," as we called him. Pete would come around all the time and even hang out with the kids in my neighborhood, always asking how we were doing and whatnot. He even played kings with us. Pete was kind and generous. We not only felt comfortable around him, he was like a friend. He genuinely seemed to care about our well-being, and we felt likewise about him.

And it wasn't just the police who would look after you; it was business owners, city workers, and anyone else whose vocation brought them into the neighborhood. It didn't seem to matter what color they were, either. But by the time I was fifteen or sixteen, this kind of community support had begun to fade. It seemed to change so fast. It wasn't long before police were riding two or four deep in their squad cars. Walking the beat became a thing of the past.

Not long after the riots in Harlem and Bed-Stuy, violence erupted in Philadelphia, Chicago, and Rochester in western New York, among other cities. Just across the Hudson River from New York City, riots broke out in several New Jersey cities, including Patterson and Jersey City. The summer of 1964 was proving to be one of the bloodiest in recent American history. The increasing tensions and violence only reinforced my own determination to find a way to make this music thing work—for my own survival.

By the time of Murray the K's Big Holiday Show at the Brooklyn Fox in September, the partnership between Little Anthony and the Imperials and Teddy Randazzo had yielded another hit with "Goin' Out of My Head." The song, which peaked at number six on the Billboard chart, was ultimately covered by dozens of artists, from Ella Fitzgerald to Shirley Bassey, Frank Sinatra to Luther Vandross. Teddy and the group followed with another top-ten hit, "Hurt So Bad." Linda Ronstadt's formidable cover of the song would also reach the top ten in 1980.

It was easy to see that Teddy's songwriting skills coupled with the Imperials' vocal abilities was a match made in heaven. With Teddy around so often, I started asking him questions about becoming a songwriter myself. Teddy was a prince of a man. He was easy to approach and even easier to talk to. I wanted to spend as much time as I could around him, gleaning all his wisdom, insight, and skills. Despite how busy he was, he was generous with his time, and before long, I thought of him as a mentor.

The Imperials, Teddy, and some of the other acts used to unwind at the bar inside the Mohawk Hotel after shows at the Fox. The Mohawk was at Greene and Washington, only a block from my old elementary school. Oh, how badly I wanted to hang out with them. But alas, I was only sixteen and couldn't join them at the bar.

The September 1964 showcase at the Fox had a spectacular and rather large lineup, and this run of shows was Motown heavy. There were always two or three Motown acts on the bill, but this time it was the entire Motown Revue. Among those performing were Marvin Gaye, the

Temptations, the Supremes, the Miracles, and Martha and the Vandellas, among other Motown acts. Other performers at those shows included Jay and the Americans, the Shangri-Las, the Ronettes, and an up-and-coming young singer from London named Dusty Springfield. Having just released her debut album, she would go on to become one of the most successful "blue-eyed" soul singers from either side of the Atlantic.

Backstage at the Fox, there were whispers that Dusty was in a relationship with another woman from England. I don't think the gossip was meant to be malicious; it was just something that others wondered about. The fact that Dusty's girlfriend was also black brought additional intrigue. I found Dusty to be rather sweet, albeit a little eccentric. During one show, she sent me on an errand to buy some dishes. It seemed a rather odd request, but she insisted that I bring her a box of dishes. So I made the short trip to Fulton Street near Flatbush Avenue, at what is today known as the Fulton Street Mall. A number of stores were selling dishes on the street, and I found a large box that contained plates, saucers, cups, and bowls. I figured this would work, and I paid the eight or nine dollars for them and hustled back to Dusty's dressing room.

She thanked me, and I headed upstairs to hang out with the Imperials in their dressing room. Suddenly, we heard a loud crash. All the dressing rooms emptied, and I ran downstairs with the Imperials to see what was going on. There was Dusty, throwing the dishes I had just bought for her across her dressing room and against the wall. Someone yelled, "What the hell's the matter with you?" Dusty, as calm as could be, said, "This is how I release tension. You should try it. It really works."

Before you knew it, other artists started throwing dishes against the wall as well. Even I threw a couple. Now everyone, including Dusty, was laughing and having a good time. It was great fun. Apparently, Dusty had been having problems with her girlfriend, which is what led to the dish toss. It turned out, as her career progressed, she would become well known for these kinds of outbursts.

Her time at the Brooklyn Fox not only helped introduce her to American audiences but enabled her to further expose some of the Motown artists to music fans back in the UK. In March 1965, she hosted a special edition of the *Ready Steady Go!* television show in London. Billed as "The Sound of Motown," the show featured the Temptations, the Supremes, Stevie Wonder, Martha and the Vandellas, and Motown's celebrated studio house band, the Funk Brothers. Dusty covered a number of Motown standards herself, including "Nowhere to Run," which she famously performed live on the BBC. I know that she struggled and suffered a lot over the years, but I thoroughly enjoyed the short time I spent around her. She was an interesting person and an extraordinary talent.

Among the other things I remember about those September 1964 shows at the Fox revolved around Little Anthony and the Imperials and Motown's female artists. Little Anthony and the Imperials had quite the reputation as ladies' men. Uncle Clarence, for instance, was dating Barbara Lee of the Chiffons, Micki Harris of the Shirelles, and Betty Kelly of the Vandellas all at the same time. Clarence and Barbara had a baby girl together, my cousin Danielle.

All the Imperials were like that. They were players, plain and simple. Several of the female acts that played the Fox would spend time in their dressing room. This was one of

the reasons I always wanted to hang around with them—
although it wasn't the only reason, of course. They were so
cool to me. They were always laughing, talking shit about
this or that. And if they weren't talking about girls, it was
because there were plenty of them in the dressing room
already. I was eager to learn as much as I could, about not
only rock and roll but also the lifestyle that went with it.

Since the entire Motown Revue was in Brooklyn for
these shows, the label's founder and president, Berry Gordy,
accompanied them on the trip. He was well aware of the
Imperials' reputation, and he made sure his female artists
knew to steer clear of them. Clarence mentioned to me that
this was especially true for Diana Ross. It was clear that
Gordy spent most of his time hovering over her, not allow-
ing her to do much of anything except perform and stay in
the Supremes' dressing room.

One day, in between shows, Diana was able to give Gordy
the slip and made her way into the Imperials' dressing room.
I was not there at the time, but Clarence told me they were
all shooting the breeze with a number of other acts when
Gordy stormed in and escorted Diana out of the dressing
room without saying a word. Clarence said that everybody
felt sorry for her. Although the Supremes had been around
a few years, their first big hit, "Where Did Our Love Go?"
had reached number one only a few weeks earlier. I think
some of the other artists wondered how long Diana would
take this kind of treatment from Gordy. As fate would have
it, the Supremes went on to become one of the most successful groups of all time and Diana Ross one of the most
influential singers ever.

As the September 1964 shows came to an end, I was disappointed to learn that Little Anthony and the Imperials would

not be taking part in Murray the K's upcoming Christmas shows. I always assumed that there would be more shows to follow. Music was becoming so central to my life, and I wanted to continually be a part of it someway, somehow.

Sometime in 1963 I joined the Blue Jackets Guard Drum and Bugle Corps, which was essentially a music and civic pride club for preteen and teenage boys based in the Sunset Park neighborhood of Brooklyn. There was also a girls' division known as the Waves, of which my sister was a member. The Blue Jackets performed at various community-based events, parades, and other gatherings. I got good at my instrument pretty quickly, and I was named Bugle Leader. A lot of the dudes around the neighborhood would stare at me when I was in my Blue Jackets uniform. It may not have looked cool to some, but I didn't care. It was cool to me. I was doing something that involved music, and I truly enjoyed it. Plus, I was able to play one of my father's bugles that I had found in his closet as a little boy, and that meant a lot to me.

I also continued to process everything I was learning from Teddy, particularly in terms of song structure, melodies, and lyric writing. I decided to pick up a guitar and teach myself to play. Before long, I was attempting to write songs in earnest. I quickly realized that songwriting could be a painful and arduous process. There was a great deal of starting and stopping. Still, I felt that Teddy had given me some key tools to forge through the process. More importantly, I was full of inspiration and determined to make music my vocation. The first song I completed was called "My Mind Is Open." I couldn't wait for Teddy to hear it.

When I gave the song to Teddy, I was so nervous, wondering what he would think of it. When he gave it back to me, it looked like someone had bled all over the paper. That was my introduction to the red-line process. I was initially devastated, but Teddy had a way of explaining things that was constructive, not critical. And the song did need a lot of work. Despite my initial embarrassment and fear that I hadn't measured up to his standards, Teddy was a guiding force. He helped me to see the changes I needed to make while instilling confidence in me. I began to rewrite the song and told him I'd have another version for him soon.

In the meantime, Teddy asked that I sit in on a recording session for the Little Anthony and the Imperials' song "Take Me Back." The song included an elaborate orchestral part, and what I didn't know when I arrived at the famous Bell Sound Studios on West Fifty-Fourth Street was that Teddy had a surprise for me.

The session lingered well into the early morning hours, and I was having a great time, soaking it all in. As it neared the time to record the orchestral part, out of the blue, Teddy says, "Pepé, you're conducting the orchestra." I couldn't believe my ears. I was like, *What did he say?* Before I knew it, baton in hand, I was conducting the full orchestra.

Part of me was so thankful that Teddy believed in me enough to pull this off. The other part of me was some strange jumble of euphoria and fear. It was four in the morning, and here I was in midtown Manhattan on one of New York City's most famous streets and at one of the most celebrated studios of the day. I was only sixteen, contributing to the recording of a track that Teddy Randazzo had written and produced for Little Anthony and the Imperials. As I put my heart, mind, and soul into conducting, I thought, *It doesn't get any better than this!*

"Take Me Back" was released later in 1965, and it spent

eleven weeks on the Billboard chart, peaking at number six-teen. It also reached number fifteen on the US R&B chart. That I had been a part of that recording, however small, meant the world to me. I felt as though I was in the process of becoming a professional musician. If the experience at Bell Sound hadn't fully cemented that feeling, another big break soon would.

I continued to work on "My Mind Is Open." After every rewrite, I shared it with Teddy, who continued to push me to make it better. When it was finally ready, Teddy shared it with Uncle Clarence and Little Anthony. They liked it and decided they would produce it. They chose Phillip James and Lloyd Campbell, who comprised the Jamaican singing duo the Blues Busters, to record my song. Formed in 1960, the Blues Busters had gained serious recognition when they were tapped to support Sam Cooke on his Jamaican tour in 1961. The Blues Busters released their debut album in 1964, and they performed at the New York World's Fair that same year.

"My Mind Is Open" was never released as a single, and I don't know if it ever appeared on an album. But I didn't care. I had written my first song, which was produced and recorded by professional artists. The entire experience was thrilling. I was starting to live my rock and roll dream.

It was difficult to contain my excitement when Clarence told me that Little Anthony and the Imperials would once again be playing the Brooklyn Fox during Murray the K's April 1965 Easter Showcase. Slated for nine days and nights, the Easter shows would once again be loaded with Motown's top acts, this time including the Four Tops but minus the Supremes. The Righteous Brothers, the Del-Satins, Gerry and the Pacemakers, and Cannibal & the Headhunters, one of the earliest Mexican American rock bands, helped to fill out the lineup.

Little Anthony and the Imperials were still riding high from their two-year run of success. In addition to "Take Me Back," the Imperials' partnership with Teddy spawned two additional hits in 1965: "I Miss You So" and a cover of the 1954 Roy Hamilton classic "Hurt," produced by Teddy Randazzo for Don Costa Productions. The group also made their debut on *The Ed Sullivan Show* on March 28, 1965, where they performed their top ten hit "Hurt So Bad."

During the Easter shows, the Imperials developed a friendly rivalry with the Four Tops, who were making their first appearance at the Brooklyn Fox. With two Top 40 hits under their belts, the Four Tops' first number-one single, "I Can't Help Myself (Sugar Pie Honey Bunch)," was released while the Fox shows were going on. I got to know the guys from the Four Tops pretty quickly, as the Imperials would send me to their dressing room before each show. My mission was to find out what the Four Tops were wearing for their next set so that the Imperials could make sure not to clash with their outfits. I might show up and say something like, "Hey fellas, what are y'all wearing tonight?" They might say that they were wearing their blacks, and I'd say thanks and head back to the Imperials' dressing room with the information. When I relayed the message, Sammy Strain would jump up and say, "All right then. We are gonna kill 'em in the whites." As the new kids on the block, the Four Tops handled the competition well, and it always remained friendly.

I often think about this when looking back at those days at the Fox: everyone seemed to get along really well, even as the lineups changed for each run of shows. A lot of the younger acts, who were hoping to get their break, knew what was at stake when they took the stage. Yet from my vantage point, nobody ever tried to undercut or besmirch another act. They were supportive, made an effort to watch each other onstage, and frequently praised one another's performances. These artists, many of whom were already stars or on the verge of stardom, showed me what it meant to be a professional. It was a really cool vibe backstage at the Fox.

After the Easter 1965 showcase, word went around that Murray the K was producing a television special for CBS titled *It's What's Happening, Baby*. The show, which was to air at the end of June, would feature performances recorded a few days earlier at the Brooklyn Fox. The lineup for the program was extraordinary and consisted of nearly twenty acts. In addition to the entire Motown Revue, the concert showcased such performers as Jan and Dean, Tom Jones, the Dave Clark Five, Gary Lewis & the Playboys, the Ronettes, the Drifters, the Righteous Brothers, comedian Bill Cosby, Ray Charles, and, of course, Little Anthony and the Imperials.

I was rather anxious for the show, not only because it was a quicker turnaround than normal, but because I would be able to observe an actual television production being recorded. In the meantime, I was having other experiences that kept my attention. I got to know some of the girls that were dating or hanging out with members of Little Anthony and the Imperials. In addition to Cheryl, who was dating Uncle Clarence, I became close to Beverly, Marvy, and Boo Boo. When Little Anthony and the Imperials were out of town on tour, which was frequently, the girls invited me to spend time with them. They all were around twenty-two or twenty-three years old, while I was still only sixteen. That didn't seem to matter to them, and they introduced me to an entirely new world that I'd only heard about: drugs. They had a little bit of everything. There was cocaine, weed, uppers, downers, all kinds of pills, even cough syrup with codeine. I think I tried just about all of it and began to use drugs pretty much every weekend.

These women also taught me just about everything there was to know about sex, at least in my teenage mind. At first, it was hard to believe. Here I was, still shy of my seventeenth birthday, spending time with these beautiful older women, getting high and having the time of my life. I was experiencing another side of the rock and roll lifestyle, one that so many artists fall victim to. I couldn't get enough of it.

Back at home, I knew my Grandpa and Grandma Willie began to sense that I was getting a little wild. I doubt they knew quite how wild, but they were concerned. They never had been the party types and didn't understand that world at all. Grandpa and Grandma Willie weren't just old school; they were old, old school. They went to church every Sunday. They believed in hard work, saving money, and the pursuit of a useful vocation in life. It was extremely important to them that I finished school, and they pushed me hard. Although there were times that I wanted to quit school, I knew I couldn't disappoint them. It meant too much to them, and they meant too much to me.

I was expected to keep up with my chores, and I made sure I did everything they asked of me. Beyond that, I was not home very often, particularly on the weekends. That time was reserved for Cheryl, Beverly, Marvy, and Boo Boo. If they were not available, I found other friends to spend time with. Although I chose to go out rather than stay home, I hope that my grandparents knew how much I loved them.

When June came around, I started to think more about the upcoming Murray the K show that was to be broadcast on national television. Several acts on the bill I had never seen before. No doubt the biggest name was Ray Charles. He had to be one of the biggest stars ever to grace the stage at a Murray the K show. By that time, Ray Charles was nearly two decades into his career and had already accomplished so much. He played jazz, gospel, classical, soul, blues, big band, rock and roll, and even country and western music.

Before the show, I was told that Ray needed me to go to the store for him. I knocked on his dressing room door to find out what he needed. Another guy answered the door, and it was pitch black inside the dressing room. I thought to myself, *Where's Ray?* The guy told me what I needed to get and quickly shut the door. As I walked away, I wondered if Ray was inside shooting heroin. He had already been arrested for heroin possession several times. A few months later, Ray Charles entered a rehab facility in Los Angeles in order to get off heroin. Within a year, he was making his comeback and was releasing Top 40 hits to round out the 1960s. That said, I will never forget the haunting feeling when I knocked on his door and realized what he must have been doing there in the dark.

A more pleasant memory from that show was my experience with Patti LaBelle. As the leader of the Bluebelles, which featured Nona Hendryx, Cindy Birdsong, and Sarah Dash—all of whom would become stars in their own right—Patti had the reputation of being a diva. However, I found her to be extremely kind, generous, and respectful. I was always happy to go to the store for her and get her whatever she needed. The Bluebelles had recorded a couple of modest hits to this point, but the group really developed their reputation through several memorable shows at Harlem's Apollo Theater, which garnered them the nickname "The Sweethearts of the Apollo." They were even selected to open for the Rolling Stones on the American leg of the Stones' 1965 tour. Patti and the Bluebelles certainly didn't disappoint during their performance at the Brooklyn Fox, but what I remember most was their singing backstage.

In her dressing room, Patti would start to sing a gospel song. The Bluebelles would then start in, and before you knew it, other groups would come out of their dressing rooms and join in. It was chilling to see Patti and her girls, along with David Ruffin, Eddie Kendricks, and Melvin Franklin of the Temptations, the Four Tops, Martha Reeves, Marvin Gaye, Little Anthony and the Imperials, and others sing in perfect harmony up and down the backstage hallways of the Brooklyn Fox. They would sing song after song, all gospel, as if they had been harmonizing together their whole lives.

That was something that initially caught me off guard. These artists, who came from different parts of the country, all knew the same songs, word for word and note for note. It didn't make sense to me. After all, my Grandma Willie used to drag me to church all the time, and I didn't know any of these songs. I must not have been paying attention, or perhaps my grandmother's church was different from other churches. What I didn't understand at the time was how these songs spoke to the power of the black church and its role in the struggle of black people in America. From that moment, I would come to better understand the history, purpose, and force of black American music dating all the way back to the beginnings of slavery.

Seeing and hearing all those extraordinary talents sing together seem like fleeting moments now. But wow, was it ever powerful. It was like a gift. And for that reason, Patti, and everyone else who was there, will always have a special place in my heart.

The June 1965 show, like all Murray the K's shows at the Brooklyn Fox, was a great success. The question now was, how would it come off when televised to a national audience? Murray the K's *It's What's Happening, Baby* aired on CBS on June 28, 1965. I don't know if it was a ratings hit or not, but it had to have been, considering how popular the Brooklyn Fox shows were with the kids of New York City. Those shows always had kids lined up around the block. I am sure that teenagers and preteens throughout the rest of the country were excited to see it for themselves, even if it was only in their living rooms.

Another thing I recall about the television broadcast was that it was produced with the support of the US Office of Economic Opportunity. Established in 1964 as part of President Lyndon Johnson's War on Poverty, the Office of Economic Opportunity implemented several service programs and initiatives, many of which targeted youth. As part of the production arrangement, Murray the K delivered public service announcements encouraging young people across America to pursue employment, educational, and career opportunities. I certainly appreciated the message promoting job training, post-secondary education, and other avenues for youth, but I had found my calling, and my school was the Brooklyn Fox Theatre.

6

NOW WHAT?

I TURNED SEVENTEEN in July 1965 and had one year at George Westinghouse High School in front of me before I could start working for Little Anthony and the Imperials full time, and maybe even travel with them on the road. The group's partnership with Teddy Randazzo yielded three more charting singles in 1966, now released under the Veep label, after Don Costa Productions was purchased by United Artists.

The Imperials also had another appearance at the Brooklyn Fox, for Murray the K's Easter Showcase of 1966. Those shows featured a smaller lineup than previous showcases and included several acts that had not appeared at the Fox before. To my delight, Patti LaBelle and the Bluebelles were back, as were Jay and the Americans. Some of the newer acts included Joe Tex, Mitch Ryder & the Detroit Wheels, the Gentrys, and the Royalettes. Although the shows were memorable, I could sense that the vibe was different. Perhaps everyone subconsciously knew that, just as the Brooklyn Paramount had a few years before, the Fox was destined to close.

In December, the Brooklyn Fox hosted its final rock and roll shows, and the following spring, Murray the K staged his final ever showcase, which was held at RKO Proctor's 58th Street Theatre in midtown Manhattan. The Brooklyn Fox, which was purchased by the Grand Opera Company, soon closed and eventually was demolished in 1970. It was the end of an era.

When I received my diploma from George Westinghouse High School in June 1966—much to my grandparents' delight, and to a lesser degree my own—I was officially a high school graduate. The only question was, *Now what?* There was no debating that I would continue to hone my skills as a songwriter and a musician while still working for Little Anthony and the Imperials at every opportunity. I wasn't sure where it all might lead, but there was no other direction I wanted to go in. This was kind of it for me; rock and roll or bust.

I knew that I would have to step carefully to avoid some of the pitfalls I'd encountered in my youth. And being just a month away from turning eighteen, I couldn't stop thinking about an even more ominous prospect that lay before me: the Vietnam War. I didn't necessarily hold any ill will toward the US military. After all, my Grandpa Willie served in the army during World War I and my father was a World War II veteran. Although I sometimes wondered how my father's experience in the military may have affected his personality and his view of the world, I think most soldiers had a good idea of what they were fighting for in those earlier wars. I don't know that war is ever a good thing, but the stakes were high back then, and many believed that the fate of the world was in doubt.

For most of the kids I grew up with, the war in Vietnam was different. Far too many young men were dying over there, and for what none of us really knew. Plenty of brothers from Brooklyn were being killed in Vietnam, including several who were close to our family. The war was killing more young American men—regardless of race or ethnic background—than gangs, drugs, or the police. And many who weren't killed in action came back messed up in one way or another. For those of us watching from afar, it seemed like a nightmare with no end in sight.

Despite that constant fear hanging over me, I needed to find a full-time job. I decided not to go on the road with Little Anthony and the Imperials, although I did work for them whenever they had a gig in town. Instead, I found a job selling magazines for a publishing company in New York. I sold fashion magazines to models working in Manhattan. I thought it might be glamorous at first, but it wasn't. I would walk into modeling agencies in lower and midtown Manhattan, scoping out models to make my pitch. I always gave them a couple of sample magazines and tried to convince them to subscribe. It didn't take long for me to realize this job wasn't a good fit. Although I got to spend time around a lot of pretty and sophisticated women, I hated the job. I just wasn't much of a salesman, and I began to look for something else.

In the fall of 1966, I responded to an advertisement for seasonal work, and within a few days I had a new job. Amusingly enough, I was going to work for Uncle Sam— as an employee of the US Post Office, however, not for the US Army. I worked at the Morgan Station in the Chelsea neighborhood of Manhattan. It was a stone's throw from Madison Square Garden and Penn Station. I can recall the excitement of being in the middle of the action, so to speak. But it was hard work. My temporary employment status soon turned into a full-time job, and after passing my postal clerk exam, I was promoted to the position of clerk carrier. I was pleased with the job and thought that it was something I could do for a while as I nurtured my songwriting career. I was still living with my grandparents, which allowed me to save up some money to get my own place.

What I was not prepared for were the events of March 12, 1967. Driving his truck home from work, my Grandpa Willie was less than a block from the house when he suffered a heart attack and crashed the truck into a signpost right on St. Mark's Place. He was gone.

At the funeral, the reverend started to talk about my grandpa's family. He mentioned his three children, which were my uncle Edmund, my aunt Sarah, and of course, my father Linster Willie. The instant the reverend mentioned my father's name, I broke down in tears. I was inconsolable, and eventually I passed out. They had to give me smelling salts to bring me to.

At age fourteen, while attending my own father's funeral, I had not shed a single tear. Less than four years later, when we buried my grandpa, the mere mention of my father's name brought me to my knees. I guess I had not reconciled my deep love for my father with the regular abuse he subjected me to throughout my childhood. Even though I knew it was wrong for him to beat me like he did, I never doubted that he loved me. My grandpa's funeral was the first time I admitted to myself how much I missed my father.

My aspirations toward music continued to be my saving grace. I put a lot of time into writing songs and playing the guitar. I wrote and wrote, and before long I had a pretty nice collection of completed songs. I was anxious to use them and waited patiently for the opportunity to arise.

In June, Little Anthony and the Imperials performed for

two nights at the Boulevard in Queens. The shows were stellar, and as always, I welcomed the chance to work for the group. It was also nice to be in an atmosphere, if only for a few days, where people had come together in harmony to enjoy great music and one another's company. However, outside of the occasional musical escape like the Boulevard shows, the rest of America, from coast to coast, felt like it was about to erupt.

In addition to a growing antiwar movement that polarized much of America, a radical shift had taken place in the black community, as more and more people were moving away from the philosophy of nonviolence, which had been a focus for much of the civil rights movement up until then, and began embracing the principles of Black Power. In addition, beginning in the summer of 1967, riots erupted in many urban communities throughout the nation, from Newark to Detroit, Boston to Atlanta, Tampa to Minneapolis. Police brutality and violence against black folks sparked many of the uprisings, but it was the tragedy of April 4, 1968, that pushed many over the edge. That evening, Dr. Martin Luther King Jr. was assassinated in Memphis. Violence broke out in cities all over the country, some of the worst of which occurred in Chicago, Baltimore, Kansas City, and Detroit and on the streets of Harlem and Brooklyn.

Just two months and two days later, Robert F. Kennedy was assassinated in Los Angeles after winning the California Democratic presidential primary. In August, protests outside the Democratic National Convention and the brutal response by the Chicago police were broadcast on national television and further elevated the national tension. And through it all, the continuing death and destruction taking place halfway across the globe in Vietnam was resonating through American homes on a nightly basis. From where I was sitting, it seemed like America had become completely unhinged.

Through it all, I tried to stay focused on my own future and what it might hold. By early 1969 I began to feel that my time at the post office had run its course. One day, by chance, I heard about some job openings at the New York Telephone Company. I went ahead and applied. It wasn't long before I was hired and entered a training program to become a cable splicer. During the several days of training, I realized that there were a number of things I would like about the job, even though it could be rather tedious and sometimes quite dangerous. The thing that I most looked forward to was the freedom it would allow me. Typically, I wouldn't even have to go to the office but rather could head directly to the work site. I would get the chance to work in many different parts of the city, and I would be able to work outside, even if some of that time was spent under the New York City streets. And of course, being outside so much made it easy to watch and talk to all the girls as they walked by.

Once my training was complete and I began working as an official telephone cable splicer, I met someone who would become a lifelong friend. Ike Paige hailed from Birmingham, Alabama, but his desire to get into the music business enticed him to New York. He was part of my team at the telephone company, and we spent just about every day together splicing cable. We worked all over the city. We might spend three or four months at a site uptown. After that, it was three or four months in midtown. From there, we might move to Greenwich Village, then the Lower East Side, and on to any number of other locales. The frequent change in scenery was always welcome, as the work itself could be monotonous. I really enjoyed the job, though, and working with Ike. We were kindred spirits and had a strong chemistry. When we weren't working, we spent much of our free time together writing songs.

At the time I was feeling like I had been away too long from the music scene I'd so thoroughly enjoyed at the Brooklyn Fox and other venues. Fortunately, in the summer of 1969, I was asked to accompany Little Anthony and the Imperials on a trip to Puerto Rico, and I was able to get time off from work. The band's stint at San Juan's famous Flamboyan Hotel drew raves from critics and audiences alike. And although it demanded a great deal of hard work and attention to detail, I was thrilled to be back in the fold.

As much fun as Puerto Rico was, it couldn't compare to what came next for me and for Little Anthony and the Imperials. The group was booked for a two-week stand at the legendary New York nightclub the Copacabana, located on East Sixtieth Street between Fifth and Madison Avenues. Long before its fame spread to a wide audience with the 1978 Barry Manilow hit song of the same name, the Copacabana was a hallowed venue for musicians. Among the musical icons who had graced the stage there were Harry Belafonte, Lena Horne, Frank Sinatra, Nat King Cole, Dean Martin, Perry Como, Sam Cooke, Jackie Wilson, Tony Bennett, the Supremes, Martha and the Vandellas, the Temptations, and Marvin Gaye. In 1964, Sammy Davis Jr. performed a historic run of shows, which is what the members of Little Anthony and the Imperials were striving for.

During their two-week run, which began on July 24, 1969, the Imperials performed two shows nightly, at 8:00 PM and midnight, from Sunday through Friday. On Saturday nights, they did three shows, at 8:00 PM, 11:00 PM, and 2:00 AM. It was clear from the first notes played on opening night that this thirty-show stand would be something special.

In his review of opening night for *Billboard Magazine*, noted critic Radcliffe Joe wrote:

> Not many artists, especially on opening night, are blessed with the dynamism needed to "turn on" the usually staid, blasé audience which frequents the Copacabana. Yet, Little Anthony and the Imperials not only achieved this at their debut performance and after only the first couple numbers but went on to receive a standing ovation at the end of the show.
>
> The group, fresh from a successful stint at the Flamboyan Hotel in San Juan, Puerto Rico, swept away speculation that they may be losing touch with today's musical trends, and established themselves unquestionably with the leading entertainers of the day.
>
> Dishing out an exciting bill of fare, which ranged from rock to pop to ballads, the group sang, danced, cavorted, and clowned its way through a tightly woven program which reached breathtaking crescendo with "Let the Sun Shine In" from the Broadway production of "Hair."

That particular arrangement of "Let the Sun Shine In," which Little Anthony and the Imperials had been performing for some time, served as an inspiration to the 5th Dimension, who were good friends of the group. The 5th Dimension recorded and released as a single the two-song medley from the musical *Hair* titled "Aquarius/Let the Sun Shine In (The Flesh Failures)." Their single not only earned platinum status but sat at number one on the Billboard charts for six weeks in April and May of 1969.

I certainly worked hard during the Imperials' stand at

the Copa, but I had just turned twenty-one and was finally able to legally partake in the party side of things as well. At the time, Don Taylor was managing the Imperials. Don later went on to manage Bob Marley as well as Diana Ross, Martha Reeves, and for a short time, Prince.

As long as I was taking care of my end on the business side, Don was fine with me enjoying myself as well. I know Clarence and the other guys in the group were cool about it too. I had been with them now for more than eight years, and I believe they enjoyed having me around and were happy to see me living it up.

Among my roles at the Copa was to escort celebrities and VIPs up the private elevator and to their seats. Not only did I get to be a guide for the likes of Ike and Tina Turner, New York congressman Adam Clayton Powell Jr., and a host of others, I was able to hang out and drink champagne with them after the shows. It was amazing. I began to feel like a celebrity myself. I couldn't imagine anything that could top this experience.

One night after one of the shows, Clarence invited me to a nightclub nearby. I don't remember the name of the place, but it was close enough to walk. It was in an older building, and as we got on the dingy, old-fashioned elevator, I wasn't sure that this was the place to be. When the elevator opened on the fourth floor, however, we walked into one of the coolest rooms I've ever seen. This club was fabulous. There were aquariums, multiple bars, funky lights and artwork, cocktail waitresses everywhere, great music, and a groovy vibe.

As we sat down at a table, I noticed some dude with psychedelic clothes hanging out in the corner of the club. I did a double take and realized, *Oh, shit! That dude over there is Jimi Hendrix!* I grabbed Clarence by the arm and said, "That's Jimi Hendrix!" Clarence said, "Where?" He started to scan the room and I yelped, "Don't look."

Incredulous, Clarence looked at me, smiled, and then mocked me by asking with a laugh, "Don't look?" Then Clarence shouted across the room, "Yo, Jimi!" Hendrix looked over and responded with a boisterous, "Hey, Clarence, my man! What's happening?"

Clarence got up from the table and made his way over to Jimi. They embraced and started to chat. I was just sitting at the table, stunned and amazed that Clarence knew Jimi Hendrix. I couldn't believe what I was looking at. Then the two of them came over to the table, and Clarence introduced me. "Jimi," he said, "this is my nephew Pepé." The next thing I knew I was shaking hands with Jimi Hendrix, one of my musical heroes.

I can't recall a single thing I said or if any of it was at all coherent. I do remember how massive Jimi's hands were. Not that I thought about it much before, but my hands are a pretty decent size. However, they simply disappeared in his.

As Jimi and Clarence continued to catch up, I sat there starstruck. That cosmic aura and vibe people always associated with the man seemed very real to me. You could tell he was a good guy, too, a genuine cat so to speak. To this day, it is difficult for me to believe that Jimi would be gone just over a year later.

Suddenly, while talking to Clarence, Jimi noticed a beautiful girl not far from our table. He politely excused himself, said goodbye, and moved in her direction. He whispered something in her ear, and the next thing you knew, they disappeared together. I thought to myself, *That is one badass motherfucker.*

It was going to take me awhile to come down from the high of meeting Jimi Hendrix. I simply couldn't believe my good fortune. And yet there would be another encounter during the Imperials' run at the Copa that proved to be one of the most pivotal moments, if not the most pivotal moment, in my life. I was about to meet someone who would change the course of my life forever, even if it would be years before I recognized their importance and their role in shaping my destiny.

7

SHAUNTEL

NEAR THE END of the Imperials' two-week stint at the Copa, I was getting everything together in the dressing room before a show. Just as I was hanging up Sammy Strain's uniform, he walked in and asked me, "Who is the girl in the waiting room with the green eyes?"

To this day, I am not sure what possessed me to do so, but I declared, "That's my girl!" A little surprised, Sammy said, "Okay, youngblood. That's cool. I was just asking." I think he added a "not too bad" to indicate his admiration for my taste in women.

Truth be told, I had no idea who Sammy was talking about. I just knew I had to find out. So I casually made my way to the waiting room, where I noticed her right away. Sammy was right. She was gorgeous. And those green eyes. I was immediately smitten.

I made my way over to her, and our eyes met. I walked up and said, "Hi. My name is Pepé." She smiled and said, "I'm Shauntel." I asked who she was there with, and she replied, "I'm here with my aunt Kahlua." Excited, I said, "I know Kahlua. She goes with my uncle Clarence."

Her friendly disposition and smile definitely helped to bolster my confidence, and I asked, "So, Shauntel, would you like to go out tonight? Do you have a curfew or anything like that?" She told me she did not have a curfew and would definitely like to spend the evening in my company.

That first night we talked mostly about her. She mentioned that she was visiting from Minneapolis, where she was born and raised. She talked a little bit about her family, including her mom Edna Mae, her mom's twin sister Mattie, as well as her siblings and her cousins. I didn't know much about Minneapolis, other than it was cold. Don't get me wrong, New York can get cold too, but Minneapolis? I couldn't see myself living there.

It didn't take long before we were joined at the hip. If someone was looking for me, there was a 99 percent chance they would find Shauntel. We were in love, and we spent nearly every second together. Although she was supposed to be staying with Kahlua, she was usually at my apartment. I had my own place in the Bronx at the time and was actually the superintendent of the building. I still had my gig at the telephone company and was moonlighting with the Imperials every chance I got. Being the building super gave me a little more cash in my pocket. The extra money allowed me to show Shauntel a good time as I guided her around the sights and sounds of the city.

This was a great time in my life. For once, everything seemed to be working. With Shauntel by my side, I was extremely happy. I had a good job. My songwriting partnership with Ike continued to grow, and we started talking about forming a band together.

It was also shaping up to be a big year for Little Anthony and the Imperials. In addition to touring the nation and playing many gigs in the local New York area, the band was preparing for another appearance on *The Ed Sullivan Show*, on January 25, 1970. It had been almost five years since they performed their top ten single "Hurt So Bad" at what was then known as Studio 50. Renamed the Ed Sullivan Theater in 1967, the studio was one of the grandest stages in all of entertainment. In addition to hosting *The Ed Sullivan Show*, it was home at one time or another to *The Jackie Gleason Show*, *The Merv Griffin Show*, and a litany of other variety and television game shows.

This return to *The Ed Sullivan Show* was a significant moment for the Imperials, particularly considering that the group would be able to perform a total of five songs, as opposed to just the one song in their 1965 debut. To prepare for the event, the group rented space at the Harlequin Rehearsal Studios on West Forty-Sixth Street, less than half a mile from the Ed Sullivan Theater.

Rehearsals were intense, and it felt like there was a lot at stake. The group had had a steady run of success since reuniting in 1963. In fact, they had charted at least one single on Billboard for seven years running, including what would be five consecutive charting releases in 1969 and 1970. They desperately wanted to maintain the momentum they had generated with Teddy Randazzo during the 1960s far into the next decade. They had become renowned for their live performances, and along with runs at the Copa and other famed venues, they wowed audiences on just about every major television show of the era: *The Merv Griffin Show*, *Shindig!*, Perry Como's *Kraft Music Hall*, *American Bandstand*, *Soul Train*, *Hullabaloo*, *Upbeat*, *The Midnight Special*, and *The Tonight Show*, among others.

Just a few years earlier, in 1967, Little Anthony and the Imperials had been afforded one of the more prestigious honors in popular music, as they were tapped to record the theme song to the upcoming James Bond film, *You Only Live Twice*. Although the song was recorded, mastered, and submitted to United Artists for the soundtrack, the influence of Frank Sinatra resulted in the producer opting to have Frank's daughter Nancy perform the song for the movie. Despite the slight, it was clear the group was on everyone's A-list.

One day during rehearsals in advance of the Sullivan show, I was asked to run an errand for the group. As soon as I got on the elevator at Harlequin Studios, I completely forgot what the errand was. To my shock, I found myself standing face to face with Muhammad Ali. By this point, I had met a number of famous people over the years, and I was starting to get used to the company of celebrities. Nonetheless, I had just recently been awed by meeting Jimi Hendrix, and now I was standing in an elevator with Muhammad Ali. I didn't know what to say other than, "Hi."

Fortunately, he was very friendly. We started talking, and he asked me what I did. I told him I was a songwriter, which was how I imagined myself regardless of my other vocations at the time. He smiled and said, "Man, that's great. I'm actually looking to record my own album. Would you write some songs for me?" With some surprise but no hesitation, I said, "Yes, I would be happy to." We got off the elevator, exchanged phone numbers, and parted ways. I was beside myself that the heavyweight champion of the world would ask for my help, writing songs for his album no less. For a split second, I wondered if he was just being polite, but the more I thought about it, I was sure he was serious.

This album wouldn't be Ali's first foray into the recording studio. In 1963, he released a spoken word album titled *I Am the Greatest*, which netted him a Grammy nomination. The next year, he covered Ben E. King's soul classic *Stand By Me*, and in 1976, Ali earned another Grammy nomination for a children's spoken word record.

Before I could pursue working with the Champ, though, I still had work to do as the Imperials finished up preparations for *The Ed Sullivan Show*. As always, their performance was exceptional. The set included four of their biggest hits—"Goin' Out of My Head," "Shimmy Shimmy Ko-Ko-Bop," "Hurt So Bad," and of course, "Tears on My Pillow"— as well as their latest single, "Don't Get Close." One of their last releases on the United Artists label, the song was composed by the Philadelphia-based songwriting duo of Jerry Akines and Johnnie Bellmon, who had penned hits for Wilson Pickett, Jimmy Ruffin, and Eddie Kendricks.

The mood in the dressing room after the show was triumphant. I was certain that the Imperials' next appearance on the show would come well before another five years passed. However, that next gig was not to be, as Ed Sullivan called it quits in the spring of 1971, and one of the most iconic and groundbreaking institutions in American popular culture exited the television landscape. (This would not be the final time Little Anthony and the Imperials graced the stage at the Ed Sullivan Theater, however, as they performed on the *Late Show with David Letterman* in the summer of 2008.)

After the appearance on *The Ed Sullivan Show*, I thought more about what my next move would be in pursuing my own career in music. I loved every moment that I worked for the Imperials. But I was approaching my twenty-third birthday and had been invited to write songs for Muhammad Ali. It could be the break I was looking for, and I was fully prepared to jump in with both feet. Then, as fate would have it, one of my longest-standing fears came to fruition.

Just before I was going to begin work on songs for Ali, I was thrown a wicked curveball. Uncle Sam finally caught up with me, and I was drafted into the US Army. I was given two weeks to report to basic training, and I used every bit of those two weeks to party my ass off. I can't say that it was the best use of my time, but I didn't know what else to do. I had dreaded this day for so long and for so many reasons.

Sure, I was scared. But more than that, I was angry. I was angry because it seemed to me that so many young black men were being sent halfway around the world to die for no good reason. I had witnessed the heartbreak and anguish of too many mothers who had lost their sons in Vietnam. Far too many families were never able to say goodbye to their loved ones. In my neighborhood, the prevailing attitude was, *Why do you want me to go and shoot the Viet Cong? I don't know them. They haven't done shit to me.* In fact, Muhammed Ali famously said, in 1966, "I ain't got no quarrel with them Viet Cong" when announcing his own refusal to be inducted into the army.

Around the time I was drafted, Shauntel and I were getting tighter, and I was considering our future. By no means was I ready for marriage, but I entertained thoughts of a successful career in music with her by my side. Now I had to break this terrible news to her. I told her, "Don't wait for me. Live your life because I might not ever come back." She tried to reassure me that I would be back and that everything would be okay. But after feeling like I was on the cusp of something special in pursuit of my musical dreams, I now feared it would be all for naught.

I arrived at basic training scared to death at what the future might hold. After basic, it was on to individual training, where my Military Occupational Specialty, or MOS, identified me as a member of the military police. When I finished MOS training, I was granted a thirty-day leave.

I went to see Shauntel in Chicago, where she was visiting relatives with her mother. I had learned when I was away at training that Shauntel had taken my advice and decided not to wait for me. In fact, she started dating my buddy Nat. I had developed a close friendship with Nat a few years earlier. At the time, Nat was who I got most of my drugs from. He was a good dude, and the two of us shared a birthday, although I believe he was a couple years older.

Their courtship didn't last very long, and I didn't hold it against either of them. Nat was my man. He always had my back. As for Shauntel, I just loved her and wanted to be with her. We had so much fun together in Chicago. Although I am New York City through and through, I recognized that Chicago had more than a few things going for it.

The thirty days went by way too fast, and before I knew it, I was on my way back to Fort Jackson, South Carolina, and the army. One thing that helped provide some level of tranquility during my time in the service was music. I took every free moment to think about, dream about, and write music. I remember writing one song in the army that I called "Paint the Clouds with Sunshine." There was no mystery there; the title speaks for itself. It was one of those songs that tried to make light of an otherwise difficult time in my life.

Fortunately, my stint in the army didn't last long. I received an honorable discharge on December 10, 1970, and was given ninety days before I had to report back to my job with the New York Telephone Company. I didn't think twice about where I would spend those three months. I headed straight to Minneapolis to reunite with Shauntel. I didn't even care that it was winter.

Minneapolis was so different from Brooklyn, so different from anything I was used to. But something about the city spoke to me. I decided that if this was Shauntel's home, I should at least give it some serious thought. After all, how bad could it be? Plus, I found a kindred spirit in Shauntel's father, Eddie. Eddie and I got along immediately. He was so cool to me. Eddie loved to play golf, and that eventually became another connection we shared. He taught me so many things about golf, wisdom I still use today. More important than the practical or strategic concepts he shared about the game, he spent an extraordinary amount of time helping me and others. Eddie would sit with you for hours while you hit bucket after bucket of golf balls, imparting his knowledge and encouragement the whole time. He was once featured in *African American Golfer's Digest* for his accomplishments at the Theodore Wirth Golf Course in Minneapolis, where he scored holes in one on two consecutive holes, the ninth and tenth holes in one of his career.

I met several other members of Shauntel's family as well, including her twelve-year-old cousin Prince. Prince and Shauntel's mothers were twins. Although their roots were primarily in Louisiana, Edna Mae and Mattie Dell were born and raised in north Minneapolis, the city's historic African American neighborhood.

I didn't pay Prince much attention at the time. To me, he was just a little kid. On the few occasions I saw him in those early years, there wasn't much to indicate what, if anything, he liked to do. He was a shy little cat who didn't say much. My clearest memory of him during that time was watching him wrestle with his cousin Chazz.

Regardless, nearly all my time and energy while in Minneapolis was directed toward Shauntel. And while I hated to leave, I had a job to get back to in New York. I wasn't sure when we would see each other again, but I knew it had to be soon. Shauntel and I discussed plans for her to come visit me in New York.

I returned to the city in February 1971, and it was nice to get back to my job at the telephone company. It was cool to work and hang out with Ike again too. I was happy to see all the people I'd missed while in the army. It had been a full year since I'd seen my Grandma Willie, my mother, my sisters, or any of my uncles, aunts, or cousins. My cousin Buddy and I started hanging out a lot, and I was thrilled to see my old friends.

After having lived in the Bronx for a year or so before I left, I moved back to Brooklyn. I rented a house at 431 Washington Avenue, which was just down the street from the Mohawk Hotel, where Little Anthony and the Imperials used to hang out after their shows at the Brooklyn Fox. The house was in the Clinton Hill neighborhood, which was bordered by Bed-Stuy to the east and not terribly far from where I went to junior high school before I moved to Park Slope to live with my grandparents. It was good to be back in Brooklyn, for sure.

I had been home a few months when I got word that my friend Angel was getting married. Angel had been one of my closest friends since high school, and I was extremely happy for him. Most important to me was that he seemed happy. I know I wasn't jealous in the worst sense of the word. Still, I was lonely, and I missed Shauntel. I wanted what I thought Angel had. So I decided to ask Shauntel to marry me.

Whether it was the right time or not, I couldn't imagine my life without this woman in it. I didn't even take the time to fly back to Minneapolis to ask her. I did it over the phone. I couldn't wait any longer. To my delight, she accepted my proposal and was on her way to Brooklyn right away.

We were married in a small church in Brooklyn. Her father and stepmother flew in, along with some other relatives from Minneapolis. It was a subdued yet elegant ceremony. My old friend Bubba was my best man. We held the reception at my grandma's house in Park Slope. Everyone seemed happy. I might have been a little scared, but I was pretty happy myself. I was crazy for Shauntel, and now she was my wife.

After the reception, we wanted to let loose and party. We headed out to one of the most legendary spots in all of New York City: Smalls Paradise in Harlem. Opened in 1925 by Ed Smalls, Smalls Paradise was the only major Harlem nightclub during the Harlem Renaissance that was both black-owned and racially integrated. Most Harlem clubs during that era were exclusive to white clientele. In 1955, the all-night club was bought by New York disc jockey Tommy Smalls (no relation). Also known as Dr. Jive, Smalls worked for the noted African American radio station WWRL. Beloved by Harlemites, he was recognized as the unofficial mayor of Harlem. Like Alan Freed and Murray the K, Smalls was an impresario who had a big influence on the early days of rock and roll in New York City. In the 1950s, he put on frequent rhythm and blues revues at the Apollo Theater and Rockland Palace. And like Freed, Smalls was later indicted in a payola scandal that effectively ended his radio career. Smalls finished out his life in music as an A&R man with Polydor Records.

By the time Shauntel and I got married, the club was known as Big Wilt's Smalls Paradise, having been owned by Wilt Chamberlain since the early 1960s. Regardless of the decade or the owner, Smalls was always a "place to be" in New York. It was renowned author and activist James Baldwin's favorite club in the city. Comedian Redd Foxx and musicians Ray Charles, Wes Montgomery, King Curtis, and Jimmy Smith all performed there. Baseball Hall of Famer Willie Mays was a regular during his playing days, and the club was a popular hangout for many NBA players. Nestled in the basement of a five-story building on Seventh Avenue, the room had a soul, and you could feel history seeping through the walls. It was more than a nightclub; it was an institution.

Today, the building where Smalls operated as a club for nearly sixty years is the Thurgood Marshall Academy for Learning and Social Change, situated between what are now Frederick Douglass Boulevard and Adam Clayton Jr. Boulevard. No disrespect to the Honorable Thurgood Marshall, but I'll always refer to the building as Smalls.

Married life started out well enough for Shauntel and me. I was still working at the New York Telephone Company, and she found a job as a secretary with a law firm in Manhattan. We would both take the subway from Brooklyn into the city, but because my work sites frequently changed, we weren't always on the same train.

One day on her way to work, Shauntel began to feel faint. It was morning rush hour, and the subway was packed full of people. Desperately needing air, she moved toward the door and at the next stop fought her way to the platform. It was too late, and she fainted right there in front of hundreds of commuters. Being New York, which for all its pluses has more than a few faults, no one bothered to help her. When she came to, she realized that she had knocked out several of her front teeth from the fall and suffered abrasions on her face and head. She was traumatized and unsure what to do.

When she finally got her wits about her, she found a pay phone and called my supervisor to find out where I was working that day. She got in a cab and headed in my direction. When she arrived at the jobsite, she was still out of sorts. I looked at her and my heart just dropped. My first thought was that someone did this to her and all I could think about was going after that person. She eventually explained what had happened. I felt so bad for her. I just wanted to hold her and make it all go away. I told Ike that I was taking her to the hospital and I would see him tomorrow.

Fortunately, her cuts and scrapes were minor, although she suffered a mild concussion. We were given a referral for a dentist to fix her teeth. Within a few days, Shauntel had a brand-new smile. There was no question that my wife was a strong woman, and she did not hesitate to return to work. Shauntel was also independent, and it was important to her to contribute to our household.

Everything seemed to be getting back to normal when I myself had an accident at work. I can't recall exactly how, but one day I injured my back while working underground. I had taken a lot of beatings in my life, whether from my father or brothers on the block, but I'm not sure I had ever felt this kind of pain. It was excruciating. Ike helped me back up to the street, and I was headed to the hospital myself. I must have wrenched my back pretty damn good, because the doctor suggested that I not return to work for a while. That sounded okay to me, considering the time I had already put in at the telephone company. After three days away from the job, my short-term disability kicked in and I started receiving full pay again.

Since I was in no hurry to return to work, I enrolled at New York City Community College. To my good fortune, the tuition was covered by the Veterans Administration. A number of my courses were taught at the NYU campus, and my swimming classes were held at Brooklyn Tech, which was not far from my home.

Although I had not enjoyed my time in high school much, I found college to be quite interesting. Still, I felt like something was missing. In addition to my passion for music, I was always interested in acting. So I joined the Bed Stuy Street Academy, which was essentially a consortium for aspiring actors. It immediately filled a void in me. I quickly became friends with a lot of the fellas in the group, as well as some of the ladies.

With college and the Street Academy, I found myself spending less time with Shauntel. Before, we had both worked normal nine-to-five schedules and generally spent the evenings together. Now I was attending classes in the evening or spending those hours honing my acting skills. After a while, it was putting some stress on our relationship. At the time, I never felt that I was neglecting her. I was just trying to make something of myself, make a better life for the both of us. I thought that was significant and didn't understand why she didn't see that. I wanted her to be proud of me.

When I reflect on it today, I imagine Shauntel was lonely and missing her family. Because of all my obligations, she spent a lot of nights alone at home. Eventually, the stress and bitterness between us escalated, and we spent most of our time together arguing. More often than not, those arguments were not about anything important. Whatever the subject of the disagreement may have been, it was just a pretext to bicker and express the resentments each of us was feeling. One night it reached a crescendo, and it ended with Shauntel putting her foot through one of my most prized possessions: my guitar.

It was the first guitar I ever owned. There wasn't anything exceptional about it, but it was mine and it meant a lot to me. Now it was no more. What infuriated me even more than the fact that she had destroyed something so important to me was the look she gave me as she did it. At the same time her foot was breaking through the nylon strings and splintering the natural wood body of my guitar into pieces, she had this smug glare on her face, as if to say, *Now what, motherfucker?!*

That was the thing about Shauntel. She could use her stunning green eyes to send the most loving gaze in your direction, or she could just as effectively send you a look that felt like she was stabbing you in the heart with a knife. It wasn't an evil or hateful look, but you couldn't help but anticipate her laughter as she twisted the knife further.

As I stood there looking at my guitar and then at her, a tremendous sense of calm came over me. I remained quiet, kept still, and tried to let this feeling of peace take over. I am so pleased that it did, otherwise I am not sure what I might have said or done. We exchanged glances, and without saying another word, we both knew we needed a break. We decided to separate, and Shauntel flew back to Minneapolis. Although I was saddened by this turn of events, I couldn't sulk over it. I didn't know what the future held for Shauntel and me. I did know, however, that I needed to forge ahead.

I was enjoying my time at the Bed Stuy Street Academy, and the college experience was also going well. After she had been gone awhile, I wondered if Shauntel was interested in reconciling. Personally, I wasn't ready to consider such a thing. That said, I didn't have any plans to replace her either, until I saw this girl on campus one day. She was so fine. As confident as I thought I had become around women, I have to admit, this one was intimidating. I told myself, *I have to get next to her*. I tried to find out as much about her as I could without her knowing.

When I first heard what her name was, I couldn't believe it. It was Lena Horne. And it was spelled the same way as the name of world-renowned and Bed-Stuy's own Lena Horne. They were not related. The famous Lena Horne was at least a decade into her career when the younger Lena Horne was born, so her parents surely knew what they were doing when they christened her with the same name.

As I continued to admire her from afar, I learned that we had a friend in common. Janeen, who was in school with us and lived just a few houses down from my grandparents' brownstone, knew Lena. I asked her to introduce me to Lena, and she agreed. Although I tried to play it cool, it was pretty clear to Janeen how enamored I was with this girl. She let out a little schoolgirl giggle when I approached her about the introduction. I think she thought it was cute.

Janeen arranged for us to meet in the cafeteria at Brooklyn Tech. From the very beginning, Lena was as easy to talk to as she was to look at. I told her I was a songwriter as well as an aspiring actor. I also talked about my days as a valet at the Brooklyn Fox and continuing work for Little Anthony and the Imperials. All of this seemed to pique her interest. Lena appeared to be rather taken with me, and we essentially began dating at the lunch table where we met. I had recently bought a sky blue Volkswagen Beetle, and although it was hardly a muscle car, it was hip. I would pick Lena up from school or home and we would cruise around town together.

Shauntel was still my wife, and she was never far from my mind, but I was so into Lena. She was so beautiful, so sweet, and so cool. I always liked to think I was cool, but with her, I felt I had upped my game substantially. We went to a lot of A-list parties together. This included parties with players from the New York Knicks, some of whom I had met before at Smalls Paradise. In the early 1970s, the Knicks were the talk of the city when it came to sports. They had won their first NBA championship in 1970 and were about to add a second in 1973. The team had more than its share of star power.

Aside from the fact that I was separated from Shauntel, these were good times for me. I was trying to make the most of every opportunity, whether it was social or career oriented. I was living it up, wondering what would come next.

8

THE EDUCATION OF PEPÉ WILLIE

BY THE SUMMER OF 1973, Shauntel and I had been apart for several months. Lena and I were still together, but I sensed that our relationship was fading too. In addition to song-writing, the Bed Stuy Street Academy kept my spirits up. There was no question that music was my principal passion, but this acting thing was wearing on me in the best possible way. I was good friends with the other students, and for the most part, we all looked out for one another. Although we were all hoping for our big break, it was not a competitive environment, and we would give each other tips during classes or rehearsals.

Toward the end of the year, I heard about auditions for a major motion picture from Paramount that was to be filmed right in the heart of Bed-Stuy. Titled *The Education of Sonny Carson*, the screenplay chronicled the life of Robert "Sonny" Carson and was based on his 1972 autobiography of the same name. *The Education of Sonny Carson* underscored what life was like for thousands of African American boys growing up in Bed-Stuy during the 1950s and 1960s.

One of the most provocative personalities ever to come out of Bed-Stuy, Carson spent his teenage years as a member of the notorious gang the Bishops and later served time in juvenile detention for armed robbery. After serving with the US Army's 82nd Airborne in the Korean War, Carson returned to Brooklyn and spent the remainder of his life as a community activist, including a stint as the director of the Brooklyn chapter of the Congress of Racial Equality, or CORE.

I had known Sonny, who was twelve years my senior, since I had moved back to Brooklyn almost three years before. He lived around the corner from my house on Washington Avenue and would sometimes hold court to some of the men in the neighborhood, including me. He would sit on his stoop and rap to us about the mistakes he had made in his life, all that he had learned, and what he believed needed to be done to improve the quality of life for black New Yorkers and oppressed people everywhere. Education was one of his big issues, in particular the substandard public school systems that served New York City. To me, he seemed like a good guy who had already gone through far too much for his age.

Sonny remained a polarizing figure well into the 1990s and was often at the center of controversy. He was even arrested during the filming of *The Education of Sonny Carson* and served fifteen months in New York's infamous Sing Sing prison. Respected and admired by many throughout Brooklyn and the other boroughs, he was otherwise unpopular in greater New York and viewed as a pariah in the press. Sonny passed away in 2002.

For me, I saw a lot of myself in Sonny, especially as a teenager. Sonny's coming-of-age story reflected many of the same overtones as my youth in Bed-Stuy. In many ways it seemed like we led parallel lives. More than anything, I wanted to avoid the mistakes he made, while learning from the ones I had already made myself. For better or worse, these are the things that made the movie project so appealing to me.

Of course, I also just wanted to act in something real. Whether it was a play, film, television show, or whatever, I wanted to be in front of a camera or onstage. Some of the guys at the academy pushed me to try out for the film, but I didn't need any extra encouragement. I willingly auditioned and was hired on the spot.

The producer on the film was Irwin Yablans, who later became known for the *Halloween* franchise and other horror films. Michael Campus, who had recently completed his second feature film, 1973's *The Mack* featuring Richard Pryor and Max Julien, was tapped to direct. I developed a rapport with both Yablans and Campus almost immediately, which helped reduce my nervousness. That wasn't the case for everyone, however, especially crew members who weren't comfortable filming in Bed-Stuy, where real-life gangs still ruled the streets. More than a handful of individuals quit during the filming, and the producers were constantly trying to fill wardrobe, production, art department, and other jobs on the set.

As a day player, I was able to spend the full eight weeks on the set at five hundred dollars per week. I never went back to work at the telephone company, and although it was temporary, I had never been paid as much as I was on the film set. I began to think that acting, in addition to music, might be at the forefront of my future plans.

Just as I had witnessed the professionalism and dedication of the top acts in the music business, I was now learning how to be a professional behind and in front of the movie camera. The film's cast included several prominent African

American character actors, including Paul Benjamin and Mary Alice, who were cast as Sonny Carson's parents. Rony Clanton, who became a close friend, was cast in the lead role. The real Sonny Carson spent quite a bit of time on set and advised not only Rony but many of the other young actors as well. Rony seemed to benefit from this tutelage and nailed the role. In fact, Rony's portrayal of Sonny Carson helped to launch a more than four-decade career in film and television.

My big scene was shot on the Staten Island Ferry as it rolled across New York Harbor. During the scene, which focuses on a romantic moment between Sonny and his girlfriend Virginia (played by Joyce Walker), I performed the song "Five Cent Ride to Freedom." I wrote the song, an original composition, specifically for the film. To me, it was a simple but elegant scene. I think I took direction from Campus very well. But this scene came so naturally to me. It was just me, my guitar, and my voice on the deck of the ferry, accompanied by the ambient sounds of the harbor and the distant noises of the city. I felt as though it was the most important thing I had ever done to that point. I was so proud of it.

Even as I started to feel like a professional, on my way to bigger and better things, I still couldn't escape the drama of my personal life. I became interested in another girl who was part of the film production, and Lena and I drifted apart. To complicate matters more, I still missed Shauntel. I called her and told her I was part of a movie that was filming in Brooklyn. She flew out to visit the next day. I got the impression she thought I was going to be some kind of movie star or something. Either way, it was good to see her.

Shauntel and the new girl I was seeing quickly sized one another up and down, and as to be expected, neither thought much of the other. Shauntel and I spent time hanging out, but we never really got back together during this period. On the other hand, the new girl, whose name I can't even remember, seemed increasingly interested in developing a serious relationship. Fortunately, I was able to keep this part of my life separate from my responsibilities on the film.

Shauntel stayed in New York for a while but went back to Minneapolis before the film premiere. Although it was clear we were still in love, it didn't feel like the right time to renew our romance. We wished each other well, and I wondered when I might see her again.

Meanwhile, my excitement for the premiere was immeasurable. I couldn't wait to see myself on the big screen. I wasn't sure what would ultimately come of it, but I felt like this could be a real start for me and my career aspirations.

The world premiere of *The Education of Sonny Carson* took place in July 1974 at the Paramount Theatre, which was located underneath the forty-four-story Gulf and Western Building near the southwest corner of Central Park. As I remember, it was a cool place to watch a movie.

Before the curtain even opened, I was buzzing with anticipation. As the film moved along toward the Staten Island Ferry scene, I had trouble sitting still. Then, at the point when I thought I would appear on-screen, I didn't. My performance of "Five Cent Ride to Freedom" had been replaced by a Leon Ware song. I wondered if perhaps they'd moved my scene to a later point in the movie. But I also noticed that I wasn't showing up in some of the smaller scenes I'd filmed either. Before long, the end credits were rolling, and it was clear I wasn't going to see my name scrolling up the screen.

My big scene, my lines, and every other moment that I was supposed to appear in the film died somewhere on the editing-room floor. I don't think I had any inkling this was even possible. Shocked doesn't begin to describe how I felt. I was devastated. I could barely get out of my seat. When I did, the first person I saw coming toward me was my friend B. T. from the Street Academy, who did appear in the film as the character "Crazy." He tried to console me. He talked how, when my scene didn't appear, you could feel the air being sucked out of the room, at least among those in the audience who were part of the production. I hadn't sensed any sort of change in the audience, but that's likely because I was caught up in my own sense of dread. I was so hurt. And after that, I could never listen to a Leon Ware song again.

Producer Irwin Yablans came over to make sure I was okay. He apologized profusely and noted that while he thought my performance of "Five Cent Ride to Freedom" was stellar, tough editing decisions had to be made. Campus also apologized, telling me not to take it personally. "These things happen with every film," he said. He assured me that the decision had nothing to do with my ability, and he told me to keep in touch.

I appreciated the kind words, but it didn't lessen the sting. Putting aside my own feelings, the response to the film was generally positive. Critical acclaim came from all over, and *The Education of Sonny Carson* was ultimately recognized as one of the cornerstones of 1970s' black cinema. Writing for *Cinema Gotham*, New York film critic Gil Jawetz would later describe the film as "one of the most vital stories ever told about the inner city. From the tough Brooklyn streets to any ghetto in the world, the struggles here are universal. What Carson and Campus did was distill the essence of this battle for the soul down to the most basic elements: sadness, disappointment, longing and fear." As disappointed as I was, I was still proud to have taken some part in what I consider a meaningful project.

After the premiere, Rony, B. T., and our friend Howard from the Street Academy convinced me to go party with them. The thoughtful words from Yablans and Campus earlier that night meant a lot to me, but nothing compares to the love and support of friends who are there for you in your darkest hours. Then a night that had already brought such heartache was about to take another absurd turn.

The four of us stayed out for an hour or so past midnight and then drove back to my house on Washington Avenue. We were all crowded into my blue Volkswagen Beetle when we saw two dudes walking out of my house. One of them was carrying a reel-to-reel machine while the other had some more recording equipment.

B. T. yelled out, "Pepé! That's your shit!" Before I could react, B. T. was out of the car and chasing after the thieves. Rony and Howard were right behind him, and there I was, hands still on the steering wheel, in disbelief. I finally gathered my faculties and jumped out to join the chase. It had been awhile since I had run like that, but I was determined to catch these fools, especially after they dropped my reel-to-reel machine.

We chased them for blocks through the back alleys and backyards of Clinton Hill. As we approached one house, we came across this dude sitting outside on the back stoop. We asked him if he had seen anyone run through here, to which he replied, "Nah, man." I noticed he was out of breath and had some sweat on his brow. I think we all suspected that he was one of the guys we were after, but before we could say anything, an older couple opened the back door to see what was going on. The guy looked at them and with a straight face said, "Mom. Dad." In hilarious fashion, the woman said, "Who the hell are you?" Right then, I yelled, "I knew it was you!" We were all ready to beat the hell out of him when the police showed up.

They had already caught the other guy up the block and placed him in a squad car. We explained to the police what happened, and they arrested this guy too. Of course, the NYPD was a different breed, especially in the 1970s. Many of them seemed to believe in retribution regardless of who delivered it. As the officer placed this dude in handcuffs, he turned him toward me in a certain way. It was the officer's way of telling me that I could hit the guy if I wanted to, without repercussion. So I did. I hit him square in the face as hard as I could. I looked him in the eyes and asked, "Who is the motherfucker that set me up?"

Then I saw the other guy who was already in the back of the police car. I moved closer and recognized him as someone who hung around my neighborhood. I said, "I know you, motherfucker." His face flushed with fear. I was so angry, and he could see it on my face. The fact that these two had been staking out my house, likely for some time, didn't sit well with me at all.

On any other night, I might not have made such a big deal out of it. I mean, it was my stuff and I needed it, but I had done my share of questionable things, particularly when I was younger. I just had a hard time getting over the fact that they had planned it, knowing enough about me and how important this equipment was to me. I am not sure how much time they got, but I hope they learned a lesson and eventually got their lives together. It wasn't lost on me that, had I followed other paths, I could have been sitting in the same place they were.

My contract from working as a day player for the filming of *The Education of Sonny Carson*, 1973

Lead sheet for the music to "Five Cent Ride to Freedom." I wrote and performed the song for *The Education of Sonny Carson*, but the scene was cut from the final film.

9

HOLLYWOOD

AFTER THINGS DIDN'T QUITE work out as I had hoped with *The Education of Sonny Carson*, I knew I had to regroup, refocus, and rededicate myself. I was more determined than ever to make it in the music business. Ike and I had talked about putting a band together for some time, but he was still more of a songwriter. He was learning the guitar but wasn't quite ready. I had this idea for a three-piece band, although not a traditional power trio like Jimi Hendrix and the Band of Gypsys. For one thing, I was more of a rhythm player, and my songwriting style leaned more toward the melodic. Jimi was my idol and I dug everything he did, but I was no Jimi. Nobody was.

The first call I placed was to my cousin Buddy, who was a skilled drummer. We rounded out the band with our friend Willie Laws, whose uncle was Hubert Laws, a well-established jazz flautist and saxophonist. Like his uncle, Willie's main instrument was the flute. So there we were, a three-piece outfit: Willie on flute, Buddy on drums, and me on guitar and vocals. I don't even remember what we called ourselves.

The three of us started rehearsing as hard as we could,

day after day. Things came together quickly, and before we knew it, our set was pretty tight. After just a few weeks, we booked our first gig, at Le Dome in Greenwich Village. This was no small deal for us, as the emcee of the show was none other than the "Chief Rocker," Frankie Crocker. Crocker came to prominence as a deejay at New York's WWRL before moving to the highly rated WBLS. He also starred in several classic black films of the era, including *Cleopatra Jones* and *Five on the Black Hand Side*. Crocker later became a staple at Studio 54 and was a longtime emcee at Harlem's Apollo Theater. Also known as "Hollywood," Crocker used his influence as a deejay to promote upcoming artists like Bob Marley, Blondie, the System, Colonel Abrams, Madonna, and Mica Paris. Unfortunately, just like Alan Freed and Tommy Smalls, Crocker was mixed up in a payola scandal in the mid-1970s. He managed to rebound in the 1980s and went on to help shape the music video revolution as a host and personality on such shows as *Solid Gold* and *Friday Night Videos* and on the VH1 network.

Our gig at Le Dome was extremely well received. As far as I was concerned, we rocked the shit out of the place. Frankie was very cool and complimented our performance. As mesmerizing as it had been for me in my youth to have a backstage pass to see amazing musicians up close, it didn't compare to the adrenaline and exhilaration of being onstage myself. I had to find a way to keep accessing this feeling. I thought maybe I had stumbled onto something, a path or a big break that would lead to something more.

To my dismay, Buddy and Willie didn't have the same level of intensity or commitment to our group. The Le Dome show would be the band's last. I found myself searching once again for new opportunities to pursue my musical dreams. I was almost twenty-six by this time. By no means was I old, but I wasn't getting any younger.

On a whim, I packed up my car and headed west, with Buddy accompanying me. Los Angeles was the final destination, but I thought some time with family would boost my spirits, so I decided to stop first in Las Vegas, where Uncle Clarence had settled. Clarence was always great to me and exceedingly generous. But if I learned anything from my father it was to be your own man. I could never take advantage of Clarence, and I wanted to pull my own weight. So after we got to Las Vegas, Buddy and I began bringing in some money by selling Kirby vacuum cleaners. After a while Buddy decided he'd had enough of the desert and went back to New York.

I, on the other hand, was enjoying myself and stayed longer than I originally planned. Clarence and I would frequently hang out on the Vegas Strip. He introduced me to his friends, several of whom were celebrities. The two people I became closest to were Louise and Nikki Goulet. The ex-wife and daughter, respectively, of singer/actor Robert Goulet, Louise and Nikki were two of the kindest, most unassuming people I had ever met. Clarence first met them through Bill Cosby, who used to hang out with Little Anthony and the Imperials so much that he was referred to as "The Fifth Imperial." During their early years, the Imperials played the "chitlin' circuit" with comedians including Redd Foxx, Moms Mabley, and Flip Wilson, not to mention countless musical acts. Now, here Clarence was in Las Vegas hanging out with the likes of Sammy Davis Jr., Liza Minnelli, and Wayne Newton. Nikki Goulet did some film and theater acting herself but was best known for her work on the daytime soap operas *Guiding Light* and *As the World*

Turns. As unpretentious as they were, the Goulets had an elegance about them. Being around them made me feel like a star. Then I met the biggest star of all.

It was August 1974 when I met up with Louise, Nikki, and their friend Andy at Circus Circus on the Las Vegas Strip. Dick Clark was putting on one of his famous rock and roll revues, and on this particular night he was featuring one of the greatest showmen in music history: none other than "Mr. Excitement" himself, Jackie Wilson. If Little Richard and Chuck Berry are considered (rightly so) two of the principal architects of rock and roll, then Sam Cooke and Jackie Wilson are, without question, two of rock and roll's preeminent voices. I had seen Jackie perform years earlier at the Brooklyn Fox, and I was incredibly excited to see him again.

Jackie was superb, and as his set ended, Dick Clark went up to the microphone onstage. At that same moment, Elvis Presley walked through the doors with a giant bodyguard on either side of him. Clark noticed him right away and announced, "Ladies and gentleman, the King." Elvis took off his sunglasses and just stood there as the audience erupted in applause. It was so cool. I thought to myself, *Now, there's a star!*

As Elvis made his way through the venue, he made eye contact with Louise and Nikki, whom he'd known for years, of course. When he arrived at our table, Louise introduced us. I could not believe I was meeting Elvis Presley. We shook hands and said hello. He was very friendly but mostly spoke to Louise and Nikki. He didn't stay long and soon disappeared into the crowd.

My mind instantly went back to my youth, when I used to imitate Elvis for my father and his friends. There was no bigger star in the world than Elvis Presley. Even when I met him, a time when some ridiculed his flamboyant Vegas showmanship and his weight gain, you could feel his fame envelop you and your surroundings. To be there at Circus Circus and see both Elvis and Jackie on the same night, I felt like I was dreaming.

Elvis and Jackie had been friends for a long time, and there is a famous photo of them together backstage from that night. Although it was decades ago, I remember that night like it was yesterday. Sadly, just as Jimi Hendrix died barely a year after I had met him, these two legends were not long for this world either. In the fall of 1975, a little more than a year after I saw him in Las Vegas, Jackie was performing at a Dick Clark revue in New Jersey when he suffered a major heart attack onstage. He essentially spent the rest of his life in a semi-comatose state, until his death in 1984 at age forty-nine. Then in August 1977, Elvis died at his Graceland home; he was just forty-two. It is still hard for me to believe that they had been right there in my presence and then were gone not long after, taken before their time.

As summer gave way to autumn and winter slowly approached, I remained spoiled by the Las Vegas weather. Of course, the weather in Los Angeles was rather nice as well, and I needed to get there and see what course my life and career might take. I also heard that Shauntel was going to be in Southern California for a family reunion. I connected with her before I left, and we agreed to catch up once we were in LA.

First things first, however. As soon as I got to Hollywood, I met with Michael Campus, the director of *The Education of Sonny Carson*. As always, he was friendly and support-ive. I asked him if he was working on any projects or knew of any that I could be a part of. He apologized and said he didn't have any work for me at the moment, but he added that if something did come along or he heard of anything, he would let me know. I left disappointed but not dejected. There had to be something out there.

In the meantime, I was anxious to see Shauntel. It had been about a year since I had seen her last in New York. We met at one of the dinners her family was holding as part of the reunion. As I recall, it was her father's side of the family. One of her aunts made the best gumbo I've ever tasted. But the real treat was seeing my wife again.

We spent a few days together and before long started to talk about reconciling. I told her I was even willing to make the move to Minneapolis. It wasn't exactly the place to go to break into the entertainment industry, but I thought maybe, just maybe, a break from the big city is what I needed. Not to mention that Shauntel was my wife, and I was committed to giving our marriage another chance.

Before we left for Minneapolis, we decided to enjoy some more time in the sun. During our stay, Shauntel asked me if I remembered her cousin Prince. I said, "Of course, I remember him," but in all honesty I didn't remember him much. The few times I had seen him he was only twelve years old. Now he was fifteen, and Shauntel informed me that he was demonstrating quite the aptitude on piano and guitar. She said he had a few questions about the music industry and was wondering if I could speak to him. I told her I would, and I gave him a call.

We didn't talk for long, maybe five or ten minutes. The subject he wanted to know about most was publishing. He wasn't sure what it meant. I told him it was important, but not something he really needed to worry about yet. I also let him know I would be arriving in Minneapolis soon and publishing rights would be easier to explain in person.

That was the end of the conversation, and I didn't think much more about it. Shauntel and I were back together, we were on our way to Minnesota, and I was thinking about the next steps on my own musical adventure. I wasn't sure what the Twin Cities had to offer, but I was ready to find out.

10

FROM THE BIG APPLE TO THE MINNEAPPLE

IN DECEMBER OF 1974, Shauntel flew back to Minneapolis while I made the nineteen-hundred-mile trek from California to Minnesota in my Volkswagen. After a few days of settling in, I went skiing with Shauntel's father, Eddie, at Trollhaugen resort in western Wisconsin. Later that night, I was looking forward to the chance to unwind at a party Eddie was throwing in the western suburbs. He had rented a room in a high-rise office building, with a full bar and a stage for live music. Among the entertainment was a group of sixteen- and seventeen-year-old musicians who called themselves Grand Central.

The band was fronted by Shauntel's cousin Prince, who sang and played lead guitar. André Anderson was on bass and Linda Anderson, André's sister, played keys. William Doughty added percussion, and a freckle-faced Morris Day was on drums. My initial impression of Grand Central was that they were quite good. They played a couple of Earth, Wind & Fire covers and some other funk standards of the day.

I didn't know it at first, but I was brought to the party to evaluate the band, at least in part. When I arrived, I thought I was there just to have fun. I came to find out that Shauntel told Prince and the rest of the group in advance that I was going to be there. I don't know exactly what she said, but they seemed to be under the impression that I was some big-time music producer from New York. That was rather funny to me. After all, I was just a songwriter trying to make it in the business myself.

As I moved closer to the stage to get a better look and feel for the band, I could sense someone staring at me. It was Morris's mother, LaVonne. I made eye contact with her and then she turned her attention back to the stage. I glanced at her again and got the impression that she might have something to do with the band. I walked up to her and said, "Hi, I'm Pepé. Are you with the band?" She replied, "Yes. I know who you are. I'm LaVonne, Morris's mother. I manage Grand Central." I told her I thought they were very good. Then, before I knew what I was doing, I said I would like to work with them. Although I felt somewhat obligated, I genuinely did want to work with the group. And, after all, Prince was family.

After Grand Central finished their set, I introduced myself to the members of the band. We spoke only briefly, but I let them know I was going to be working with them, and we set up some rehearsal time for the following week. I certainly did not want to mislead them, but if they were expecting a top-notch producer from the big city, I thought I should at least try to become that. It's not as if I didn't know what I was doing. I had been entrenched in the world of rock and roll for more than a decade at that point. I had experienced so much, learned so many lessons. I was ready to share my knowledge and experience, just as so many had shared with me. My new life in Minneapolis was about to begin.

Shauntel and I were living in her apartment at 3310 Nicollet Avenue South in Minneapolis's Lyndale neighborhood. During my previous visit to the city, I hadn't seen much of the south side. Shauntel's family had long been settled in the city's historic African American community on the north side, or "over north" as it is referred to locally.

Although he lived over north, Prince attended junior high and high school in south Minneapolis, not far from our apartment. During his teenage years, Prince became familiar with the Uptown section of Minneapolis, which was only about a mile or so from where we lived and he went to school. Uptown was known for its counterculture vibe in the late 1960s and 1970s. Aside from maybe Dinkytown, which straddled the University of Minnesota campus, Uptown was the closest thing the Twin Cities had to a Haight-Ashbury or Greenwich Village. Uptown and its free-thinking ethic would later become a theme in Prince's musical vision.

At that moment, however, our business was on the north side. As I made my way to the first rehearsal with Grand Central, I wondered what was in store. Having seen the group live, it was clear to me that they were talented. But in order to be great, a band has to put in a lot of work offstage. Practice is essential. My experience watching Little Anthony and the Imperials toil through hours and hours of rehearsals taught me that there is a steep price to success. And that price is paid through sweat.

The band was rehearsing at Morris's family home, a nice A-frame house on the north side. The house had a roomy attic, which was a decent space for them to practice in. The band had experienced some recent turnover, as Terry Jackson and Charles "Chazz" Smith had been let go from the group. Chazz, who was Prince's cousin, had helped to establish the band with Prince and André. One day, Chazz showed up at rehearsal only to find his drum kit had been moved to the side and replaced by Morris's. Chazz later told me it had happened a couple weeks before I arrived in town.

I didn't know what to make of the departures of Terry and Chazz from the band, but at the time I didn't concern myself with that. It's not uncommon for band members to come and go. Prince, André, Linda, William, and Morris were the five individuals I had in front of me. They're the ones I had to work with.

My initial approach was to hang back and get a feel for what they were doing. I wanted to give them the freedom to start rehearsals as they normally would. They ran through a series of cover songs, including a few more by Earth, Wind & Fire, which was a clear influence. There was no question that the band was tight, but I wanted to hear something original. I made that known and said, "Show me what you got!" The first song they played was an original composition by Prince called "Sex Machine." Borrowing its title from James Brown's "Get Up (I Feel Like Being a) Sex Machine," the song was pretty good and demonstrated Prince's mastery of the guitar. The song needed a little editing and some more structure, but it was definitely funky. The strange thing is, I don't remember ever hearing that song again.

Next they performed André's song "You Remind Me of Me." As was the case with Prince's song, André's piece clearly revealed his talent. And likewise, the song was too long. Much of the band's original material featured long solos and far too often failed to come back to the hook. It was easy to forget the names of the songs. With André's song in particular, I noticed that everyone in the band was singing different lyrics. There was a blackboard in the attic, so I asked André to write down the lyrics to get everyone on the same page.

After that, I showed them how to construct a song. I talked about intros and outros, verses, the hook, the chorus, the bridge, and everything in between. I was impressed with how well they took direction. It didn't take but another rehearsal or two to see them get the hang of it— not just with their songwriting and musicianship, but with their whole approach to learning new things. Their attitude delighted me. They were young and hungry. You could see it in their eyes. The way they walked. The way they talked. These kids were serious.

I was especially impressed by their willingness to learn and take direction because it wasn't as if the band hadn't already had some success. They were one of the go-to groups for gigs at community hubs like The Way and Phyllis Wheatley Community Center, after-school parties, and other neighborhood events. They had already won a number of "Battle of the Bands" competitions.

That wasn't enough for Grand Central. They wanted more. I told myself, *There's a lot to work with here.* Grand Central had tons of talent. What's more, they had ambition and lots of it. I was thrilled to be working with them. Sometime later, I got confirmation that the feeling was mutual. Apparently, Grand Central had already tried out a few other people to help them get to the next level. For whatever reasons, none of those folks worked out. After I arrived, I learned that André told the rest of the band, "Pepé knows what he's doing. We got to keep him around."

Even though I was committed to Grand Central, I hadn't

given up on my own musical aspirations. I needed to do my own thing as well. By chance, an opportunity presented itself during a stroll along Nicollet Avenue. I was just a few blocks from home when I noticed a storefront up from Twenty-Sixth Street. The awning above the door read "Cookhouse Studios." It looked like a decent outfit, so I went inside and a receptionist greeted me right away. I felt I needed to assure her that I wasn't some crazy dude off the street. I began to tell her my rock and roll story. I mentioned I had been a teenage valet for Little Anthony and the Imperials and some of the biggest acts of the 1960s. I added that I was an aspiring musician and songwriter looking to record some of my own material.

She was friendly, but I got the impression she didn't believe a word I was saying. Nevertheless, she gave me a business card and I was on my way. A week or so later, I came back and talked to her some more. Again, she was nice, but nothing much came of our conversation. Finally, on a subsequent trip to Cookhouse, a gentleman named Dik Hedlund recognized me from one of my previous visits. Dik, who was the house engineer, asked if I wanted to take a tour. Naturally I said yes, and he showed me around. I liked what I saw and mentioned that I wanted to book some time to record. He gave me an idea of what the rates were, and I said I'd be back as soon as possible.

Before I left, Dik introduced me to Dale Menten, who was the president and owner of Cookhouse Studios. Dale was a songwriter himself and had a number of credits writing for labels such as Atlantic, MCA, Mercury, and United Artists. I could tell Dik and Dale were good guys. I sensed that they trusted me, and I felt that, through my persistence, I had earned my way into the studio.

During this time, I once again got a job with the US Postal
Service, again as a clerk carrier. I worked at the central facility on Washington Avenue, one of the main thoroughfares
that connects downtown Minneapolis to the city's north side.

When I had saved up enough money, I reserved some
studio time at Cookhouse in June 1975. I went in with just
my voice, my guitar, and three songs I had written back
in Brooklyn. Not that I needed much attention, but they
took good care of me and set up microphones for both
me and my guitar. I recorded the songs "I'll Always Love
You," "Games," and "If We Don't." When I was done, I
thanked Dale, Dik, and the rest of the staff, and in return,
they handed me some tapes from the session. I was pleased
but not completely satisfied. My first thought when I left
was how could I get more money so I could get back in the
studio.

I picked up a second job as a teacher's aide at Bryant
Junior High School in south Minneapolis at the corner of
East Thirty-Eighth Street and Third Avenue South. Bryant,
which is now the site of Sabathani Community Center, was
where Prince had attended middle school. His school at
the time, Central High, was only three blocks away, which
allowed me to catch up with him after school on occasion.

Not long after my initial experience at Cookhouse,
Shauntel's cousin Genene introduced me to her boyfriend,
who was a musician as well. His name was Wendell Thomas,
and we hit it off right away. I told him I had just finished
recording at Cookhouse, which caught his attention. Wendell asked me what I played. I told him guitar, and he said,
"Cool. I play bass and my brother Dale plays drums." Years
later, in 1987, Dale played drums for Prince's jazz-infused
side project Madhouse, but at the moment he was helping

to fill out the group Wendell and I were forming. Wendell next reached out to his friend Pierre Lewis, who played keyboards. Once Pierre was on board, we had ourselves a band. I gave Wendell, Dale, and Pierre cassettes from my session at Cookhouse and asked each of them to come up with their own parts.

Back at rehearsals with Grand Central, I was learning more about these kids, especially Prince. He was clearly advanced on the guitar for his age, and though quiet, he exhibited an extraordinary level of confidence. What I didn't know was how skilled he was on multiple instruments. One day during rehearsals Prince stopped the band in the middle of a song. As it was still my approach to give them the freedom to run things on their own, only interjecting when necessary, I sat back to see what was happening.

I don't recall what song they were working on, but it was a Prince composition. Prince first went over to Linda on keys. He explained to her exactly what he was looking for and played it note for note on her keyboard. I thought, "Wow, I didn't know he could play the keys like that."

Next, he walked over to André. He asked André for his bass and said, "This is how I want you to play it." I couldn't believe it. Not yet seventeen, Prince was also a master on the bass. Before he finished showing André what he was looking for, André said he understood. Prince handed him the bass and André played exactly what Prince wanted.

I always thought that, in many ways, André was as talented as Prince. Not only that, but sometimes it seemed as if they shared the same mind. The bond between them was special. It made sense when you considered how their friendship had developed. Not long after they met, Prince and André learned that their fathers, John L. Nelson and

Fred Anderson Sr., were once in a band together. Perhaps it was destiny that the two of them would join forces on the north side of Minneapolis on their way to conquering the musical world. By this time, Prince had also been living with André's family for the better part of his teenage years. When his parents divorced when he was much younger, Prince initially stayed with his mother, Mattie. Sometime after she remarried, Prince went to live with his father. And when that didn't work out, he bounced around from house to house until finding a home with the Anderson family.

I couldn't believe Prince could play multiple instruments as well as he did. To me, he was still a youngster, but musically, he was well beyond his years. I wondered where he found the time to do it all. It was becoming clear to me that I was working with a teenage prodigy. He was also family, and I wanted to help him in any way I could. I approached him after rehearsal one day and asked, "Prince, have you ever been in a recording studio?" I was pretty sure the answer would be no, but he had already surprised me plenty, and I didn't want to assume anything. He confirmed that he hadn't, and I invited him to Cookhouse to record with the band I had just put together. He immediately accepted, and although he was somewhat subdued, I could tell he was excited about the opportunity. As I had with my other bandmates, I gave Prince a cassette of my songs and asked him to come up with his own lead guitar part for each of the three songs.

That was one major difference between us. Prince had demonstrated that he could teach his bandmates what and how he wanted them to play. On the contrary, my approach was to have each member bring their own feel to a song. It was important to me that they had some buy-in, some ownership in what we were doing. As Prince got older, he would afford similar latitude to some of his bandmates.

But before we could go any further, I needed to come up with the money to get us back in the studio. While Prince and the other guys were learning my songs, I was counting every dollar and looking for any viable opportunity to make more.

To complicate matters, my home life was again in shambles. Shauntel and I really tried to make it work, but we just weren't able to pull it off. We moved to a new place on Thirty-Ninth and Garfield in south Minneapolis. After a short time, she moved out, and we agreed to divorce. I know it was for the best and allowed us the freedom we needed. That said, there were definitely hard feelings, and I was bitter for some time. I thought the best way to process our breakup—while keeping my focus on my music career—was to write a song about it.

So that's exactly what I did. Titled "If You See Me," it was by far the most personal thing I had ever written. For me it was therapy and, at least in my mind, one of my better compositions. I knew that whenever I made it back to Cookhouse, "If You See Me" would be part of those sessions.

11

94 EAST

IN THE FALL OF 1975, I heard about a casting call for the musical *Nettie* being produced at the Landfall Theater in St. Paul. I auditioned and was cast in a small role. A chance to add a little cash to my Cookhouse fund was all I was looking for. What I didn't expect to find was a lifetime collaborator, much less two, in the play's leading lady and her best friend. I developed a fast friendship with Kristie Lazenberry, who was starring as the play's namesake, jazz vocalist Nettie Hayes Sherman. A picture of Sherman in her twenties showed that she was the spitting image of Kristie. Kristie was no doubt talented, but her resemblance to the real Nettie Hayes Sherman played a big part in her getting the role.

Sherman, a St. Paul icon, was the first African American woman in the United States to host her own radio show. She was also a frequent performer at St. Paul clubs during the Prohibition era of the 1920s and 1930s, when the city was known as a "gangster's paradise" and several of the nation's most notorious mobsters used it as an alternate base of operations and safe haven. As a result, Sherman became a favorite performer of famous underworld figures like Al Capone, Baby Face Nelson, John Dillinger, and Machine Gun Kelly.

Sherman was in her mid-seventies at the time of the Landfall Theater performances, and she participated in the production by singing lead and playing piano. So, while it was clear to me that Kristie could act, I didn't know if she could sing. Either way, she quickly became a good friend, as did Marcy Ingvoldstad, whom Kristie introduced me to during the production of *Nettie*.

Kristie was born and raised in St. Paul, whereas Marcy, whose father was an officer in the navy, was born in Patterson, California. The Ingvoldstad family moved frequently, as is common among military families, until they settled in the inner-ring Minneapolis suburb of Golden Valley for Marcy's high school years. Kristie and Marcy met as students at St. Olaf College in Northfield, Minnesota. The three of us started spending a lot of time together, mostly at Kristie's childhood home on North Chatsworth Street in St. Paul. I told them I was getting ready to go back to Cookhouse Studios to record five songs with my band. They thought that was cool. Neither of them mentioned that they were both singers. All I knew is that they were exceptionally good people, and the three of us got along famously.

Another very special person I met during my first year in Minneapolis was André's mother, Bernadette Anderson, who had also been a kind of foster mother to Prince. Any reason I had to visit the Anderson family home on 1244 Russell Avenue North was all right by me. It was one place in Minneapolis that reminded me of growing up in Brooklyn. Everyone was welcome there. Friends and family would come and go freely. There was always music in the air and always good food. People could be themselves and enjoy one another's company.

Affectionately known on the north side as "Queen Bernie," Bernadette was more than just a mother to her own six children and to Prince; she was a matriarch to the whole community. Born and raised on the south side of Minneapolis, Bernadette was the rare individual who was loved and cherished by just about everyone who was fortunate enough to know her. Through her activism and her career with the Minneapolis Public Schools, YWCA, Minneapolis Urban League, and KMOJ community radio, Bernadette had a profound impact on the lives of thousands of north side residents, especially young people.

In Bernadette and the Anderson family, I believe Prince found stability, after a tumultuous childhood during which he moved around a lot. She treated Prince as if he were her own son, giving him love and respect. Of course, she also expected him to excel in school, complete his chores, respect others, and demonstrate self-respect and discipline. Prince, for his part, seemed able to toe that line while offering love in return. I can only think of one incident when I saw Bernadette get on Prince's case.

Once I had saved enough money to get the band, including Prince, into Cookhouse to record, I scheduled a couple of weeks of intense rehearsals. One day, I arrived at the Anderson home to pick up Prince for rehearsal just as Bernadette was getting home from work. She noticed that Prince was in the basement getting dressed. Thinking something was amiss, she questioned Prince as to whether he had been to school that day. He replied, "No, ma'am." Bernadette then asked him if he had spent the day in the basement with a girl. With a glum look on his face, Prince confessed, "Yes, ma'am."

All I can say beyond that is, Bernadette indeed treated

Prince like he was her own son. That was the first time I ever saw him cry. Although it was his senior year and he didn't have much school left, I am certain he never skipped class or snuck a girl into Bernadette's house again.

Despite the embarrassment this episode caused Prince, he was all business by the time we arrived at rehearsal. The two weeks we spent preparing for the Cookhouse sessions went smoothly. The decision to let each player create his own part worked out well. Our sound was tight. We were ready to record.

When we arrived at Cookhouse Studios in December 1975, Prince fit in just like one of the guys. And despite how young he was, he approached the session like a seasoned professional. During the recording, I didn't focus much on what anyone else was doing. I was mostly concerned with making sure my own parts were perfect. I trusted everyone else to take care of their own parts, and they did.

After we left the studio and I had a chance to listen to the tapes, I was even more impressed by Prince. Wendell listened to the tracks too, and he called me up right away and nearly shouted into the phone, "Pepé, did you hear what Prince was playing?" I countered, "Yeah, I know, man. The kid is something else!" I didn't know what else to say. Prince was special.

At this point, I was hoping to relax and unwind a bit after all the rehearsals and the recording session, so I joined Kristie and Marcy at a party in the western suburb of Plymouth. On the drive back home, rolling down State Highway 55 in my beloved sky blue Volkswagen, LaBelle's "Lady Marmalade" came on the radio. Instantaneously, the three of us began singing along in perfect harmony. I thought, *Oh, my God. These girls can sing*. When the song ended, we all looked at one another and realized we'd stumbled upon something special.

I asked them, "Why didn't I know this about you two?" They said I had never asked. Fair enough. It turns out Kristie came from a pretty successful musical family. Her mother, Norma Stokes Lazenberry, was a talented percussionist, and cousins Butch and Michael Stokes had founded a popular local band at St. Paul Harding High School in 1961 called the Galaxies. Later known as the Mystics, they toured throughout the Midwest during the 1960s and recorded on different record labels. Considered one of the top acts in the Twin Cities during this era, the Mystics opened locally for a litany of renowned artists, including Wilson Pickett, Aretha Franklin, Sly and the Family Stone, Dean Martin Jr., Desi Arnaz Jr., the Who, Three Dog Night, and Strawberry Alarm Clock.

Marcy also had a strong musical background, and her mother, Marcella, was an accomplished singer as well. Once I learned about their musical pedigrees and their own talents, I knew I had to have Kristie and Marcy in my band. So I planned a return to the studio so they could put some vocals on the songs we had recorded.

I booked a date at Cookhouse a couple of months out, as I wanted to give them time to rehearse. They had no idea what they were in for. I worked them so hard. Kristie and Marcy complained, cried, and then complained some more. But I wanted to make sure they were ready and understood the time commitment and discipline this required.

By the time the three of us walked into Cookhouse Studios in March 1976, they were ready. These women were tough, they were serious, and they could sing. Once Kristie's and Marcy's voices were added to the mix, I knew we had something to present to the labels. Wendell and I decided it was time to go to New York.

There had been one change in the band's roster between the time we left Cookhouse in December and when we recorded the vocals from Kristie and Marcy. Dale, who was a great drummer, had a habit of showing up late to rehearsals and other band functions. It was critical to me that everyone in the group had the same level of commitment and loyalty. For whatever reason, Dale couldn't live up to those expectations, and as much as I hated to do it, I let him go.

To find a replacement, we ran an advertisement in the newspaper. Among those who auditioned was an extremely gifted multi-instrumentalist named Sonny Thompson, who would later become the bassist in Prince's New Power Generation. After auditioning a few more people, we picked a twenty-year-old kid from nearby St. Louis Park by the name of Bobby Rivkin. Soon known to the world as Bobby Z., he fit in right away. Like Prince, Bobby had been playing music since he was very young and had started his own band back in junior high school.

With the band's lineup complete, I had a few more things to get in place. From everything I had learned watching the Imperials and others, I understood the importance of publishing, production, and artistic control. To that end, I established Pepé Music Incorporated, or PMI. Going through this process would also serve well when it came time to help Prince establish his own publishing company years later.

Now our band needed a name. To be honest, a name was one of the last things I considered during this journey, and I asked Kristie and Marcy for their thoughts. They suggested 94 East, after the interstate that runs through the Twin

Cities and connects downtown Minneapolis and downtown St. Paul. I suppose the name could just as easily have been 94 West, but we settled on 94 East since it was the route I took whenever I went to visit Kristie, not to mention that it was a nod to my roots back east in Brooklyn.

Interstate 94 also represents a difficult part of St. Paul's past and fostered deep wounds that linger today. When the Minnesota Department of Highways was planning construction of I-94 through the Twin Cities in the 1950s, the route it chose went directly through St. Paul's Rondo neighborhood and the center of the city's African American community. As a result of the construction, black families were forced from their homes and many black-owned businesses were shuttered. The Rondo community was obliterated.

Kristie experienced the destruction of Rondo firsthand, having grown up less than a block from where Interstate 94 now traverses the city. I don't know if any of this history was considered when we decided to name our band 94 East. For us, the name had inherent symbolism outside of politics, yet the symbolism stands even larger today when considering what the Interstate 94 episode represents to the history of African Americans in Minnesota.

12

BACK TO THE BIG CITY

IN APRIL 1976, Wendell and I left the Twin Cities for New York City with our Cookhouse demo in hand. I had no intention of leaving New York until I had a record deal secured. I ended the lease on my apartment in Minneapolis, unconcerned about where I might live when it was time to return.

In New York, Wendell and I stayed with my grandmother in South Brooklyn. It was so nice to spend time with her and be back in the house where I spent some of my most formative years.

Meanwhile, back in Minneapolis, Prince was keeping busy with his own pursuits. He spent the early part of 1976 recording a demo with André and Morris, produced by Bobby Rivkin's older brother, David Z. Not long after that, I learned that Prince had left Grand Central after a disagreement with Morris's mother, LaVonne. The band reformed as Shampayne, and Prince went about doing his own thing. I was somewhat disappointed, as Grand Central seemed to have so much potential. But it was clear Prince was on a mission, and I knew better than to bet against him.

It was also during my time away that Prince befriended Chris Moon, a British transplant who operated Moon Sound

Studios out of his home in south Minneapolis. After working with Prince for a while, Moon approached Owen Husney, a local businessman who had experience in the music
industry. Owen took an immediate interest in Prince and
began devising a plan to get him a record deal.

While I hoped to get back to Minneapolis quickly and help
Prince, I was consumed with my own quest at that moment.
My first order of business when we got to New York was to
call Teddy Randazzo. I was hoping he would put some string
and horn parts on one of the songs we had recorded, "Better
Than You Think," cowritten by Kristie and me.

Always a gentleman, Teddy agreed to help. He hired
some players to record the parts in his home studio. I wasn't
really feeling the horns, so I edited them out. But I kept the
string parts that Teddy played himself. With five completed
songs in hand, I was ready to make my pitch to the record
companies.

I called various labels to try to get in front of them with
my tape. I arranged to meet with Brunswick first, although
I had no intention of signing with them. To me, it would
serve as a rehearsal or trial run, a chance to get used to
talking to industry people. Not that I had any disrespect
or ill will toward Brunswick, whose roster included at one
time or another Count Basie, Al Jolson, Duke Ellington, Bing
Crosby, Cab Calloway, Louis Armstrong, Nikolai Sokoloff,
Arturo Toscanini, and Buddy Holly. At the time, the label,
which fashioned itself as "the heart and soul of R&B," was
home to Jackie Wilson and the Chi-Lites.

Brunswick said they liked what they heard, but that it
was not what they were looking for at the time. Still, the
meeting accomplished what I had hoped for: getting a
chance to practice my pitch to industry executives. Now I

was ready to move on. Over the following weeks, I met with Columbia, Arista, and RCA. They were all encouraging and made positive comments about the material, but none of them expressed full interest.

Undeterred, I scheduled a meeting with Polydor Records, which by this time was a subsidiary of PolyGram. Just before our meeting, I got word that they needed to reschedule. Then they canceled again, and then again. All told, the meeting was rescheduled five times. Wendell was frustrated by the lack of progress and flew back to Minneapolis.

I was finally able to meet with Polydor in July. I told Teddy the appointment was scheduled, and he graciously agreed to come with me. I was so happy. I thought it would be cool to walk in with the one and only Teddy Randazzo at my side. The meeting was with Rick Stevens, who was vice president of Polydor's A&R on the East Coast. Rick was new to Polydor but had previously been with CBS Records, where he worked with such artists as Johnny Cash, Sly and the Family Stone, Billy Paul, and the O'Jays. Rick was extremely gracious and apologized for the string of cancellations, which, he said, was why he wanted to be the one to meet with us personally. He told me he loved the songs, but they needed to be remixed. Teddy agreed with his assessment and told Rick he would be happy to remix them himself. To my amazement and delight, we walked out of Rick Stevens's office with a verbal agreement that 94 East would be signed to Polydor Records.

When I saw the actual offer, I realized it was by no means a great contract, and there was no serious money attached to it. Still, it was a record deal, and it was with a major label. Teddy was so happy for me. I must have thanked him a thousand times for everything he'd done—not just for his help during this process, but for all the ways he supported me from the time I first met him.

I called Kristie and Marcy right away. I got ahold of Kristie first, and I simply said to her, "Guess what: 94 East is officially a member of the Polydor family." She freaked out. Everyone else was equally excited when they heard the news.

I stayed in New York a little longer to get to know Hank Cosby, who was assigned to work with us by Polydor. He was to be our producer, with me coproducing. Hank was already a living legend as one of the original members of the Funk Brothers, Motown's famous house band. Among numerous other credits, Hank cowrote and produced Stevie Wonder's "My Cherie Amour" and "Tears of a Clown" for Smokey Robinson and the Miracles. These are just two among the dozens of hits he helped to write. Hank's accomplishments ultimately earned him a place in the Songwriters Hall of Fame. Things seemed to be falling into place for 94 East, and I headed back to Minneapolis in September.

Although I would have loved to have him, it was clear Prince wasn't going to be a part of 94 East moving forward. He was destined to have his own thing, and he was working with Chris Moon and Owen Husney to make it happen. Prince introduced me to them, and I was pleased with the arrangement. I might have been a tad suspicious at first—after all, Prince was family, and I was determined not to let anything interfere with his development—but Chris and Owen seemed to have Prince's best interests in mind.

As they were preparing to make another demo and get Prince in front of record labels, I started on some new tracks for 94 East. The first two songs I came up with were "Warp Seven" and "Disco Booty." I thought they were pretty good, but seven songs was still not enough, so I went back to work.

Soon, another song came to fruition. I called it "10:15." Hank also gave us the song "Fortune Teller," which he wrote specifically for 94 East. I felt even better about these two songs and couldn't wait to get back into the studio to record.

Since I had given up my apartment before I left for New York, I also needed to find a place to live. Kristie was kind enough to let me stay with her in St. Paul when I first got back in town, but I didn't want to impose any further on Kristie's family. I looked into renting a place in Minneapolis and found a small but charming house at 3809 Upton Avenue South, less than a block from the south shore of Lake Calhoun, now known as Bde Maka Ska.

One of five urban lakes that make up Minneapolis's Chain of Lakes, Bde Maka Ska is the largest lake in the city and affords a scenic view of downtown. It is a recreational haven in the urban landscape. Having spent most of my life in Brooklyn, I thought this location was fabulous. I had never lived anywhere with so much usable, open space. The neighborhood was perfect. Plus, the house had a large basement that was well suited for rehearsals. I said to myself, *I can work with this. This is home.*

I also came to realize how much I had come to depend on Kristie and Marcy. They were not only dear friends, but in essence they had become my business partners. So I invited them to live and work with me in my new home, an invitation they readily accepted. I couldn't have found two better people than Kristie and Marcy to share my musical journey with.

As 94 East spent a few weeks rehearsing the new material, I was looking to get us back into the studio. I booked time at Sound 80 on East Twenty-Fifth Street in south Minneapolis. Sound 80 was established in 1969 by Tom Jung and Herb

Pilhofer, both of whom had worked at Kay Bank Studios, which later became Cookhouse. Sound 80's claim to fame at the time was as the studio where Bob Dylan recorded several songs for his 1975 opus, *Blood on the Tracks*.

We arrived at Sound 80 in March 1977 ready to record "Fortune Teller" and "10:15." As we walked into the studio, the first person I saw was Prince, who was on his way out. He had been there working on his demo tape. I was happy to see him, as it had been a couple of weeks since we had talked. He was so busy pursuing his own deal, it was hard to keep up with him. He asked what we were doing there, and I told him we were recording a couple of songs for our deal with Polydor. He asked, "Can I play with you guys?" Without hesitating, I replied, "Are you kidding? Absolutely! Let's do this."

Prince didn't know the songs, but I knew he would catch on quickly. He ended up playing lead guitar on both tracks, and as always, he killed it. Not yet nineteen years old, the kid was so bad, it didn't make any sense. I already loved the songs, and they only got better with Prince's involvement.

On "Fortune Teller," I sang lead while Kristie, Marcy, and Prince did backup vocals. The girls were exceptional, and mixing their voices with Prince's was pure magic. Still, I thought the song needed something more. I wanted to find another singer to handle lead vocals, and I had my heart set on an up-and-coming talent named Colonel Abrams, whom I had met in New York. Originally from Detroit, Colonel was a year younger than I was and had already been in some bands on the New York club scene. He became an underground legend in the early 1980s and then broke big after signing with MCA Records in 1985. Colonel was a multi-instrumentalist, but his voice is what set him apart. It was equal parts smooth and authoritative. There was no doubt in my mind, Colonel was the perfect lead vocalist for "Fortune Teller."

I went to New York and reached out to Colonel, and he was excited to help. I told Hank about my plans, and he started to laugh. Coincidentally, Hank had just met with Colonel when Colonel was approaching labels for his own deal. Hank thought Colonel was a wonderful choice for "Fortune Teller."

The sessions started out great. Both Hank and I felt Colonel's vocals took the song to another level. There was another issue that I didn't anticipate, however. Hank said we needed to replace the drum track, as our drummer didn't deliver the right feel to the song. My heart broke for Bobby Z., but I trusted Hank. I asked him who he had in mind. Hank mentioned Buddy Williams, a phenomenal session player who had worked with such jazz and soul artists as Grover Washington Jr., Lee Ritenour, Nat Adderley, Joe Sample, and Valerie Simpson. Buddy came into the studio, laid down a stellar drum track, and we were done.

I was pleased with how things ended up, but I still had to tell Bobby what happened. I thought about it all the way back to Minneapolis. When I finally told him, I could tell he was really hurt. I felt devastated for him. I wanted to encourage him and let him know that it was okay, that these things happen in the business. I wasn't sure if any of it helped; I just didn't want him to lose his confidence.

More unsettling news came shortly thereafter for everyone in 94 East. In June, we learned that Hank had been let go from Polydor. Turnover in the industry was exceedingly common during this time. It was so bad, in fact, that *Billboard Magazine* started a column called "The Turntable," in which they kept readers up to date with the hirings, firings, and personnel moves in the record industry.

Panicked, I called Hank and told him I was sorry to hear the news. He was already entertaining offers from other labels, however, so he was going to be all right. Those of us in 94 East, on the other hand, were freaking out. I asked, "Hank, what do we do?" He said he thought it would be fine and that whomever they brought in as a replacement would get in touch with us soon. I hung up the phone not knowing what the future held for the band.

While things remained tense for 94 East, not all was bad in Minneapolis. At the end of June, just a couple of weeks after his nineteenth birthday, Prince signed a deal with Warner Bros. Owen had been able to get Prince in front of several major label executives, some of whom, remarkably, passed on the young artist. In the end, there was a bidding war between three companies, and Warner Bros. came out on top. The deal was extraordinary for someone Prince's age, in terms of both the money and the freedom it allowed him in the studio. It is especially amazing when you consider that Owen touted him to the labels as a seventeen-year-old wunderkind, shaving two years off his age. Regardless of Prince's age, he was unquestionably a prodigy. Still, that was a pretty shrewd move by Owen, one that went a long way in spawning the mystique that surrounded the early years of Prince's career.

Despite my own worries, I couldn't have been happier for Prince. He told me how he got to hang out in Los Angeles and meet with Mo Ostin, president of Warner Bros., as well as other top executives like Russ Thyret, Lenny Waronker, and Barry Gross. He was even introduced to some of the artists already on the label. I told him I thought Warner Bros. was the perfect place for him since they had a solid reputation as an artist-friendly label. It had been a real good summer for Prince.

In the meantime, my summer was growing colder. When August rolled around, we received more bad news for 94 East. The nightmare that I had feared for the better part of two months was reality. Word came from Polydor that there was no longer any interest in us from their end. They did not want to move forward with 94 East, and we were dropped from the label.

I went numb when I heard the news. I wasn't sure if I could get off the couch. I couldn't contemplate our next move. Three years earlier, following the disappointment of having my scenes cut from *The Education of Sonny Carson*, I had experienced a groundswell of resolve to not let my dreams be dashed. But this was a kick in the gut like I had never felt before. I didn't know what to do. But then, a couple of pairs of helping hands reached out to me.

When Prince found out that we were let go from Polydor, he went to André and said they had to do something, considering all the support I had given them earlier in their careers. They approached me with the idea of going back into the studio and recording some new material. That Prince and André wanted to help meant the world to me. I will never forget it. Their love and support was exactly what I needed to get me off my ass and back to work. This overture was especially meaningful when considering that Prince, now signed to Warner Bros., was not supposed to participate in any projects outside their purview.

I pulled some songs together, including a ballad titled "Lovin' Cup" that I had written with Ike Paige in New York. Another track I'd recently written and wanted to record was called "Dance to the Music of the World." Lastly, Prince and I wrote a song together, which became "Just Another Sucker." It was a bright, up-tempo jam that came together rather quickly. I thought we were close to done with it, but Prince insisted that it was missing something. I said it sounded cool to me, and we could revisit it in a day or two. It had been a long day, and I went home to get some sleep.

At about three or four in the morning, the phone rang. Still half asleep, I picked up the phone and before I could even utter a hello, the voice on the other end said, "Pepé, I finished that song." I was like, "Prince? Is that you?" He said yes and repeated that he had finished the song. I didn't know what to say other than, "Man. That's great."

To my mind, this news could have waited until morning, but I didn't want to discourage him or make him think I didn't appreciate his efforts. What this episode did display, as if there was ever a doubt, was Prince's singular drive for perfection. When Prince set his mind to something, nothing would get in his way. This is a trait that all those who worked with him will testify to.

In the fall of 1977, Prince, André, and I, along with Kristie and Marcy, went back to Sound 80 to record these three new songs. Because Prince's contract with Warner Bros. didn't allow him to record with us, we had to keep it a secret, and our comings and goings had to be discreet. In the studio, André provided exceptional bass work, but Prince just tore the place up playing guitar, keyboards, drums, and synthesizer on all three tracks. I added some acoustic guitar and percussion, and Kristie and Marcy handled vocals. Still, it was clear Prince had the ability to be a one-man band. And in addition to his abilities as a musician, his increasing mastery of the studio put him miles ahead of so many others.

When we finished, I thanked Prince and André for everything they had done. I was thoroughly pleased with the songs and felt it was time to go back to New York and try again. Nothing much came of my trip, however. I was able to catch up with some friends and family, but that was about it. The new songs didn't garner any serious interest from the labels.

Prince and André, meanwhile, were off to the West Coast, where Prince would start recording his first album for Warner Bros. Warner executives suggested the Record Plant in suburban Sausalito, across the Golden Gate Bridge from San Francisco. Prince was excited about the studio, which had recently hosted some of his favorite artists, including Sly and the Family Stone, Stevie Wonder, Fleetwood Mac, and Tower of Power. Although I sensed that Prince might have been the slightest bit scared before he left, I knew his determination, work ethic, vision, and, above all, talent would serve him well in California.

From the very beginning, Prince insisted that he be allowed total control over the creative process in the studio. Warner Bros. pushed hard for Maurice White, founder of Earth, Wind & Fire, to produce the record. Though Prince was heavily influenced by Earth, Wind & Fire, he pushed back. He told me, "I've studied Maurice White and I admire him. I know what he does and how he does it. That's great and all. But that is not what I want to do." Prince ultimately agreed to let veteran engineer and producer Tommy Vicari serve as the album's executive producer. But it was still Prince's show from top to bottom, beginning to end. The phrase "Produced, Arranged, Composed, and Performed by Prince" would become a familiar refrain in the music industry.

13

FOR YOU

BY LATE 1977, I was back in Minneapolis, and Prince returned from the West Coast. His first album, *For You*, was in the can and slated for an April 1978 release. He was eager to talk about how he met some of his heroes while he was in San Francisco, folks like Sly Stone, Chaka Khan, Stevie Nicks, and Carlos Santana. I could sense that he was in a good place, and he could hardly contain his excitement. He told me he put everything he had into *For You* and thought it was a "perfect record."

As I struggled to figure out my own next move, I considered focusing all my attention on helping Prince. After all, he was the one who was signed to a record deal and had an album coming out. I told Kristie and Marcy, "94 East had its chance." And while I hoped that another opportunity would emerge for our band, at that moment it was all about Prince. I let the girls know, "We have to make sure what happened to us doesn't happen to Prince."

Around this time, I received a call from an old friend in New York, Tony Silvester. Tony, a native of Panama, was a founding member of the renowned soul group the Main Ingredient. Established in Harlem in 1964 as the Poets, the Main Ingredient featured Donald McPherson and, subsequently, Cuba Gooding Sr. on lead vocals. The group released several top-selling albums on RCA in the 1970s and had a string of hit singles, including "Everybody Plays the Fool." In 1975, Tony released a solo record and began a production career that allowed him to work with such artists as Stevie Wonder, Martha Reeves, Ben E. King, Marlena Shaw, and Sister Sledge. In early 1978, he was preparing to produce a few tracks with the Imperials for Power Exchange Records, a subsidiary of EMI.

Tony called me because he needed some top-notch musicians for these sessions and wanted to know if I knew anyone. I said, "Sure, Tony. I got two guys for you, and I promise you these two guys are all you'll need." He didn't believe me, but I assured him it was true. He said, "Okay. I'll see you when you get here."

As soon as I hung up the phone, I realized that I had just committed Prince to another project even though he was under contract with Warner Bros. Nevertheless, I knew how much he loved to play, not to mention that he was his own man and pretty much did whatever he wanted. I asked Prince and André if they were interested, and they both said yes without hesitation.

This would not be the first time I hung out with Prince in New York. When I was in the city working on "Fortune Teller" the summer before, Prince had made a trip to New Jersey to visit his sister Sharon. We connected, and I invited him to come hang out with me and Ike Paige at Ike's place in Harlem. The three of us started writing a song together, which we called "ABC, 123." Prince finished his part much faster than Ike or I finished ours, so he went out on the balcony to take in the sights and sounds of the big city. As Ike and I sat inside the apartment completing the song, I called out to Prince to see if he had any more input on the song. He said, "No, I'm cool. Go ahead and keep it." I said, "Are you sure?" He said, "Yeah. It's cool." Then he asked Ike if it was okay for him to sleep on the balcony. Ike replied, "Sure."

The next day, Prince, Ike, and I went to the Village and stopped in at a guitar shop. I could sense that the owner thought we were up to no good. I pulled Ike aside and said, "Watch this." I then called over to Prince, "Hey, man. Come here and check out this guitar." Prince grabbed the guitar, sat on a stool, and immediately began to tear it up on the guitar. Every head in the store turned toward Prince. People started to gather outside to hear this kid play. They couldn't believe it. It was like nothing they had heard before. When he finished, everybody applauded. I made sure to stare in the owner's direction as we walked out of the store, without buying anything.

When Prince, André, and I arrived in New York in February 1978, Don Taylor, who was still managing the Imperials, put Prince and André up in the New York Hilton, all expenses paid. While Prince and André were living it up in midtown Manhattan, I stayed with Ike in Harlem. I couldn't wait to introduce Uncle Clarence to Prince and André, since I had been telling him about them for nearly two years. I was also excited to see Clarence, as it had been a while since I had seen him.

We met him at Sound Palace Studios in Manhattan for the recording. By this point, Anthony, Sammy, and Ernest had all left the Imperials to pursue other opportunities, leaving Clarence as the only original member from the group's classic 1960s lineup. Anthony went solo again, while Ernest became a member of the Platters. Sammy left the business for a few years before joining up with the O'Jays in 1975. The Imperials now consisted of Clarence, Bobby Wade, and Harold Jenkins. Tony Silvester had already recorded a string of non-album singles and B sides with the group for Power Exchange Records, including "Where You Gonna Find Somebody Like Me," "Who's Gonna Love Me," "Another Star," and "You Better Take Time to Love."

The Sound Palace sessions went well, and Prince and André more than held their own. Tony conceded that I was right—all he needed were these two musicians. He said to me, "Man, you weren't lying. Those cats can play."

Roller disco was a big deal at that time, and one of the songs the Imperials recorded was a collaboration between me, Tony, and Ike called "Fast Freddy the Roller Disco King." Prince played guitar, keyboards, synthesizers, and even the clavinet on the song. It was released as a twelve-inch single in 1979 by Tammi Records. The B side was a remake of my song "10:15." Clarence and Bobby added some new elements to the song and retitled it "I Just Wanna Be Your Lovin' Man." Along with the songs that Tony had produced for Power Exchange, "Fast Freddy" and "I Just Wanna Be Your Lovin' Man" were the last original recordings the Imperials released until the classic lineup of Collins, Gourdine, Wright, and Strain reunited in 1992.

A few years after the Sound Palace session, Tony, Ike, and I reworked "Fast Freddy" without the vocals and added some overdubs to create what became "One Man Jam." And nearly thirty-five years after its original release, the Imperials' "Fast Freddy the Roller Disco King" appeared on a disco compilation by UK label Soul Jazz Records.

Before we left Sound Palace, I asked Prince and André to help me record a song of mine called "If You Feel Like

Dancin.'" An extended instrumental jam, it featured André on bass, me on keys, and Prince on lead guitar and synthesizer. Prince's guitar drives the song from beginning to end. It was quite extraordinary and another reminder of how gifted he was.

We still had time to kill in New York, so I suggested that we put it to good use. We booked time at another studio, Music Farm, on West Fifty-Fifth Street. Prince and André both had some original material they wanted to try out. Prince recorded a demo of "I Feel for You," which appeared on his self-titled second album and, in 1984, became a number-one hit for Chaka Khan, for which Prince received a Grammy Award for Best R&B Song.

André was working on a song called "Thrill You or Kill You." I remember how funky it was, featuring a driving bass line. The song was eventually recorded in Colorado during the summer of 1979 as part of an unreleased Prince side project called the Rebels. The Music Farm sessions was also when I first heard the ballad "Do Me Baby." André was the one who introduced it to me, and it seemed to be his song. Later, when it appeared on Prince's 1981 album *Controversy*, André reached out to me. He said, "Pepé, that's my song. Don't you remember?" I told him that I did recall it being his song. I know he was upset about it for some time, but as is André's personality, he took the high road and let it go.

When we finished up at Music Farm, the engineer gave us a reel-to-reel tape with "I Feel for You" and "Thrill You or Kill You." He must have overhead someone mention that Prince had a record deal. However, he assumed that Prince was Prince Phillip Mitchell, which is what he wrote on the tape box. Prince Phillip Mitchell is a singer-songwriter who has written for the likes of Sam & Dave, Millie Jackson, Bobby

My parents, Agnes Collins Leake and Linster Herbert Willie Sr.

The apartment on Grand Avenue in Brooklyn where I lived with my father growing up

Me and my "Irish twin" sister, Carol, in Brooklyn, 1950s

Looking sharp as a teenager
in Brooklyn in the early sixties
(with my uncle Lionel)

My uncle's band, Little Anthony and the Imperials, performed alongside many legendary artists at the Brooklyn Fox Theatre for Murray the K's 1965 Easter Showcase.

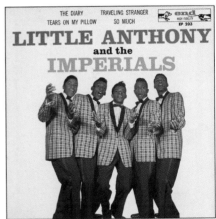

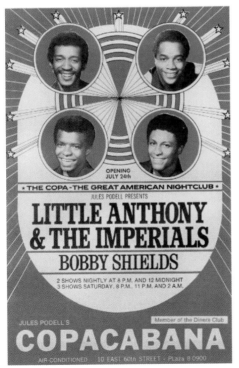

Above: This seven-inch EP released by End Records in 1959 featured the classic Little Anthony and the Imperials hit "Tears on My Pillow."

Left: In the summer of 1969, Little Anthony and the Imperials did a two-week run at New York's legendary Copacabana nightclub, where I worked hard as their valet and rubbed elbows with some big-name stars.

When Little Anthony and the Imperials reunited in the 1990s, they looked as sharp as they had thirty years earlier. Here they're performing at Fantasy Harbour near Myrtle Beach, South Carolina, February 1996.

Backstage at Fantasy Harbour with Ernest Wright, my uncle Clarence Collins, "Little Anthony" Gourdine, and Sammy Strain of Little Anthony and the Imperials

In New York with my mother, Agnes, my sister Pearl, and my nephews Brian and Jason

With my Grandma Anna Willie in Brooklyn, late seventies

Chillin' in Brooklyn in the early 1970s

Shauntel Manderville and me shortly after we started dating in New York. Meeting Shauntel changed the direction of my life forever.

With my new bride, Shauntel

A few days after arriving in Minnesota, I went skiing with Shauntel's father, Eddie, in Wisconsin. Welcome to the snowy Midwest!

With Bernadette Anderson, the matriarch of the Minneapolis Sound

My new partners in music and business: Kristie Lazenberry and Marcy Ingvoldstad

Playing around on the fiddle with our dog, Rince, at my feet

Images from the first photo shoot for 94 East, taken by LeRoy Lazenberry near Walker Art Center in Minneapolis

Right: Cookhouse Recording Studios on Nicollet Avenue in Minneapolis

Below: In the Cookhouse Studios with engineer Dik Hedlund (and his son) at the mixing board, and Marcy and Kristie behind

At Eddy Grant's Blue Wave Studios in Barbados, making the *Minneapolis Genius* album, 1985. Coproducer Tony Silvester is seated to the left in the image.

Wendell Thomas, Marcy, me, and Kristie at Cookhouse

PR photo of 94 East, 1980s

94 East with the Revolution at the Revolution's reunion show at First Avenue in February 2012. From left to right: Marcy Ingvoldstad, Dez Dickerson, Wendy Melvoin, me, Lisa Coleman, Bobby Z., and Kristie Lazenberry

With Jimmy Jam, Terry Lewis, Morris Day, and Jerome Benton at the album release for the Original 7ven (formerly the Time) at Mall of America in November 2011

Catching up with Morris Day backstage at the annual United Negro College Fund gala in May 2017

94 East rehearsing for the Regal Swan Foundation benefit at Lake Eola in Orlando, Florida, in October 2008

94 East, with Matt Fink on keyboards and Geoffrey Castle on fiddle, at the after-party for the Second Annual Benefit Concert for the Rock and Roll Hall of Fame in Raleigh, North Carolina, 2009

With my beloved daughter, Danielle, 1990s

Womack, Candi Staton, and the Average White Band. He is also probably about fifteen years older than Prince, so the engineer clearly didn't know who either of them was. Prince, André, and I had a good laugh over that.

We returned to Minneapolis, and I reflected on all that we accomplished in New York. I marveled at how Prince had come so far so fast. In the three years that I worked with him, he had grown to demonstrate an extraordinary mastery of his craft. You only had to tell him something once and it was committed to memory. And there were a lot of things that you never had to tell him at all. He either figured it out or somehow knew it instinctively. He was a monster on just about every instrument. He could sing, write, produce, whatever. Prince could do anything and everything, and he still had not yet reached his twentieth birthday.

While he was in LA preparing for the release of *For You*, Prince asked me to look after the house he had purchased in the posh Minneapolis suburb of Edina. He had moved out of the apartment that Owen found for him on Aldrich Avenue South, nestled between downtown and Uptown Minneapolis. His new house at 5215 France Avenue South was smallish, but it suited his immediate needs. He told me to go ahead and use his four-track home studio while he was away, and I put it to good use. He had a brand-new Korg drum machine, which at the time was the Cadillac of drum machines. It served me well. I worked on two songs at Prince's studio: "You Can Be My Teacher" and "Love, Love, Love," the latter of which I'd written back in New York and featured Colonel on lead vocals. When Prince was back in town, I asked him to put a bass line on both songs. He also added a real nice guitar track to "Love, Love, Love."

It was good to see Prince at home in Minneapolis, especially with how excited he was about the upcoming release of his debut album. Although he was anxious about what might lie ahead, Prince seemed to be in a good mood. I did, however, upset him a bit around this time, albeit unintentionally.

Prince had been dating this girl named Nadeera, and I assumed they were serious. I ran into her one day and she asked me for Prince's new phone number. I thought it was odd that he hadn't given it to her, but I figured it must have slipped his mind, with everything else going on. After she called him, he confronted me: "Pepé, why did you give her my number?" I could sense he was annoyed when I replied, "Well, aren't you dating this girl?" Prince said he was seeing Nadeera but he didn't want her to have his number. I looked at him, a bit puzzled, and said, "Then you need to tell me this kind of thing ahead of time."

Our exchange wasn't that big of a deal, and we both quickly forgot about it. Although it may have been the first time I did something to upset Prince, it certainly wouldn't be the last. What I learned most in that particular moment, however, was that Prince was becoming a player when it came to the ladies. I guess I should have expected this time would come, but I had never viewed Prince in that light before. In spite of his self-assuredness as a musician, he came off as pretty shy around women. I later found out he used that shyness and a sort of faux innocence to his advantage during this time. It turns out, Prince would tell a lot of girls that he was a virgin as a means to get them to sleep with him. Of course, I couldn't be too critical of Prince. I was twenty-nine years old at the time and had spent at least half of my life in pursuit of the affections of the fairer sex. But more than anything I didn't want Prince to hurt anybody, nor did I want anyone to hurt him—be it a broken heart or something worse, like a beatdown from a bitter husband or boyfriend.

As much as I may have wanted to protect him, the reality is, stardom is a difficult thing to manage. Prince was about to take a giant step into the public eye. I felt I needed to continue teaching him everything I had learned in my many years observing musicians and the industry. I hoped his intelligence, focus, and instincts would help to keep him out of trouble. A lot of us had lofty expectations for Prince, but his own expectations soared well above everybody else's. I wanted to make sure he gave himself the chance to reach them, no matter how high they might be.

When *For You* was released on April 7, 1978, it was a pretty big deal around north Minneapolis, although it took some time for the album to catch on elsewhere in the city. The *Minneapolis Tribune,* one of the two daily hometown newspapers, didn't even publish a review of the album until more than three weeks after its release. Warner Bros. had held a big prerelease reception in Los Angeles in March, and I remember a press photo from the event that went around, featuring Prince and Owen Husney standing alongside Warner Bros. executives Mo Ostin, Russ Thyret, and Barry Gross. I thought this photo and the reception would make people take notice and help generate buzz, but the response was slower than Prince expected. I think one thing that worked against him was that the first single off an album often was not released until after the album dropped. Most of the time that initial record is designed to help drive album sales. In Prince's case, *For You's* first single, "Soft and Wet," didn't hit the stores or radio stations until two months after the album was released. But when it did come out, "Soft and Wet" became a hit on the Billboard soul chart and cracked Billboard's Hot 100. It was time to take this show on the road.

I drove to Chicago with Owen and his wife, Britt, to do a small promotional tour on Prince's behalf. We stopped by a few radio stations, record stores, and a school auditorium while distributing posters and other promotional materials all over the city's South Side. One of the items people really went crazy for was a schoolbook cover that featured one of the more recognizable photos from Prince's Warner Bros. press kit.

Although it was a short trip, I thought the time we spent in Chicago would serve Prince well. When we returned to Minneapolis, I suggested that he call all the radio stations we had visited to thank them for playing his record. To my dismay, Prince said he had no interest in doing that. I tried to explain to him that it was a smart public relations move and would demonstrate appreciation toward the deejays. I told him they might even want to record some promos that they could run before they played his stuff.

Prince looked at me and asked, "Pepé, do you think the record is a hit?" I said, "Yeah, I do." To which he replied, "Then don't worry about it." While I was mad at him for his stubbornness, he was clearly confident in his ability and his music. We all were. Even so, I felt that he squandered an opportunity to show some grace.

After the Chicago trip, I was also asked to accompany Prince on a promotional visit to Charlotte, North Carolina. Warner Bros. flew us out there and put us up in a nice hotel. The itinerary included a radio station interview and an appearance at the Soul Shack record store downtown.

In addition to this being a good thing for Prince, I personally was looking forward to visiting North Carolina. Both of my parents had been born there, yet I had spent very little time there.

On our way to the radio station, we were listening to the disc jockey who would be interviewing Prince. He was really hyping Prince up, and he played "Soft and Wet" right before we arrived. The interview went well, and it seemed as though the people of Charlotte were pretty big on Prince and his music. That feeling was confirmed when we arrived at the Soul Shack for an in-store autograph session. As we pulled up, there must have been two thousand teenage girls and young women in line to see Prince. Although he was new to this life, Prince never wanted to disappoint his fans, and he had already made it a habit to sign every last autograph that was requested of him. It was clear we were in for a long afternoon.

In addition to Prince, Tomi Jenkins of the band Cameo was also making an appearance at the store. Cameo was about to release its third album, *Ugly Ego*, and had already placed a handful of singles on the R&B and dance charts. Still, there was no doubt that nearly everyone was there to see Prince. The store had set up tables for both of them, and there were never more than a handful of fans in Tomi's line. In contrast, Prince's line ran back out the door and onto the street. I felt bad for Tomi. He was a real good guy and a great artist.

I focused my attention on Prince and made sure things didn't get out of hand. I thought back to the time when I was thirteen and was mobbed by all those girls at the Brooklyn Fox simply because they heard I was running an errand for Chubby Checker. I wasn't about to let these girls besiege

Prince. From the moment we got there, I felt as though security was lax. As these young women got increasingly rambunctious, I put my hand on Prince's shoulder and whispered to him that it was about time to go. He insisted that he continue signing, but I told him, "The next time I lean over and whisper something, we are out of here."

Second by second, the girls got a little more out of control. I felt the enthusiasm in the room had escalated enough, and I grabbed Prince by the shoulder. He hopped up and we were quickly out the back door and in the car. Prince didn't say much on the drive to the hotel, and I was trying to gauge his mood. Back in his hotel room, Prince got upset and started to complain. He said, "Pepé, I feel like a piece of meat." I assumed he would have expected this reaction from his fans, but the more he talked, the more I felt like he was becoming unglued. On the one hand, I am sure he was flattered by all the attention from thousands of girls at once. On the other hand, I could understand his unease at being objectified, not only by fans but by industry types as well. It's not an easy situation, but I needed him to come down to earth and relax a bit. This is the kind of thing rock stars are subjected to, and it wouldn't be the last time he would experience it.

About an hour or so after we got back from the Soul Shack, Tomi from Cameo knocked on the door. He wanted to make sure Prince was okay, and the two of them started talking. During their conversation, Tomi mentioned that he was living in New Jersey. Prince said, "Oh, my sister Sharon lives in New Jersey. What part?" Tomi responded, "I'm in Rahway." Prince started laughing and said, "No kidding? Sharon is in Rahway too." As they continued down this road, Tomi asked Prince what his sister's last name was. "Nelson,"

Prince said. It turned out, not only did Tomi know Sharon, but they lived in the same building. Prince thought this was so funny, and talking to Tomi settled him down quite a bit. Things were seemingly back to normal, and Prince and I got ready to return home.

14

THE BAND

WHEN PRINCE AND I got back from Charlotte, it was time to focus on the crucial next task: putting his band together and getting ready to take this show on the road. It seemed automatic that André would be involved, or at least to Prince it did. However, despite their strong sense of brotherhood, André wasn't interested in being in someone else's band. He wanted his own thing. André shared many of the same qualities as Prince, and it was clear he would front his own group at some point. By this time, he was fashioning himself as André Cymone (a play on his middle name, Simon). In the end, André relented and told Prince he would stay around and help him get established. André was determined to eventually venture out on his own, but for now, he would play the bass, and play it well, alongside his best friend.

When it came to the other half of the rhythm section, there were plenty of talented drummers to choose from. The obvious choice seemed to have been Morris Day, a remarkable drummer who already had a rapport with Prince and André, but Prince went with 94 East's drummer, Bobby Z. I'm not sure what went into that decision. I know that the Rivkin family had long been close to Owen Husney. At the time Prince chose Bobby as his drummer, Bobby was running errands for Owen on behalf of Prince.

Also, Bobby's brother, David Z., had played in a band with Owen years before, and he would go on to become an accomplished producer and engineer, working with Prince and many others. Among David's contributions to Prince's catalog were engineering the *Purple Rain* soundtrack and winning a Grammy Award for his work on Prince's third number-one single, "Kiss." He produced several Paisley Park artists as well, including Jill Jones, the Family, Sheila E., and T. C. Ellis. David also did production, writing, and mixing work for such major artists as Etta James, Buddy Guy, Joe Cocker, Elvis Costello, Billy Idol, Jody Watley, and Nu Shooz and for the locally based Lipps Inc., Jesse Johnson, Paul Peterson, the Jets, Jonny Lang, the Steeles, and Prince's sister, Tyka Nelson.

Prince acknowledged Bobby and André in the liner notes of his second album, *Prince*, as his "heaven sent helpers." So I guess it was a natural fit. I also think Prince's vision was similar to what mine had been with 94 East. He wanted his band to be in the mold of Sly and the Family Stone, which meant, among other things, a mixed-race, mixed-gender lineup. Bobby helped to make that vision a reality, which is not to disparage his drumming ability in any way. Although he wasn't the flashiest drummer in the world, he could really keep the beat, which was a particularly demanding task when working for Prince. Moreover, Prince seemed to trust Bobby, which shaped their friendship for decades to come.

For the remaining auditions, Prince rented out rehearsal space from Steve Raitt in the back of Del's Tire Mart in the Seven Corners neighborhood of Minneapolis, near the

University of Minnesota's West Bank campus. Steve, the brother of blues legend Bonnie Raitt, was an accomplished local sound engineer and musician. He got a lot of use out of Del's over the years, and it was the perfect space for Prince to get started.

When auditioning musicians, regardless of the instrument, Prince wanted them to learn the material from *For You*. After one guy auditioned for guitar, Prince complained to me that he was taking shortcuts and not playing the music as it was written. I told him that anyone who took shortcuts just made his decision easier, and he would find the right someone. Prince mentioned that he knew a guitarist from St. Paul who was coming to audition, and he was hopeful he would be the one. That guy turned out to be Dez Dickerson. Dez, who was a little older than Prince and André, was a veteran on the Twin Cities rock scene, most recently having fronted the band Romeo. Not long after Dez's audition, I asked Prince, "So, was he any good?" Prince swiftly replied, "Oh, yeah!" He noted that Dez's chord placements on some of the songs were different from his, but it worked. Prince was impressed with pretty much everything about Dez. It was hard not to like Dez. Not only was he a good guy, but he came with experience, charisma, and skills. I always thought Dez was a good influence on Prince too. And, just like André, Dez was extraordinarily talented and a natural front man. The fact that he and André were able to suppress their egos in support of Prince and his career says a lot about them both.

For the finishing touches, Prince added a pair of keyboardists to the band. Prince's cousin Chazz brought a friend of his, Gayle Chapman, to Prince's attention. Gayle could more than hold her own on keys and had a great singing voice. She and keyboardist Matt Fink rounded out the first lineup of the band that would eventually become the Revolution. Matt, or Doctor Fink, as he would come to be known, brought a lot to the table musically. He translated his jazz and classical background to become one of the funkiest keyboard players in popular music.

With the band in place, rehearsals started in earnest. I occasionally stopped by Del's to check in on Prince and see how things were going. On one visit early in the summer, I was greeted by rather glum faces. Someone had broken into the building and stolen all the band's gear. Other than some large speakers that I had lent to Prince, everything was gone. Everyone was mad. I'm not sure that anyone was madder than André. At that moment, André thought this guy named Joey was responsible. Before I realized what was happening, I was driving André's car with him in the passenger seat holding a rifle he had taken from home.

As André was directing me through north Minneapolis to get to Joey's house, I was praying that we wouldn't find him. I was terrified about what might happen if we did. I had spent most of my adolescence as a gang member in two of the toughest neighborhoods in New York, so this kind of thing wasn't new to me. But there was so much at stake here, not just for me but for Prince, André, everybody. If this didn't end well, we would all lose. Fortunately, we never found Joey, and it turned out he wasn't responsible for the robbery anyway. To my relief, André realized that it wasn't worth pursuing this any further, and he let it go. To this day, I am not sure anyone knows for certain who robbed the band.

Once everyone got over the initial shock and anger, they had to find another rehearsal space. I told Prince and

André not to worry. "You are coming to my house," I said. "You will rehearse in my basement. And I promise you that nobody is coming up in this motherfucker."

The first order of business once Prince and the band agreed to move rehearsals into my basement on Upton Avenue was to replace the equipment that had been stolen. Ever since high school, Prince had a favorite local music store in Uptown called Knut-Koupeé, which supplied and delivered most of the new gear to the house.

A few years later, prior to the filming of *Purple Rain*, Prince called on Knut-Koupeé luthier Dave Rusan to custom build what would become one of the most recognizable instruments in rock history: the cloud guitar. Dave was also one of the guitarists who had auditioned for Prince at Del's Tire Mart, but he didn't get the job, of course.

Once the band settled in and rehearsals started up again, Prince worked them like crazy. The schedule was twelve hours a day, from ten in the morning until ten at night, seven days a week. I remember Marcy and Kristie—particularly Marcy—being a little salty about it at first. They were budding songwriters in their own right, and yet they had to move all their equipment upstairs into their bedrooms in order to accommodate Prince. And even when Marcy and Kristie did find time to work on their own music, they couldn't hear themselves think, much less write anything, with the band rehearsing downstairs all day long and well into the night. Marcy is rather self-deprecating about it today, mocking herself at being put out by the band— considering that none other than Prince was in her basement planting the seeds of what was to become one of the most prodigious careers in music history.

In the end, Marcy and Kristie were extremely helpful to

the band. They performed a variety of tasks that helped both the music and business ends of the operation. To keep Prince from having to deal with some of the minutiae and day-to-day tasks at his place, all his mail was rerouted to my house. He was spending half his life there anyway, and when something needed his attention, I could take it right to him.

Prince struggled with the content of some of his fan mail. As you might expect, he received a plethora of gifts from female admirers that included jewelry, trinkets, undergarments soaked in perfume, and photos, often showing them scantily clad or completely nude. Kristie begged me time and again to let her see some of Prince's fan mail. I refused until I couldn't stand it anymore. I let her see one piece of mail, which she found considerably shocking. She never asked to see Prince's fan mail again.

While he received many letters that were suggestive and blurred the lines of good taste, there were also a sundry of love letters that were sweet and heartfelt. Regardless of the tone, one thing was clear: nearly everyone who took the time to send mail was quite enamored with Prince. And that is something he couldn't fully grasp. He confided in me about this and asked, "Pepé, why do they say they love me? They don't even know me." While I acknowledged that some of the stuff might seem over the top, I reminded him of the adoration he'd received in Charlotte. I wanted him to remember that these women and girls were his fans. I said, "They love your music. They love what you are doing, what you are about." Even though Prince's image would embrace elements of hypersexuality later in his career, at the time he was still only twenty-one years old and a relatively shy young dude. I think he always possessed a sort of boyish modesty. There is no doubt that Prince was a sensitive soul.

As rehearsals progressed that summer, I thought back to the first time I ever spoke to Prince, just prior to my move to Minneapolis, when he had asked me about publishing, and I told him it wasn't something he needed to worry about then. We discussed the subject some more over the ensuing three and a half years, and now it was time for him to get serious about it and register with one of the organizations that protects the publishing and royalty rights of songwriters. The two primary organizations that did this were BMI, or Broadcast Music, Inc., and the American Society of Composers, Authors and Publishers, also known as ASCAP. I sat Prince down and talked him through the process. We contacted BMI's New York office, which sent along the requisite paperwork. On the form, Prince had to submit three options of potential names for his publishing company. I don't remember the other two, but one of the names he chose was ECNIRP, which was Prince spelled backwards. We completed the forms, stuck them in an envelope, and sent the package off to New York. Days later, Prince's first publishing company, ECNIRP Music, was officially incorporated.

About fifteen years later, as his relationship with Warner Bros. soured, Prince established himself as the foremost insurgent in the battle over publishing rights and waged a crusade for complete ownership of his catalog. Although he faced criticism from many circles during that contentious process, Prince remained true to his convictions, and he inspired other artists, both young and old, to fight for their rights. This was Prince at his best. He was a teacher, an activist, a revolutionary, sharing many of the lessons he learned along the way with his fellow artists.

Prince learned one such lesson himself just three weeks

after establishing ECNIRP Music. One day, an envelope arrived from BMI's office in Los Angeles. Inside was another set of blank registration papers, identical to the ones we filled out barely a month before. Attached was a letter from Prince's attorneys along with a bill for nine hundred dollars. I immediately showed him the bill and said, "See, this is what I'm always talking to you about. Your lawyers are trying to charge you nine hundred dollars for something that you already took care of by yourself for the price of a stamp!" It was a huge lesson for him. By this time, Prince seemed sufficiently impressed by many of the things I had told him and everything I had done to protect him, and this incident reinforced that.

I also tried to offer advice and guidance to the members of Prince's band. They all worked extremely hard and wanted to be part of this journey, but things weren't always easy for them. Not only did Prince demand more of them physically, emotionally, and mentally than they could have imagined, but everything had to be Prince's way. This isn't unusual, especially with artists of Prince's caliber, but it wore on his bandmates.

One by one, they unburdened themselves to me. I sensed that none of them felt comfortable bringing this directly to Prince and thought I could talk to him on their behalf. Even Dez, who was becoming somewhat of a mentor to Prince, and André, who was essentially Prince's brother and considered himself an equal, were reticent to approach Prince with their concerns. I thought they had legitimate complaints and that it was only fair to bring them to Prince's attention, so I said I would facilitate a meeting where they could air their grievances. One morning before rehearsal, I gathered everyone in the basement and said, "Prince, the

band has some issues they would like to discuss with you."
I first called on Matt to speak. Dead silence. He didn't say
a word. Then I called on someone else and got the same
response, or lack thereof. This continued; no one would
talk. So I said, "Oh, well," and went back upstairs.

There were no complaints from the band after that. And
not that he needed it, but I am sure this episode further
crystalized in Prince the sense of power he held over his
band. He didn't necessarily abuse that power in any significant way; he was simply the boss. I tried to make the band
understand this as well. I told them, "Look, Prince is the one
who's signed to Warner Bros. And he's the one who signs
your checks. So you must protect him. You've got to have
his back." I wanted them to know in no uncertain terms
that they had a big part to play in Prince's success, and if he
was successful, they would have the chance to be successful
as well, both in support of Prince and, if they so chose, on
their own. From what I could tell, they took this advice to
heart and gave their full support to Prince.

Aside from the band keeping my house full of people all
day, every day, there were other frequent visitors as well.
Owen often came by to see how things were going. Chazz
also hung out from time to time, as did a talented young artist that Prince knew from over north named Sue Ann Carwell. Sue Ann was notorious for helping herself to whatever
she wanted in the kitchen, which baffled Marcy and Kristie.
Still, she was a sweet girl and a great singer. With the help
of Owen and David Z., Sue Ann recorded an unreleased version of my song "Lovin' Cup" and became a labelmate of
Prince's, releasing her first album on Warner Bros. in 1981.
She later signed with MCA and went on to work exten-
sively with Jesse Johnson. Sue Ann is a terrific singer who

can perform in virtually any genre of music, but like so many great talents, her success as a solo artist never matched that talent. It's a shame, really, as she was so much better than many others who have made it big in this business.

Another repeat visitor to the house was Jon Bream, an up-and-coming music writer with the *Minneapolis Star*. Jon was relentless in his pursuit of an interview with Prince. I tried to reassure him that it would happen soon enough, yet he kept coming around. One day I walked outside to find him waiting again, and I said to myself, *Okay, today's the day*. And Jon got his interview.

Jon would become a dear friend of mine, and in many ways his career parallels Prince's. When the *Minneapolis Star* and the *Minneapolis Tribune* merged in 1982 to become the *Star Tribune*, Jon was the natural choice to be the paper's chief music critic. I am sure he interviewed Prince more than any other writer, and he was Prince's first biographer, releasing *Prince: Inside the Purple Reign* in 1984. Though Jon and Prince had their ups and downs over the years, they are no doubt linked, and each one impacted the other's career.

While many people came and went, Matt Fink never seemed to want to leave. Marcy, Kristie, and I all thought that, after spending twelve hours a day in the basement, the last place anybody in the band would want to be was at the house. Still, Matt would come up from rehearsals, and as everyone else left, he would find a chair or a spot on the couch and just hang out. He would stay so long sometimes we'd have to kick him out. I am not sure why he liked being around so much, but we took it as a compliment, even if it drove us crazy.

Although it seemed like the days in my basement were never-ending, there were occasional breaks in the rehearsal schedule. When Prince was out in Sausalito recording *For You*, he attended a concert by renowned jazz singer and Warner Bros. labelmate Al Jarreau. It was there that Prince met a teenage percussionist from the Bay Area named Sheila Escovedo.

I remember first meeting Sheila sometime later at a warehouse space that Prince rented on East Lake Street in Minneapolis. She couldn't have been more than twenty-one or twenty-two at the time, and she reminded me of Prince in so many ways. She was standing by herself in a corner, and I went over and asked, "Why are you over here all alone? There are plenty of chairs to sit in." She just smiled and didn't say anything. She was painfully shy, like Prince.

In mid-1978, some months after Prince and Sheila met at Al Jarreau's San Francisco concert, Jarreau's tour rolled into Minneapolis for a show at Northrop Auditorium. Prince was a big fan of Al's and desperately wanted to see him again. After the concert, Prince introduced himself to Al, who of course already knew who he was. The next night, Prince, Owen, and I had dinner with Al in downtown Minneapolis. Al was and always has been a pro's pro. He was genuinely interested in everything Prince had to say and was ready to offer any wisdom he could. I remember Prince asking him for advice on how to nurture and protect his singing voice. Al shared with Prince a few trade secrets and some of his own. I could tell it meant a lot to Prince that Al was so forthcoming and kind.

Later that summer, during another break in rehearsals, I escaped to New York for a few days. I was able to catch up with former Imperial Sammy Strain, who was now a member of the O'Jays. Sammy is one of a small number of artists to be inducted into the Rock and Roll Hall of Fame with more than one group, as the O'Jays were welcomed in 2005 and Little Anthony and the Imperials in 2009. At the time, the O'Jays were riding high on their hit single "Use Ta Be My Girl," which hit number one on Billboard's R&B chart and number four on the Hot 100.

I saw Sammy at Nassau Coliseum in Long Island, where the O'Jays were sharing a concert bill with the band Heatwave. Backstage, the members of Heatwave were extremely friendly. They seemed unaffected by their rising fame and were happy to just hang out. A musically diverse and interracial band consisting of members from the United States and United Kingdom, Heatwave had been dominating charts all over the world with songs like "Boogie Nights," "Heatwave," and the lush ballad "Always and Forever."

As expected, the O'Jays and Heatwave both gave everyone their money's worth and more. It was also great to see Sammy again after all those years. Although I didn't think much about it at the time, I now reflect on the fact that if Sammy had never mentioned the "fine girl with the green eyes" that night at the Copacabana, I probably would have never met Shauntel. Were that the case, there probably would not have been a twenty-year-old musical genius from Minneapolis sowing the seeds of superstardom in my basement. Prince still would have made it, and made it big, but I wouldn't have been a part of the journey. I can never forget that night at the Copa and Sammy Strain's unwitting role in my own musical destiny.

When I returned to Minneapolis and Prince had finished up some other things, rehearsals picked up where they had left off. I have so many beautiful memories of those days, musical and otherwise. I still smile about the day we unexpectedly added another member to our household on

Upton Avenue. I was riding my bike around the lake one beautiful summer morning when I came across a guy with a litter of German Shepherd and Samoyed mixed puppies. He asked if I'd like to buy one, and I couldn't say no. They were so adorable, just little white balls of fur and energy.

A few minutes after I brought the puppy home, Prince walked in for the day's rehearsal—the first to arrive, as usual. He immediately started playing with our new dog and asked what his name was. I hadn't even thought about a name. Then it hit me: "His name is Rince. Prince without the P." Prince laughed and said, "Oh, yeah. I like that. I like that a lot."

Prince and I also had a lot of serious conversations around this time. I was still messing around with drugs then, and one day when it was just Prince and me hanging out, I started to snort some cocaine. I am not sure why I did it in front of him. I guess I figured it was my house and I didn't care. After doing a line, I looked up, and Prince looked at me with inquisitive eyes. He said, "Does that hurt?" I paused for a second and replied, "No, it doesn't hurt. And I'll tell you what else. If I ever hear about you doing something like this, I promise you that I will kick your fucking ass!" We never spoke another word about it.

The irony was that a lot of us—me, André, Morris, and others—used to make fun of Prince for being such a square. He didn't drink, take drugs, or do any of that stuff, and for that I was so thankful, even if we may have made fun of him behind his back. Music was his drug of choice, and to that end, his discipline and determination served him well. So even though I felt the need to remind him of certain dangers, Prince was miles ahead of the rest of us when it came to this kind of thing.

I often read him the riot act about any number of potential pitfalls or land mines he might encounter in this life and career. I was fond of telling him, "Prince, you have the opportunity of a lifetime. Don't fuck it up." He heard me say repeatedly to be watchful of attorneys, accountants, and other industry types. Far too many artists, legends even, have been taken advantage of and died broke. I also told Prince to be wary of friends and family—not close family and friends, but those he might not be real close to, or people who just show up out of the blue. We may have bumped heads from time to time, but Prince was a good listener and always respectful. Regardless, Prince was about as strong-willed a person as I've ever met, and he was always going to do what he thought best for him.

15

THE MINNEAPOLIS STORY

AS WINTER APPROACHED in 1978, Prince and the band had been rehearsing in my basement for the better part of six months. The band was real tight, and Prince was dying to show the world what he was building. One day he said to me, "Pepé, we're ready. I want to do a show." He expressed his interest in performing live to Owen Husney as well, and we all agreed it was time. Owen started conversations with Warner Bros. about setting up a showcase for some of their top executives.

I was charged with finding a venue, and the first place that came to mind was the Capri Theater on West Broadway Avenue in north Minneapolis. With about five hundred seats, the Capri seemed to be about the right size, and it was something of a historic cornerstone of the neighborhood. Originally one of several movie theaters on the north side, it is the only one still around today.

I went to meet with a guy named Ira "Smitty" Smith, who owned the Capri at the time. Ira was a funny dude whose signature phrase was, "You know what I mean-o!" It didn't take much to convince Ira to agree to a deal, and we scheduled three consecutive gigs on January 5, 6, and 7.

The Capri had some limitations for live performances, and we had to bring in proper concert lighting for the show. In the Twin Cities, a place called the Naked Zoo was the standard-bearer in that regard, so I arranged to rent lights from them. Established in 1970, Naked Zoo provides local entertainment and event services still today and, in addition to Prince, has supported a who's who of rock and roll acts over the years.

Kristie, Marcy, and I were responsible for all the concert promotion, and Kristie even designed and printed the tickets for the shows herself. We charged $4.00 in advance and $4.75 at the door. If each show were to sell out, that would mean more than $2,000 per night. Of course, making money wasn't the priority; this was an opportunity for Prince to show Warner Bros. he was ready.

The middle show, on Saturday, January 6, was to be the showcase for the label executives. The Friday night show, which served as a dress rehearsal of sorts, went well. The only negative thing I remember was that the Capri staff tried to control the ticket revenue at the door. That was not the arrangement we agreed upon. I had seen these kinds of tricks before, and I made certain we were in charge of the money.

After the Friday show, I could tell Prince was confident the execs from Warner Bros. would be duly impressed the following night. I believed so too, but unfortunately things didn't quite go as planned. I don't recall if Mo Ostin was there or not, but I remember that Russ Thyret, Barry Gross, and a few others made the trip. It was a typically cold January night in Minneapolis, and the building, which was more than half a century old, was not exactly well heated. Still, I was sure the energy and excitement Prince and the band would bring could more than make up for that.

Things started well enough, and the emcee for the show, the venerable KMOJ disc jockey Kyle Ray, was downright prophetic in his introduction when he proclaimed to the Capri Theater audience, "The Power. The Glory. The Minneapolis Story. Prince." The local reviews were generally good, and Jon Bream reported that Prince was an "extraordinary talent."

However, issues with the sound and the equipment created some problems during the concert. I think Dez was trying out a wireless amp that malfunctioned, and there was some feedback that annoyed the hell out of Prince. All in all, it was an uneven performance. Although they had to recognize Prince's skill and showmanship, Warner Bros. told him after the show that he wasn't ready to tour.

Prince was devastated. The best way I can describe his response was equal parts mad and sad. He didn't agree with Warner Bros., and frankly neither did I. But there wasn't much we could do about it. I remember Chazz hanging around after the gig trying to cheer Prince up, without much success. I simply told Prince he should get back to work and prove them wrong. But I don't know if anyone could have gotten through to him that night. He decided not to proceed with the final show scheduled for Sunday night.

As wounded as he must have been from the experience, there's no question in my mind that it elevated his vision, motivation, and resolve even higher. Rehearsals stopped in our basement at 3809 Upton Avenue as Prince wanted to work alone in his own home studio in Edina. I thought this was a good idea. Even though most of the time the band spent rehearsing in my basement was pleasant, and everyone seemed to have fun despite the long hours and exhausting work, I think everybody needed a moment to relax and regroup as they went back to the drawing board.

A week or so after the Capri shows, Prince complained to me that he was uncomfortable in his basement studio. It was the dead of winter and he was having trouble getting the heat right. I told him it was his manager's job to take care of that sort of thing and Owen needed to provide him with space heaters or something. Prince made such a request of Owen, but apparently Owen seemed disinterested in helping. I think tensions already had been mounting between them, and this was the last straw for Prince. So Prince sent me to Owen's office to fire him. I didn't have the authority to fire Owen, but I was acting as a messenger for Prince, who was reticent about doing it himself. I wasn't particularly excited about the mission, but I knew something had to be done.

I went to Owen's office at the Ad Company, one of several businesses that Owen ran, and told him, "Prince is not happy. He's cold in his basement and needs some space heaters." Owen was visibly irritated, as if he didn't have the time or the request was somehow beneath him. He said, "So I'm supposed to leave my company and do all this for someone who probably won't even make it in this business?" After processing what he just said, I responded, "Owen, I came over here to let you know that you're fired." He looked at me and said, "You manage him then." I told Owen that I was not a manager, but I was going to make damn sure Prince didn't get screwed over in this business.

Owen's recollection of our meeting is different than mine. He says it didn't happen that way and that he decided to quit on his own. People often remember things differently and through their own lens, but I am certain that it happened as I described: Prince sent me to fire Owen, and that's what I did. Due to legal and other matters, Owen wasn't officially let go from his contract until 1980. But effectively, he was done as Prince's manager.

Unfortunately, Owen and I would have other differences even after his time with Prince ended. Owen was also Sue Ann Carwell's manager, and using the same formula that helped him secure Prince's deal with Warner Bros., he began to package her for presentation to the labels. As that was going on, Sue Ann mentioned to me that she was not comfortable with the agreement she had signed and asked if I could help. So I arranged a meeting at my house with Owen, Sue Ann's father, David Z., and Cliff Siegel, an associate of Owen's.

When I reviewed the management agreement, I said straight up, "This is not fair. You guys have to tear this up immediately." Everybody got a decent percentage of the deal, even Sue Ann's dad. I told them, "When you add this up, Sue Ann is the one left with nothing." To their credit, they all agreed and recognized my point. They ripped up the contract and began to work on a new one. I don't think they were trying to take advantage of her; they just didn't think it through. Nevertheless, I know Sue Ann appreciated that I was looking out for her.

Although she used to hang out at our house all the time, and even recorded a version of 94 East's "Lovin' Cup," I never had the opportunity to work with Sun Ann myself. Her recording of "Lovin' Cup" came about from an occasion when Prince, André, and I were in the studio together at Sound 80. As we were leaving, Sue Ann was coming in to record a demo with David Z. and Owen. We must have left a tape behind with "Lovin' Cup" on it, because that was the session when she recorded the song. I likely would have never even known about it, but Terry Jackson, who played in the original lineup of Grand Central with Prince, André, and Chazz, knew about it. When Terry told me, I couldn't believe Owen would do that without asking. I would have happily granted permission. As it was, we had to contact our attorneys, who sent cease-and-desist letters to Owen and instructed him to destroy all copies.

I asked Owen, "If you were going to record it, why didn't you consider it for Sue Ann's debut album?" He told me they already had enough songs and didn't need it. I thought, *Yeah, okay. Whatever.* Still, my gut told me that they didn't destroy all the copies. This was confirmed years later. Owen and I were hanging out and for some reason he mentioned Sue Ann's recording of "Lovin' Cup." On a hunch I said, "You know, Owen, I would love a copy of that." He said sure and soon forwarded a copy of Sue Ann's recording. In truth, she did a great job with the song, and had things gone down differently, I would have loved to see it released.

Despite our differences, Owen and I have maintained a close friendship to this day. Even after the cease-and-desist order, he would still sometimes invite us to his parties on Forty-Fourth and France Avenue in the Linden Hills section of Minneapolis. Kristie, Marcy, and I always enjoyed his hospitality and were happy to see him on those occasions. We'd make small talk about what Prince was up to and how his other artists were doing. 94 East even recorded some tracks at Owen's American Artists Studios, the same place where André recorded his first two albums. Even though things didn't end well, I can't deny that Owen played a big role in the early stages of Prince's career and had a big impact on the local scene in general. In addition to Prince, Owen managed and helped secure record deals for Sue Ann, André, and Jesse Johnson.

After I told Prince I had fired Owen, he asked me to be his manager. I told him straight up, "Prince, you know that I would do anything for you. But I am not a manager. It just wouldn't be right. You need someone who's a pro." Still, he insisted, so I agreed to take over the reins temporarily until I found someone better suited to the task. I only had one favor to ask of him. In the whole time I had been around Prince, I never took a dime from him, not even as his interim manager. And just as I had sacrificed for him, Prince was always there for me, especially when I needed him most. At this point, there was little doubt in my mind that he was poised to receive a lot more exposure in the months and years ahead. So I said, "Prince, all I ever need you to do for me is say my name in public, just once." I knew an endorsement from Prince would open doors for me as I pursued my own career. Prince didn't hesitate. "Sure," he said. "I'll mention your name." And that was our agreement.

When considering what manager to pair with Prince, the first person I thought of was Don Taylor. In addition to having a stable of impressive clients that included the Imperials and Bob Marley, Don was well respected in the industry, and I thought he would work well with Prince. They had met before, back when I took Prince and André to New York City to record with the Imperials and Tony Silvester. Don liked Prince and immediately recognized his extraordinary talent. Prince signed off on the idea of working with Don, and Don flew the two of us to his base of operations in Miami.

With Prince about to record his second album for War-ner Bros., we were certain that some sort of tour would be in the works later that year. Don's first act as Prince's man-ager was to call the label and have them double the tour budget. Prince seemed impressed, and things looked to be on the right track.

In April 1979, Prince made his way to Alpha Studios in Burbank to record *Prince*. André and probably Bobby were there with him, but as had been the case with *For You*, Prince controlled the recording from start to finish, produc-ing every track, playing all the instruments, and performing nearly all the vocals.

With half the band gone for most of the spring, I approached Dez with an idea. I told him I knew how talented he was and that I wanted to produce some original material of his. I suggested that we split the publishing equally, and he immediately took to the idea. Within a few days, the two of us were on our way to the Sound Palace in New York City. For his part, Dez had no intention of doing anything behind Prince's back. Although he had been around for only a year or so, Dez was fully committed to Prince. Nonethe-less, I knew he was interested in developing his own music. Moreover, he had the talent, the look, and the attitude to go solo someday, and like Prince and André, Dez was a multi-instrumentalist and quite the showman. He also had more experience than anyone in the band, including Prince. He had played with the Minneapolis-based outfit the Lit-ter, who released an album on ABC/Dunhill Records, and he fronted a couple other popular rock bands in the Twin Cities, most notably Revolver and Romeo.

At the Sound Palace, we recorded three original songs by Dez: "Livin' for a Reason," "Get Off on the Music," and

"Honest Emotion." Dez took the sessions very seriously, and his skills and his knowledge of the studio were even greater than I had thought. Dez had a cool about him too, and I knew he and André were the perfect duo to stand on either side of Prince onstage—and that both of them were destined to do their own thing.

Of course, regardless of where he was or what he was doing, Prince always seemed to know what was going on with those around him, and he found out about our excursion to New York. He called me to express his dismay. "Pepé," he said, "what do you think you're doing? Dez is my guitar player. He's in my band." I told him I knew that, "But what I'm doing for Dez is the exact same thing I did for you. It is exactly the same thing I promised to do for André. There's no difference. I don't see what the big deal is."

Prince wasn't satisfied with my explanation, but I think he recognized that I had a point and that Dez needed to spread his wings as well. Plus, it wasn't as if I had pulled Dez out of rehearsals. With Prince in Los Angeles and Dez sitting idle in Minneapolis, it was time well spent. I understand that Prince was just trying to protect his group, but he had to know that I would never try to undermine him. I was just trying to help Dez. By the time Dez and I made it back to Minneapolis, it seemed as if all was forgotten.

Shortly after he returned from Los Angeles, Prince took the band to Boulder, Colorado, for a few weeks in July to work on a side project that he dubbed the Rebels. The now-famous sessions featured original compositions from Prince, André, and Dez, with each of them generally handling lead vocals on their own songs. I believe Gayle Chapman provided vocals on one or two of Prince's songs as well.

As I recall, Prince wanted to release these sessions

anonymously, similar to what he did with the Madhouse recordings in the late 1980s. Unfortunately, Warner Bros. wasn't interested in taking such a risk. I thought the sessions were spectacular and especially highlighted the talents of André and Dez, but no one else would hear the Rebels until it was bootlegged years later. Among André's contributions to the project was "Thrill You or Kill You," which he had demoed a few years earlier at Music Farm Studios in New York City. Dez's offerings included "Too Long" and "Disco Away," which was a nod to his hard-rock roots in St. Paul. Prince's songs from that demo included "The Loser," "Hard to Get," "You," and "If I Love You Tonight." The first two were never released, but "You" and "If I Love You Tonight" were recorded and released in the early 1990s by Paula Abdul and Mica Paris, respectively. André and Dez also contributed a couple of instrumental tracks.

I always felt that, in some way, Prince's decision to go to Colorado was a validation of me taking Dez to New York a couple of months earlier. The Rebels may have been an opportunity for Prince to let his two sidemen start coming into their own a bit. Regardless of his reasons for the venture, I believe the Rebels would have been a big hit had it been released, anonymously or otherwise.

While Prince and the band were out west, I was spending time writing new songs and hanging out with friends. The activity I was indulging in probably more than any other, however, was drug use, especially cocaine. Having been around the music business for nearly two decades, I found that drugs were always part of the landscape. I wasn't casual about it; I knew drugs were a big deal and that I wasn't doing myself any favors by using. On the other hand, I guess I always assumed that I could keep it under control.

However, as time went on, the drugs were starting to get the better of me. I couldn't concentrate on music. I'd try, but I'd wake up in the morning with drugs on my mind, thinking about how I could get some money to support my habit. At the time, it seemed to be the only thing that mattered.

At the same time, as Prince's star was continuing to rise, my role in his life and career was changing. For the better part of five years, Prince and I had been almost a daily part of each other's lives. That was less and less true by now, and in many ways, I had been the one who set that in motion. After all, Prince had asked me to manage him, and I turned him down. Still, to this day, I know it was the right decision. Prince needed a skilled and experienced manager, and that wasn't me. I don't think I could have evolved into that role either. I haven't got the patience to be a manager. Moreover, Prince was family, and I never wanted a manager-artist relationship to get in the way of that.

Things started to look very good for Prince in late August 1979 when the lead single from *Prince* was released. Unlike "Soft and Wet," the first single from *For You*, "I Wanna Be Your Lover" was released nearly two full months before the album. This gave Prince some momentum, and "I Wanna Be Your Lover" eventually reached number one on Billboard's R&B chart and second on the dance chart. It peaked at eleven on the Billboard Hot 100. Prince had his first bona fide hit.

By the time *Prince* was released in October, Don Taylor was already out as manager. I wasn't even aware of it until I read the album's liner notes, which listed Tony Winfrey and Perry Jones as Prince's management. Technically, Bob Cavallo and Joe Ruffalo were his senior management team at Warner Bros., and they appointed Winfrey and Jones to handle day-to-day operations. Winfrey and Jones provided him with a lot of support during the recording of *Prince*, so I assume he felt comfortable with them at the helm.

I never found out what happened with Don, whether it was him or Prince who wanted the change. Maybe it was mutual. I know there was a lot of turmoil in Don's life at the time, including a well-publicized falling out with his top client, Bob Marley.

Another thing that caught my eye in the liner notes to *Prince* was my inclusion in the "thank-yous." What was notable about it, however, was that whoever transcribed Prince's notes must have assumed he was referring to two people, and the listing read "Pepé, Willie," in between two other names. I was so appreciative that he included me, and the error didn't really bother me. I just thought it was funny, as it reminded me of my youth when everyone either told me I had two first names or assumed my name was Willie Pepé.

With the release of the new album, Warner Bros. scheduled a short club tour to kick off in late November at the Roxy Theatre in West Hollywood. After an extended break, the tour would resume with another hometown showcase at the Orpheum Theatre. As Prince and the band rehearsed for the upcoming gigs, Winfrey and Jones came around from time to time to hang out. They were really cool and always kept me up to date on what was coming up next for Prince. They mentioned that following the January release of the album's second single, "Why You Wanna Treat Me So Bad," Prince would be making his first national television appearances with visits to *The Midnight Special* and *American Bandstand*. It was a memorable milestone for the rising superstar in more ways than one.

16

HOMECOMING

ON THE AFTERNOON of January 26, 1980, just three months after the release of his second album, Prince and the band appeared on Dick Clark's *American Bandstand*. Prince made his true national television debut on *The Midnight Special* a couple of weeks earlier, but this was bigger. Much bigger. I had been looking forward to it ever since Tony Winfrey and Perry Jones had told me about it a few months before.

The *American Bandstand* performance had been recorded in mid-December, but nobody warned me about what I was about to witness on my television screen. And what I saw, I could not believe. Things started out great, with Prince and the band performing "I Wanna Be Your Lover." As was customary on the show, they were to perform two songs, with a brief interview with Dick Clark in between. After they finished the first song, Clark went over to Prince and asked him where he learned to play this kind of music, adding, "this is not the kind of music that comes from Minneapolis, Minnesota." Some have suggested that this offended Prince and soured him on the interview. However, Dez has maintained that Prince's evasive and lackadaisical attitude toward Clark was deliberate. Whatever his motivation, I was pissed.

Whether he was answering a question with his hand, giving circuitous or even nonsensical responses, or coming off as overly bashful, I thought it was a bad look. This was Prince's first opportunity to speak directly to a large national audience. I couldn't believe he would squander such a big opportunity. The band went on to perform "Why You Wanna Treat Me So Bad," and if nothing else, Prince confirmed to America his exceptional talent and showmanship.

A few days after the show aired, Prince came over to my house. I didn't wait to flip out on him. The moment I saw his face I shouted, "What the fuck happened to you? What were you doing?" Prince didn't so much as blink. He calmly responded by saying that when Clark first opened his mouth, "I realized that millions of people were watching me." He then added, "I will never let that happen again." I reiterated to him that he needed to keep the media on his side. I believe his experience on *American Bandstand* was one impetus for why Prince vigorously controlled the interview process for the rest of his career.

By February, the *Prince* album and its debut single, "I Wanna Be Your Lover," were both nearing platinum status, and "Why You Wanna Treat Me So Bad" was racing up the Billboard R&B chart. Prince and the band were preparing to take the stage at the Orpheum Theatre for another hometown showcase. I always believed that Prince's shows at the Capri a year earlier, although a bit uneven and plagued by technical problems, were otherwise quite impressive. I rationalized Warner Bros.' decision not to let him tour on the heels of those gigs as them simply flexing their muscle. Maybe they didn't want his head to get too big too soon.

Either way, I was confident Prince was ready for a much bigger stage. He had received good press for his club gigs in

Hollywood, Denver, Dallas, and New Orleans. More than anything, I knew he refused to lose. Warner Bros.' decision to keep him off the road a year earlier didn't sit well with Prince, and to my mind, it all but guaranteed that he would tear up his hometown stage this time around. And neither I nor the twenty-six hundred or so others in attendance at the Orpheum were disappointed.

Prince had been on the road for the better part of two months prior to the show, so I hadn't seen or spoken to him much. I was excited to catch up and talk some more after the concert. As I headed backstage to Prince's dressing room (where several scenes from *Purple Rain* were later filmed), I could sense a buzz in the air in the wings of the Orpheum. I am sure the executives from Warner Bros. were pleased with what they had seen. Everyone seemed to be amped with excitement. The only person whom I got a funny vibe from was Prince himself.

I could never have anticipated the scene I found in the dressing room that night. Prince was sitting in a chair with two guys standing on either side of him. I had never seen them before, but they were acting like they were Prince's handlers. I expected Prince to jump up and greet me or any number of others who came backstage to see him. That was generally how he reacted to people close to him. But he never got up from the chair. I realized there was some sort of greeting line, with people walking up one by one to say hello or whatever. He sat there like he was a king or the Godfather exchanging niceties with an adoring public. When I reached the front of the line I said, "Hey, Prince. Great show!" He sort of nodded and muttered a subdued, "Thanks." He almost acted like he barely knew me. He was like that with everyone that night. Prince was usually at his most uninhibited when he was performing and then hanging out after a show. But this environment was anything but relaxed. The whole aura was strange. He was like a different person. *What the fuck is going on?* I asked myself.

I also noticed that Tony Winfrey and Perry Jones were nowhere to be seen. As it turned out, they had been let go several weeks before. I had talked to Prince a couple of times since they'd been fired, and he never mentioned anything about it to me. Of course, I also had found out secondhand when Don Taylor was fired, so I guess I shouldn't have been surprised.

Winfrey and Jones were replaced by another protégé of Cavallo and Ruffalo named Steve Fargnoli. The three of them, who jokingly referred to themselves as Spaghetti Inc., together would represent Prince for the better part of the 1980s. Nevertheless, I didn't see Steve there that night either. I had no idea who was in charge.

The two guys surrounding Prince acted as though no one was allowed to talk to him beyond a brief hello. Prince clearly was okay with this and was completely detached from everyone who was there. I made my way around the room for a little bit, making small talk with André, Dez, Bobby, Matt, and others. Then I left, feeling rather cold and confused.

I thought back to a conversation I'd had with Prince a few months earlier. It was just after *Prince* had been released, and the two of us were hanging out at Sam's, the club that would soon be renamed First Avenue. During our conversation, he looked at me and said, "Pepé, I want to go where people can't find me." I asked what he meant, and he essentially repeated himself without further explanation. I wasn't sure why he would say something like that. I often told Prince to be wary of family and friends, but I never expected him to say those things or to exhibit the kind of behavior he did backstage at the Orpheum.

It seemed to me that his new people were trying to set up a wall around Prince. Not long after the Orpheum gig, Chazz told me a similar story. He had seen Prince at a department store in downtown Minneapolis and went up to say hi to him. Prince's handlers intervened, like he was some sort of crazed fan. Chazz told me, "Pepé, they wouldn't even let me talk to him. I couldn't believe it." I couldn't believe it either and hoped it was just a phase Prince was going through.

After the Orpheum show, Prince did another week on the club circuit, including two nights at New York City's famous Bottom Line. The big news, however, was that Prince had been tapped to open for Rick James on his *Fire It Up* tour, which ran through the spring of 1980. I thought this was great, as the opportunity would expose Prince to a much wider audience and much bigger venues, including large theaters and arenas. Critics and concertgoers alike said that Prince upstaged James during the tour, which reportedly fueled a long-standing feud between the two.

Prince also began to coax Vanity over from James's camp, which must have only twisted the knife further into James's side. Prince had first met the beautiful young model/actress from Canada named Denise Matthews in early January at the American Music Awards. Soon rechristened Vanity, she not only would become Prince's girlfriend but ultimately was tapped to be the lead singer of his girl group, Vanity 6. James had intended all along to form his own female group, which he later did with the Mary Jane Girls. Prince also lured another member of James's musical empire to his own when he brought Jill Jones, a background singer for James protégé Teena Marie, into the fold.

Despite the real-life tensions that existed between Prince and James in the early 1980s, I am pretty sure Prince ultimately moved beyond it and no longer saw it as a rivalry. I am told he rarely if ever mentioned James; he certainly never spoke about him to me. Yet, in his posthumous autobiography *Glow*, James had some disparaging things to say about Prince. For his part, Prince just let it go. I imagine that, in his heart, Prince respected James regardless of what James said about him.

With Prince on the road for much of the spring of 1980, things were quiet back in Minneapolis. In April, our household received some devastating news, however, when Kristie's father, LeRoy Francis Lazenberry, unexpectedly passed away at the age of seventy-two. To say that Mr. Lazenberry was a great man would be an understatement. He was kind, thoughtful, and caring. He opened his home to me and was extremely supportive of everything 94 East did. Unfortunately, I was so messed up on drugs around that time that I don't think I gave Kristie and her family the emotional support they needed. I spent much of that period in a daze, and I regret that I was not more attentive.

As I look back, I think not only about the tremendous support we received from Mr. Lazenberry but also the encouragement and assistance from Marcy's mother, Marcella Ingvoldstad, or "Mama Marcy," as we affectionately called her. The impact of these two on 94 East, and on my own life, was indelible. And I have no doubt that their generosity and devotion positively affected Prince and his band during those early years.

As someone who came of age in the late 1960s and early 1970s, I am reminded of all the nameless and faceless individuals who contributed so gallantly to the civil rights struggle and other movements of the era. There are always those who receive the lion's share of the credit and attention, and often deservedly so, but there are an uncountable number of anonymous souls working in the shadows whose dedication drives the movement and its success. I think the notion of the everyday yet unknown hero is a common theme in any field, be it business, social, artistic, or otherwise. Mr. Lazenberry and Mrs. Ingvoldstad were two such people, and their contributions during the early days of the Minneapolis Sound can never be minimized.

Marcy's mother, Marcella Ingvoldstad, was a strong believer in 94 East from the start. She was also a talented singer in her own right.

Marcy and Kristie with Kristie's father, LeRoy Lazenberry. Mr. Lazenberry was always supportive of me and 94 East.

17

NEW BREED LEADER

ALMOST IMMEDIATELY AFTER finishing the Rick James tour, Prince began work on his next album. Instead of spending time in a California studio, he planned to record it at home. Prince had since moved from Edina and was renting a house in Wayzata not far from Lake Minnetonka. His studio in the new house was much better suited to record an album than that in his old digs.

I had not seen Prince perform in a while, aside from the television appearance and his hometown show, and I heard that his set had become more risqué. From the beginning, sex played a big role in the mystique that surrounded Prince and his music. Personally, I thought the way Prince infused sexuality into some of the songs on his first two albums was rather creative. Double entendre and sexual innuendo were certainly in the tradition of a lot of rock and roll and blues artists, yet Prince's use of these devices struck me as unique. He was fearless when it came to pushing the envelope, whatever it might represent. And although I sometimes thought he was too forceful in his approach, I admired him for taking risks, especially at such a young age. Prince was an innovator when it came to blurring the lines of race, sex, gender, and societal norms. That said, I was not prepared for how much the next record would blow these artistic subtleties out of the water.

One member of the band already had become disillusioned with the overly suggestive stage show and the new material that was being developed for the *Dirty Mind* album. Gayle Chapman, who held strong religious convictions, found the overt sexual themes to be more than she could handle. As a result, she decided to leave the band. I think everyone was a little shocked by this. Gayle had come into Prince's camp as a huge fan, having nearly worn out her copy of *For You* before she even auditioned. Plus, in addition to being a talented singer and keyboardist, Gayle played a key part in fulfilling Prince's vision of a multiracial, multigender group.

Although he was upset, I know Prince respected her and her decision. I certainly did. Gayle was and still is a beautiful person, inside and out. And, as Prince and I used to say, she's one of the "funkiest white chicks" you'll ever meet.

Gayle's replacement arrived in the form of another talented woman: Lisa Coleman of Los Angeles. Classically trained, Lisa came from a musical family, and her father was a member of the Wrecking Crew, a well-regarded collective of Hollywood session musicians who recorded with stars across musical genres. Though she was only nineteen at the time, Lisa herself came into Prince's camp with solid experience. In addition to some television work, she had been part of a group called Waldorf Salad, which had been signed to A&M Records and included her siblings and a close family friend, Jonathan Melvoin.

Notwithstanding the rather controversial themes on the album, *Dirty Mind* was released in the fall of 1980 to widespread praise. The critics acclaimed not only the music but also Prince's uncompromising, in-your-face sexuality. There had been internal struggles at Warner Bros. over whether to even release the album, but Prince stood his ground as always, and Warner Bros. conceded. Whereas *For You* introduced him to the world and *Prince* brought him some early commercial and critical success, *Dirty Mind* served as his musical and political manifesto. The songs were so raw, so funky. Songs like the Morris Day–penned antiwar anthem "Party Up," and "Uptown," Prince's vision of a free-spirited, antiestablishment, multiracial utopia, spoke directly to his view of the world. Some other tracks on *Dirty Mind*, however, albeit every bit as funky, dealt with controversial subject matter like incest, oral sex, and other suggestive themes. As such, the album did not perform particularly well on the charts, nor did any of its singles. Nevertheless, Prince made the statement he wanted to with *Dirty Mind*, which foretold his musical, spiritual, and sociopolitical evolution.

I, for one, struggled with *Dirty Mind*. I thought the music was fabulous. And I championed the concepts of freedom, individuality, and rebellion that were explored on the record. But I had trouble getting past songs like "Head" and "Sister." I was nearly ten years older than Prince and came up in a different era. To be sure, sex had always been an archetype in popular music, and I was no prude, but to me, Prince took it too far with this album. I never talked to him about my feelings, as I didn't want to question his artistic expression. It was just a little too much for me to process.

In December 1980, Prince went on a short three-week tour in support of *Dirty Mind*. Among the stops was an appearance at the Ritz, a club that had recently opened in New York City's East Village. On December 6, just four days before Prince was scheduled to play the new club, U2 made its American debut on the same stage. And right between those historic shows by two artists who would rule the coming decade and beyond, the world lost one of its most iconic figures. On December 8, John Lennon was gunned down in front of his apartment building on Manhattan's Upper West Side. That was one of those, *Where were you when . . . ?* moments. It hit me hard, not only because of what Lennon meant to the world of rock and roll, but for his role as an activist as well.

After the first leg of the tour, which concluded at Chicago's Uptown Theatre on December 26, Prince spent the next couple of months in Minnesota. He kicked off the second leg of the *Dirty Mind* tour with a show at Sam's, which would soon become First Avenue, in downtown Minneapolis on March 9. Then Prince hit the road for another four weeks. We were a few months into the presidency of Ronald Reagan, and anyone who heard Prince's music or saw him perform live recognized that he was the antithesis of Ronald Reagan's America. Not that it mattered who the president was—Prince's vision had long been set in motion—but in the eyes of many, Prince was the perfect antidote.

I could see that Prince was really coming into his own as an artist and a live performer. The ability had always been there, but his confidence was growing exponentially. The band was also getting tighter, and each member seemed to be increasingly sure of themselves. It was clear to me that Prince was on a mission. I know that he knew I would always be there for him if he needed or wanted help, but I began to wonder, *Maybe he doesn't need me anymore. Maybe I've done everything I can for him.* It was terribly difficult for me to consider this, but again, I had been the one to decline his invitation to become his manager. After

I helped him through that transition period and the subsequent challenges with other managers, Prince had built a stable organization around him, which is all I ever wanted.

My struggles with some of the themes on *Dirty Mind* led me to drift further away from Prince's world. I still felt close to him, and we would hang out from time to time and talk on the phone. I called him quite a bit when he was on the road just to check in and see how life was treating him. Back then he would register at hotels under the name Groucho. If I knew where he was staying, I'd dial up the hotel switchboard and ask to speak to Groucho. If he happened to be in his room, we would chat about any number of things. Prince was always family to me, and I would love, support, and defend him no matter what.

As far as my own career, it was pretty obvious that 94 East wasn't going anywhere. Other members of the band were already pursuing other projects. In 1979, Pierre Lewis had released a record with his own group, the Lewis Connection, which featured Sonny Thompson on lead vocals and bass. Prince contributed guitar and backing vocals to the song "Got to Be Something Here" on the band's eponymous debut album. Wendell Thomas was also pursuing his own thing, and of course Bobby had already been with Prince for three years. That basically left me, Kristie, and Marcy.

Still, music was my life, my career. Even if I didn't have a band, I still had a business in PMI, and I could still help others. In the summer of 1981, we purchased a new home in suburban Maple Grove, which would become the new headquarters and, in my mind, the beginning of a new chapter for PMI. As soon as we moved in, Kristie, Marcy, and I set out to build the company. We installed a recording studio and got right to work.

That first summer we didn't have air conditioning in the home, so we usually left all the windows open. Coupled with the fact that our studio wasn't fully soundproofed yet, our neighbors could easily hear when we brought artists in for recording sessions. Maple Grove, which sits about fifteen miles northwest of downtown Minneapolis, was a relatively small, quiet suburb of about twenty thousand residents at the time, nothing like the sprawling hub of seventy thousand that it is today.

For the most part, our neighbors didn't take too kindly to the noise, and the police were called to our house on numerous occasions that summer. The police were generally cool about it, though. We let them know that we were just working, that music is what we did for a living. Fortunately, we were never fined or cited for disturbing the peace. Eventually, we did get air conditioning and moved the studio to the basement. We had no problems after that, and we became good friends with many of the neighbors as well.

In addition to working with local artists at the new PMI, we also launched a publication titled *The Music Outlet*. The slogan we used for *The Music Outlet* was the same as our corporate motto: "The music may be different, but the business is the same." I think we charged something like seven dollars for a one-year subscription. *The Music Outlet* was designed, in part, to educate young artists on the nuances, challenges, etiquette, and potential pitfalls of the music industry. The publication also addressed such topics as songwriting, recording, publishing, artist rights, and resources available to aspiring musicians. We had a question-and-answer column called "Getting It Straight from Pepé." In the premier issue, we included a get-well wish to Teddy Randazzo, who was ill at the time, as well as a "special message" to record company executives. The goal of this particular column was to address financial, production, public relations, and other critical issues as a strategy to foster better working relationships between artists and management types. *The Music Outlet* also covered local events, workshops, and showcases, and it frequently featured interviews with managers, attorneys, educators, and union leaders.

Putting out this type of publication was really important to me. It was something I always wanted to do, and now that it was a reality, I began to feel useful again. I had renewed hope for the future and my life in music.

Meanwhile, shortly after the *Dirty Mind* tour ended in the United States, Prince and the band made their first venture to Europe, playing gigs in Amsterdam, London, and Paris in June 1981. These turned out to be the last shows André ever played with Prince. André had made clear from the beginning that he would stick around for three albums and then go out on his own. And that's exactly what he did. Still, I know the timing of his decision was not totally as planned. In fact, had things between him and Prince been different, I think he might have stayed a little longer. I never spoke to Prince or André about it, but I heard that they had been at odds for some time. Although he is extremely laid back, André, just like Prince, is an alpha male. In spite of their brotherhood, they were bound to bump heads. Someone told me that they had a rather heated argument in Paris, and that was all André could stand.

One issue between them was Prince's new side project: the funk legends who came to be known as the Time. It's my understanding that the concept for the group actually came from André. Whether that was the last straw for him, I am not sure. André had already known for months that the Time's first record was getting ready to come out. I guess it was probably a culmination of things that made it difficult for him to stick around any longer. Either way, André soon left to start his solo career. He eventually signed a contract with Columbia Records and hired Owen Husney to be his manager.

If the mood was somewhat somber after the band returned from Europe, it didn't take long before it turned joyful. Dez married his longtime girlfriend, Rebecca, the day before Prince's twenty-third birthday. I don't know if the wedding was a last-minute thing, but I didn't find out that Dez had even gotten married until the day after. That was the day Prince held a birthday party at one of the industrial warehouses he rented during the 1980s. Located on Highway 7 in St. Louis Park, the building was used as a recording and rehearsal space. By this time, Prince had also moved to the famous "purple house" on Lake Riley in Chanhassen, which featured an upgraded home studio. Everyone seemed to be in a jovial mood at the party, including Prince, who for whatever reason had painted his face white.

As I mingled with friends and family, I noticed Shauntel out of the corner of my eye. The two of us had not spoken for quite some time, but I still loved and cared about her, so I wanted to say hi. She smiled as I approached, and we began to talk. I made sure to keep the conversation pleasant and platonic, and we hit it off great. I will always feel a bond with her; we just weren't good as a couple.

As we were talking, I noticed Prince and Morris in the corner laughing at me. When Shauntel and I finished our conversation, I decided to have a little fun at their expense. I made my way over to them, maintaining eye contact with them the whole time. When I reached them, I shouted, with feigned but convincing indignation, "What are you mother-fuckers laughing at?" They both froze, and Prince's face turned even whiter than the white makeup. I am sure they knew they had no reason to feel afraid of me, but I could tell they thought I was really pissed off. I waited a few seconds for dramatic effect and then just busted out laughing. They followed with their own laughter, and Prince admitted, "Yeah, Pepé, you got us good."

The three of us talked for a while, and I was taken back to those first days after I arrived in Minnesota. Whether it was rehearsals in Morris's attic, parties at the Anderson home, or the Cookhouse sessions, there were so many wonderful memories to recall. Things that happened five, six, seven years earlier seemed like just yesterday. Now, Prince was a big deal at home and, increasingly so, everywhere else. Morris was about to make his own move toward fame and celebrity with the Time. I felt some sadness about how things went down with André, but it was time for him to go out and make it on his own.

With another album and tour on the horizon, Prince needed a new bass player. From what I heard, Prince's first choice to replace André was Sonny Thompson. Sonny had been a contemporary of Prince and André's growing up, and he had fronted a group known as the Family that had a friendly rivalry with Grand Central. Not long after I arrived in Minneapolis, I told people that Prince and André were the two most gifted musicians in the city, but Sonny was right there with them. That became clear to me when he auditioned to be 94 East's drummer years before. Of course, Prince knew that long before I did. Truth be told, Prince idolized Sonny, even though they came up at the same time.

Sonny, like Prince, can play multiple instruments and is a monster on bass and guitar.

Sonny later said that Prince offered him the gig but wanted him to lose a few pounds first. I don't know that you could call Sonny fat, by any means; he was a big, strong dude. Still, Prince was looking for a certain image. As Sonny was diligently working the weight off, he was disappointed to find out that Prince went in another direction. Prince chose a nineteen-year-old bass player from nearby St. Louis Park named Mark Brown, whom he would rechristen with the stage name Brownmark. Mark was a phenomenal player. With the band's lineup complete once again, Prince continued his quest to conquer the music world.

18

WHAT TIME IS IT?

IN JULY 1981, just a few months before Prince's fourth album, *Controversy*, was to hit the streets, Warner Bros. inconspicuously released the eponymous debut album by a band from Minneapolis called the Time. Everyone around town knew that this was the first new act launched by Prince, but he went out of his way to keep that fact quiet at first.

As was the case with his own records, Prince wrote all the songs, with some help from Dez and Lisa. He also played just about every instrument, with some help from Matt on synthesizers, and added backing vocals. He produced the album under the pseudonym Jamie Starr.

Everything happened pretty fast. Originally, Alexander O'Neal was considered as lead singer for the group, as was Sue Ann Carwell. Alex, who was an exceptional talent in the tradition of the great soul singers of the 1950s and 1960s, was a veteran of the Minneapolis scene and fronted several bands, including Enterprise, which featured Morris Day on drums and Jesse Johnson on guitar. When first approached by Prince, Alex was with Flyte Tyme, having replaced Cynthia Johnson after she left to join Lipps Inc. Most of the musicians Prince wanted for the Time were already part of Flyte Tyme. Prince and Alex couldn't agree on financial terms, however, so Prince decided to look elsewhere. He didn't have to look far.

Like the legend of "Do Me Baby," which was included on *Controversy*, another famous song Prince "borrowed" from a friend came into play when he was putting together the Time. "Party Up," the final track on *Dirty Mind*, belonged to Morris Day. Prince told Morris that if he could have the song, he would help make Morris a star. It was time to make good on that promise.

Somebody once told me that Prince was influenced by the 1980 film *The Idolmaker*, which tells the story of an entertainment manager who takes young, raw musicians and turns them into rock stars. In a sense, Prince's creation of the Time was life imitating art, or perhaps art imitating art, if you will. Perhaps André got his idea from *The Idolmaker*. Either way, it was Prince's show now.

In addition to Morris, who despite some initial reticence proved to be a natural front man, Prince plucked Jesse Johnson from Enterprise. The original lineup of the Time was rounded out by Flyte Tyme members Jimmy "Jam" Harris and Monte Moir on keys, Terry Lewis on bass, and Jellybean Johnson on drums. The one and only Jerome Benton began as their valet and soon joined the band as well. Two others from the Flyte Tyme camp, David Eiland and Tony Johnson, were not brought over for the Time.

I felt especially bad for David, as this was the second time he was left out of a Prince project. Known around Minneapolis as "Batman," David is an amazing saxophonist. Chazz tells the story of how, during the early days of Grand Central, he and André went to Prince with the idea of adding David to the band. Prince wasn't interested, and that was that. Fortunately for David, he was able to fashion a distinguished career as a studio musician playing with the likes of David Bowie, Thelma Houston, and Junior, as well as the renowned roster of artists on the Jam and Lewis Flyte Tyme label from the mid-1980s through the 1990s.

The Time's debut album was very successful, especially when you consider that most of the music-buying public was initially unaware of Prince's involvement. It peaked at number fifty on the Billboard 200 album chart and cracked the top ten on the R&B album chart. Two of the album's three singles, "Get It Up" and "Cool," were top ten hits on the soul chart.

Prince was pleased with the early success of the Time, and as fall 1981 came around, he was anticipating the release of *Controversy*. A tour, with the Time as one of the opening acts, was scheduled to start in November, about a month after the album was to drop. Before that, however, Prince received what, at the time, must have felt like a huge blessing and opportunity: an invitation to open two shows for the Rolling Stones in Los Angeles.

Mick Jagger was a big fan of Prince's early work, and this would be a chance for Prince to significantly expand his audience. I know that Dez, being a rock and roll guy to his core, was extremely excited about the opportunity. I was hopeful, too, and I appreciated what the Stones saw in Prince, but I wasn't sure how the Stones crowd would respond to Prince's look or his material.

Still, I wanted Prince to know I supported him and was happy that things were going well for him. I went to visit rehearsals one evening at his warehouse space in St. Louis Park. As I walked into the building, Prince was in the middle of saying something to the band. I walked right up on the stage and started saying hi to everyone. I said hello to

Morris, and made my way around the stage, stopping to chat briefly with Matt, Bobby, Lisa, and Dez. It might have been the first time I met Brownmark. As I turned to say hi to Prince, he was standing there glaring at me. He had this half-smile, half-smirk on his face, and he asked, "Hey, Pepé, are you done yet?" Everybody broke out laughing, including Prince who was now sporting a full smile. I said, "Oh. Yeah, man. I'm sorry," and I went to take a seat. From the first time I saw him in action, I recognized that Prince took rehearsals seriously, more so than any other artist I have ever been around. That said, he also had a sense of humor and liked to have fun. It was nice to see neither of those things had changed even as his star was rising.

As Prince and the band got back to work, they were as tight as ever. Just like he was famous for doing onstage, Prince would employ an array of signals to keep them on point. In front of an audience, it became a regular part of the show, but in rehearsal it was almost like he was intentionally trying to mess them up. He made all these crazy noises, hand gestures, vocal changes—you name it. He would even wander out of sight of the band while still directing them. It was pretty cool. I can't imagine the band members enjoyed it much, but it worked. He had them finely tuned. Prince's level of discipline and the mastery of his band reminded me of James Brown. Contemporaries like Springsteen and Bono often commented on how extraordinary Prince was as a band leader. Seeing Prince live, particularly from the mid-1980s onward, was more than just witnessing the influence of Jimi Hendrix or Jackie Wilson; it was like reliving the days of great orchestra leaders like Count Basie and Duke Ellington.

Unfortunately, many of those in attendance at Los Angeles

Coliseum when Prince opened for the Rolling Stones didn't have the same appreciation for Prince. More than a few of them were likely shocked by his appearance and hyper-sexual stage show. Not that they would see much of it. Within minutes of Prince and the band taking the stage for the first gig in Los Angeles on October 9, 1981, the audience started pelting them with trash, food, bottles, you name it. After ripping through a few songs, Prince had had enough and left the stage. He went directly to the airport and flew home, leaving the band behind in California. After tele-phoned pleas from Dez and Mick Jagger, Prince flew back to LA for the second show, held two days later. After more of the same from the crowd, he cut the set short once again.

I never talked to him about it, but I know the experience was demoralizing. One thing that stuck out to me after-ward, though, was how supportive the band was through it all. Despite being left behind, both onstage and in LA, they stood up for him in the press, and more importantly, they let Prince know they had his back. In retrospect, I think going through such an experience may have been good for Prince, as it motivated him even more and helped bring the band closer together. And I am sure Prince was confident he would ultimately win over more than a few of the fans who had been at those gigs.

A few days after Prince and the band returned from Cal-ifornia, *Controversy* was released. Picking up where *Dirty Mind* left off, Prince continued to push the envelope with a provocative blend of rock, funk, and soul, and some other things mixed in. While sexual themes were still ubiquitous, Prince expanded on many of the social, political, and spir-itual motifs he had introduced on the previous record, fur-ther advancing his mystique.

The tour started on November 20, 1981, and it would keep Prince on the road for roughly twice as long as he'd ever been before. Fortunately, they were out of town for most of that winter, which saw record snowfalls in Minneapolis. This tour also saw Prince graduate to larger venues. Whereas the *Dirty Mind* tour was performed mostly in theaters, with a few clubs and small arenas mixed in, the *Controversy* tour brought Prince's act to midsized and larger arenas across the country. Some of the largest venues included Detroit's Joe Louis Arena, the Omni in Atlanta, Cincinnati's Riverfront Coliseum, and Kemper Arena in Kansas City.

On March 7, 1982, a week before the end of the tour, Prince and the band played the Met Center, the Twin Cities' premier concert venue at the time. Located in suburban Bloomington, the Met Center was home to the NHL's Minnesota North Stars and had a capacity of about sixteen thousand. (Today, it's the site of an Ikea.) The Met Center had sentimental value to me personally, having been home to the ABA's Minnesota Pipers in 1968–69 when my cousin Connie Hawkins was on the team.

Around the time the *Controversy* tour rolled into town, I was looking for some musical inspiration to help me come up with new material of my own. More than anything, though, I was looking forward to catching up with Prince and seeing him perform in a big venue. Not only was it a big deal for Prince to play at this major hometown arena, but it was a huge coming-out party for the Time, whose only local show had been a date at Sam's the previous fall. The Time had been lauded with critical acclaim during the tour, and the seats at the Met Center were filling up earlier and faster than they normally would for an opening act. I got to the arena early myself, picked up my backstage pass and my ticket, and found my seat in plenty of time to see Morris and the fellas.

As I was eagerly waiting for the Time to take the stage, a friend tapped me on the shoulder. "Shauntel and Mattie Dell are outside," he said. "Security won't let them in." I looked at him and asked, "What, now? Are you kidding me?" He wasn't, so I got up and headed to the ticket office to find them. Most of the Met Center staff knew me because I was there all the time, and I knew it wouldn't be difficult to get Shauntel and Mattie in. I opened the door, motioned for them to come inside, and then announced to anyone who was within earshot, "This is Prince's mom and this is Prince's cousin. They are coming in!" Despite feeling a bit humiliated, Mattie and Shauntel were thankful to get inside. I found some seats for them and told them I'd see them later. I then made my way backstage to Prince's dressing room.

On the way, I couldn't help but wonder why Prince hadn't made proper arrangements for his mother and cousin. He wasn't new to touring, and he should have known better. Maybe he figured this was his hometown and it wouldn't be an issue, or perhaps he assumed his people had taken care of it. When I walked into the dressing room, Prince smiled and said, "Pepé, what's up, man?" I was pleased to see the Prince that I had always known, and not the guy I saw backstage at the Orpheum a year earlier. I told him the Met Center staff wouldn't let his mom and cousin in the building. Prince instantly became agitated. "What?" he shouted. I told him I had taken care of it and they were good, but I just wanted him to know. He thanked me and said, "Cool." I said I would see him after the concert and went back to my seat.

Both Prince and the Time were phenomenal that night. Prince and his band were getting better and better with each tour. As for the Time, they were so much fun to watch. It goes without saying that they were all incredible musicians, but the image Prince had fashioned for them came off perfectly as well. I think Prince probably wondered to himself more than once, *Are these guys* too *good?*

The next night, Prince put on a surprise gig at First Avenue, his first appearance at the club since it had been renamed a few months before. He and I talked a bit that night, and he was telling me about the people around him. "Pepé," he said, "people have stopped listening to me." I responded by saying, "Then now is the time to fire everyone." I wasn't referring to the band, of course, but rather the managers and hangers-on. Either way, he didn't take my advice then. Later in his career, however, Prince would completely clean house on more than one occasion.

Despite his worries, the First Avenue gig went off great. At one point during the first set, Prince invited Sue Ann onstage to sing "Still Waiting" from his second album. Sue Ann's debut album had been out for a while by this point, and she had released two or three singles of her own. After a break, the Time took the stage for a few songs before Prince and the band returned. Prince asked Morris to sit in on the drums for a spirited rendition of "Party Up." There was no doubt the past few nights had been a triumphant homecoming for Prince and the Time.

With a handful of dates still left on the current tour, Prince already had his sights set to the future. It amazed me how he was always thinking a step or two ahead when planning his vision or charting his next course. I'm not sure if it was because he got easily bored or if he just had so much he wanted to share with the world. I imagine it was a little of both. Regardless, without fail, Prince would be onto the next project even before the current one had ended. This model obviously served him well, because each new album and each new tour seemed to generate more positivity than the one before, from critics and fans alike. Prince was not yet where he wanted to be, but he was getting closer. He was standing on the verge of something massive.

19

IF YOU SEE ME

ONE NIGHT in the summer of 1982, Morris and I were hanging out, driving around downtown Minneapolis. He had bought his first car, a Ford Mustang, using some of the money he made from the tour. I am sure we were looking to get high, and we were parked along Washington Avenue when we saw Prince walking toward us. The first thing that went through my mind was, *What in the world is he doing down here?* Then I thought, *Oh no, Morris and I are looking for weed and here comes this square who's just gonna get in the way.* As ultracool as Prince was and always will be, he was almost nerd-like in some ways. And I say that in the most complimentary way possible.

As Prince approached the car, Morris rolled down his window. We exchanged greetings, and then Prince reached across the driver's side of the car, handed me a cassette, and said, "Check this out, Pepé!" I inserted it in the tape deck and these funky, up-tempo drums kicked in. After a few bars came the synthesizers, then bass and guitar. Whatever it was, I knew I liked it. When the lyrics came in, they sounded different from anything I'd heard him do before. He seemed to be playing a character, taking on a different persona. Of course, this would be a common motif in some of his later work, but he hadn't done much of that at this point.

Before the first verse ended, Morris shouted, "Hey, Pepé! That's your song!" I didn't even recognize it at first. I must have been high already. But then I realized, "Yeah, man. That's 'If You See Me.'" Prince's version of the song has a much faster tempo than the original, and he changed the title to "Do Yourself a Favor." At the end of the song, he included a long monologue in which he's talking to his woman, which is absolutely hilarious. Among the priceless lines: "You know, honey, I ain't rich or nothin.' I ain't claimin' no miracles, but I am a bachelor now, baby. You know what I'm sayin'? Look out. Whooo! So just do yourself a favor, baby, and just walk on down the street."

Morris and I were cracking up, and I could tell Prince was pretty proud of himself. He obviously had a lot of fun recording it and was pleased with our response. It was real clever what he had done with the song. Prince said, "I'm going to put it on one of my albums." Excited, I replied, "Ah, man, that's great. I really appreciate that." I was truly flattered.

We chatted for a few more minutes and then parted company. I still wondered what he was doing there in the first place. We were parked at the north edge of downtown, near the post office along the Mississippi River. It didn't seem like a place Prince would be hanging out. Later, I learned that Kim Upsher, a close friend of his from Central High, lived in a new high-rise apartment building nearby called the Towers. So he was probably on his way to visit Kim.

In *Purple Rain*, Kim plays the waitress who serves Morris and Apollonia before Prince performs "The Beautiful Ones." I didn't know Kim well, but by all accounts, she was a great person. Chazz and others told me how crazy Prince was about her in high school. I know she and Prince dated off and on for a while. Even though it may not have worked out in the long run, they maintained a special bond.

One day, Prince asked me to do him a favor. Kim wanted to take a shot at becoming a singer, so at Prince's behest, I had Kim record one of my songs, the title of which escapes me now. I mixed her vocals and then let Prince hear the track. Although Kim wasn't the greatest singer, Prince and I agreed that the song worked for her. That was the last I ever heard about it, though. Kim went on to become an active and respected member in her community, working for the Minneapolis Public Schools and supporting neighborhood-based initiatives. Kim passed away unexpectedly in the fall of 2015. Her untimely death saddened and shocked the entire north side. I am sure it deeply affected Prince.

During the summer of 1982, Prince finished recording his next album, primarily at his home studio in Chanhassen as well as at Hollywood's famous Sunset Sound. A month or so before the album's release, the title track came out to less fanfare than I expected. Everyone I knew thought the song was mesmerizing. To my mind, "1999" was groundbreaking and destined to revolutionize popular music. It was the perfect single to lead with. Yet for some reason, it stalled outside the Billboard Top 40.

Meanwhile, Prince was preparing to embark on tour with the Time and his latest brainchild, Vanity 6, as the opening acts. Vanity 6 consisted of Denise Matthews, better known as Vanity; Minneapolis native Susan Moonsie; and Brenda Bennett, whose husband, Roy Bennett, was Prince's lighting designer. The Time's second record, *What Time Is It?*, and Vanity 6's debut album both had been released in August, and both went on to chart high on the Billboard 200 and reach the top ten on the R&B album chart.

Toward the end of pre-tour rehearsals, Prince decided to shoot music videos for three songs from the *1999* album: "Automatic," "Let's Pretend We're Married," and the title track, "1999." Prince invited Kristie, Marcy, and me to the shoot, and he made a point of making sure we accepted his invitation. The video shoot was at the Minneapolis Armory downtown. Prince was in a good mood when we arrived, and we had a great time. It was interesting to witness the making of a video firsthand. Music videos weren't exactly a new concept, and Prince had done a half dozen or so for his previous records. But MTV was new, and the advent of a prominent outlet for artists to release videos to the public was a game changer.

The video shoot for "1999" also marked the first time I saw Jill Jones. Jill had started in the business as a teenage vocalist for Teena Marie, and she met Prince when Teena opened for him on the *Dirty Mind* tour. Although not formally a member of the Revolution, Jill remained in Prince's camp for the better part of the decade. She appeared in the *Purple Rain* film alongside Kim Upsher as waitresses at First Avenue. Jill also played a significant role as Prince's girlfriend in the sequel to *Purple Rain*, 1990's *Graffiti Bridge*. Jill's 1987 self-titled debut album was one of the most critically acclaimed records ever released by an artist on Prince's Paisley Park label. In addition to providing vocals on *1999*, Jill was a backing singer on the tour, which would commence just days after the video shoot at the Minneapolis Armory.

The performances on "The Triple Threat Tour," as it was billed, were incredible. I first caught the tour during a three-night stand at Chicago's Auditorium Theatre in December.

In addition to Prince and the Time, I was excited to see Vanity 6 perform. Today, a lot of critics write off Vanity 6 as one of Prince's scantily clad female protégés, but that is unfair. Vanity, Susan, and Brenda all came from artistic backgrounds and were very talented. Prince wouldn't have hired them were they not.

The first leg of the tour ended just after the new year, and the bands took a nearly monthlong break before kicking off the second leg. During the time off, Kristie, Marcy, and I were charged with planning a big party for Prince in Minneapolis. It was mostly Marcy's baby, and she was in charge of just about everything—catering, lighting, invitations, prizes, giveaways, and the overall budget. The theme for the party was "A Lion in My Pocket," after a line from the song "1999," and there were plans to give away little stuffed lions. I don't remember why, but plans for the party ultimately were scrapped.

The night before the *1999* tour resumed in Florida, Prince filmed the video for "Little Red Corvette" at Lakeland Civic Center. The song would be released to radio as *1999*'s second single, and it quickly became Prince's biggest hit to date. The song's meteoric rise also resulted in the video receiving regular airplay on MTV, which helped to make Prince, along with Michael Jackson, among the first black superstars in the music video age.

On the heels of the success of "Little Red Corvette," the studio rereleased "1999" as a single, and it didn't take long for the song to crash the top ten on the Billboard Hot 100. It also charted well in the United Kingdom, Ireland, Canada, Germany, the Netherlands, Belgium, New Zealand, and Australia. The album reached number nine on the Billboard 200 and number four on the R&B/hip-hop albums chart.

The *1999* tour got bigger and bigger as it crisscrossed America, and it included a glorious return to Bloomington's Met Center and a stop at New York City's legendary Radio City Music Hall before coming to a close in Chicago. In all, the tour made stops in more than seventy cities across the United States between November 1982 and April 1983.

Over the course of his first five albums, Prince had steadily expanded his audience while honing his artistic vision. The success of *1999* left him poised to take things to yet another level, which seemed part of his master plan all along. He was looking to tear down the walls that had restricted black artists for decades. Prince would do everything on his own terms. No matter how hard executives at Warner Bros. might push back, Prince would push back harder. His dream for the next phase of his career was in place, and there was no chance he was going to fail—he simply wouldn't allow it.

One bump in the road came after the *1999* tour ended, with another key departure from the band. I always knew that Dez, like André before him, would ultimately pursue his own career, but his decision to leave still hit me hard. And although his departure was not particularly surprising, the reasons for it were. Like Gayle before him, Dez was becoming increasingly troubled by the overtly sexual nature of Prince's music and stage show. Dez had found solace in religion, and he could no longer reconcile the music he was performing with his Christian beliefs. Prince and Dez had a great deal of respect for each other and had been through so much together, and Dez undoubtedly had been a crucial influence on Prince during the early years. It appeared to me that Dez and Prince parted on good terms, and I was happy for Dez that he was able to follow his heart and go it alone.

Prince didn't have to look far to find a replacement. Wendy Melvoin, who had been friends with Lisa Coleman essentially since birth, had been hanging around Prince and the band for some time. Barely nineteen years old when she joined the band, Wendy had contributed to the *1999* album and would sit in for Dez on sound checks from time to time during the tour. Prince loved her sound, and the chemistry that she and Lisa brought to the group would heavily influence Prince's music in the coming years.

The other big news centered on Prince's most ambitious aspiration to date. I started to hear talk about Prince doing a movie. I am not sure how long he had the idea in mind, but it must have been awhile. Over the years, I have heard some people erroneously suggest that he wanted to one-up Michael Jackson's video for "Thriller." In fact, by the time "Thriller" was released, *Purple Rain* was already nearing its post-production phase. The story was that Prince had been jotting down film ideas in a purple notebook for the better part of a year. Furthermore, while I am sure that on many occasions he gained motivation from what others were doing, Prince always operated from his own vision. To their credit, Cavallo, Ruffalo and Fargnoli were supportive of Prince's desire to make a full-length motion picture, and despite some hesitation from the top brass at Warner Bros.' film division, plans for the film soon began.

Sometime during the summer of 1983, I got a call from Prince, and I asked him, "What is this movie I'm hearing about?" Prince replied, "That's why I'm calling. I have the perfect part for you." He wanted me to play the owner of a nightclub, which turned out to be First Avenue, of course. I told him that sounded great and I was looking forward to it. I didn't exactly jump for joy about it, partly because I had no idea how big this film might be; I don't know if Prince sensed disinterest on my part. We talked a little longer and then said our goodbyes.

The summer rolled on, and Prince became consumed in the filmmaking. Still, I expected to hear from him, but the call never came. I guess I was being stubborn and decided I wasn't going to call him about it. To my thinking, Prince was the one who offered the part, and he would contact me at the appropriate time.

Shortly after Prince's legendary performance at First Avenue in August 1983—a benefit for the Minnesota Dance Theatre at which he debuted five songs from *Purple Rain*— I started to hear about auditions for the film. Yet I still had not heard from Prince. A few more weeks went by, and I saw another ad for auditions. I knew my way around a film set, so I decided to go about it on my own. I went down to First Avenue to audition and was cast as a day player, just as I had been on *The Education of Sonny Carson* about a decade before. I wasn't sure what happened with the role Prince originally offered me, but I was happy to be a part of the production.

When filming got underway, I saw Prince on the set and we talked for a minute or two, but he never mentioned the part during our conversation. As it turned out, Prince gave the role to Billy Sparks, a well-known Detroit-based promoter whom Prince had known since the early days of his career. I often wonder if I had swallowed my pride and called Prince over the summer, would the role of club owner have gone to me?

During production, I made a point to stay close to the director, Albert Magnoli. I knew that being there, being on time, and being attentive might increase the number of scenes I was pulled into. The biggest scene I filmed was at First Avenue with Morris. The two of us were sitting at a table while a juggler performed onstage between musical acts. Neither Morris nor I had any lines during what was meant to be a filler scene, but we were directed to laugh at the juggler. Looking back, it's not hard to understand why this scene was cut. In fact, all the scenes I appeared in as an extra ended up on the cutting-room floor, except for one. Near the end of the film, after Prince performs "Purple Rain" and makes his way through the backstage area to his motorcycle, he runs by me. I was the last person he passes on the right side of the hallway.

Even though I didn't get much screen time, the experience of being on the set day in and day out was reward enough. I got to spend time around some old friends and met a few new ones as well. Shortly after auditions were complete and all the background roles had been cast, I noticed a young woman crying along the wall at First Avenue. Her name was Wendy Pridgen. Wendy certainly had the "look" of a star, and I soon found out that she had the talent too. When she was originally cast for the film, I think she had the impression that her role would be more significant. When she learned that she was basically an extra, it brought her to tears. I struck up a conversation with her and encouraged her to take advantage of the opportunity. I told her, "This might not be what you expected, but you're here. Make the most of this experience, as it can lead to bigger and better things." We became fast friends, and I enjoyed spending time with her on set.

The person I kept my eyes on the most, however, was Jill Jones. I had a huge crush on Jill ever since Prince brought her to Minneapolis in early 1982. There was something about Jill that I found almost intimidating. The entire time she was on the scene, I never got up the courage to tell her I was crushing on her. I knew she had been one of Prince's girlfriends, and I thought it best to admire her from a distance. Years later, I found the opportunity to come clean with Jill about my previous enchantment with her. We had a good laugh about it, and we reminisced about that time in our lives. I am sure it was life-changing for her to have been on that remarkable journey with Prince.

The *Purple Rain* album was due to be released on June 25, 1984. Having heard most of the music while on the film set, I had little doubt it would cause quite a stir. Nevertheless, I don't imagine anyone, other than maybe Prince himself, thought the motion picture *Purple Rain* would become the box office hit it was, not to mention one of the greatest rock and roll films of all time. Behind the scenes, however, the process of making the film was not without its unrest. Tensions had been brewing between Prince and Morris for some time. I hung out with Morris quite often during those days, and although he didn't talk to me about it much, I could see he felt mistreated by his childhood friend. Whether it was the maniacal control that Prince exerted over the Time, the miniscule wages he paid them, or kicking them off the concert bill in major cities like New York and Los Angeles, Morris and his bandmates had had enough.

Things really started to crack when Prince fired Terry Lewis and Jimmy Jam from the group for moonlighting as writers/producers for the Atlanta-based SOS Band. Monte Moir quit shortly after that, and the band's lineup for the movie was filled out by bassist Gerry Hubbard, keyboardist Mark Cardenas, and recent high school graduate Paul Peterson, also on keys.

Prince and Morris had only a few scenes together in the movie, but the friction was evident on set. I suppose their differences played well for the purposes of the film, as their onscreen characters were intense adversaries. But toward the end of filming things went so far that they nearly came to blows.

On the final day of shooting at First Avenue, I was sitting at a table with Morris and other people, and Prince walked up to Morris and declared, "You owe me!" I am sure this was Prince's way of letting Morris know that he was the one responsible for getting Morris to this point in his career. Incredulous, Morris responded by shouting, "I owe you? If anybody owes anybody, you owe Pepé!" I couldn't believe what I was hearing. I said to them, "Look, keep me out of this." In no way did I want to come between them, but it appeared that the damage had been done. The two of them stared each other down without saying a word, and then Morris turned and walked out the door. I wouldn't see him again until the next summer when he called me out to Los Angeles before the premiere of the film.

It was really hard for me to see Prince and Morris come to such an impasse. They had been close friends for a long time, and I had watched them grow together over the years. I thought it might do them some good to have an extended break from each other. The problem was, from a business perspective, Prince still controlled Morris and his future.

The night after filming completed in Minneapolis, there was a wrap party at First Avenue for the actors and crew. I don't remember seeing Prince there, but the mood at the party was spirited. It felt as though everyone involved in the film sensed that something special had been accomplished. How it might be received by the rest of the world wasn't foremost on people's minds at that moment. The fact that Prince had the vision, ambition, and determination to make *Purple Rain* was most important.

Toward the end of the evening, Wendy Melvoin, whom I had not met before, came over and introduced herself. She had been an official member of the Revolution for only a few months, but she had been around the band for some time. She said to me, "Pepé, I want to thank you for everything you have done for Prince." She continued by telling me that Prince would often tell the band stories about how I had been there to protect him and helped him sidestep a lot of the land mines that many young artists stumble upon. She nearly brought me to tears. I guess I had come to not expect such sentiments from Prince. At least I didn't think he would share them openly, with me or anyone else. Although it would have been nice to hear it directly from Prince, I was touched. During his career, Prince earned a reputation among many of his associates for being aloof, insensitive, and even downright cruel on occasion. But there was always another side to Prince. I've heard multitudes of stories that substantiate Prince's remarkable capacity for thoughtfulness and expressions of thanks.

Despite our agreement that Prince only had to mention my name when he made it big, I didn't require validation from him or anyone else about the role I played in his career and what would become the Minneapolis Sound. I assumed by this time that he was never going to say my name in public. And that was fine. After that conversation with Wendy, I was thrilled to know that Prince, in his heart of hearts, felt that way about me and all that I did for him.

20

MORRIS

MAKING SURE THAT PRINCE had everything he needed had been a priority for me for many years, but when Morris called me in the summer of 1984, I knew I had to help him even if it meant upsetting Prince. Within the first few days of arriving in Los Angeles, I was able to make sure Morris had a ticket to the world premiere of *Purple Rain*, courtesy of Warner Bros. president Mo Ostin. Regardless of their differences at the time, it would have been rather sad if Prince had prevented Morris from witnessing what was, in essence, Morris's coming-out party.

As Morris, his mother LaVonne, and I walked into the Hollywood night following the star-studded premiere at Mann's Chinese Theatre on July 26, 1984, two things were evident to me. One, Prince would secure his status as a household name as soon as the film was released nationwide the next day. And, two, Morris E. Day was about to become a bona fide star in his own right.

Fortunately, in the days before the premiere, Morris and I were able to put together a team for him. Representing the best of the best in the music industry, this included attorney David Braun; the accounting firm of Gelfand, Rennert & Feldman; Triad Artists, Inc.; and Sandy Gallin as manager.

As the reviews of his performance in *Purple Rain* started coming in, Morris was well positioned to set out on an extensive media tour. Gallin immediately began setting up interviews for Morris with outlets such as *People Magazine*, *Rolling Stone*, *CBS News Nightwatch*, *The Merv Griffin Show*, and *Late Night with David Letterman*. All told, by the end of the summer Gallin scheduled Morris for some eighty interviews with media outlets across the country.

I also secured an interview for Morris on the CBS newsmagazine *Entertainment Tonight* through Dixie Whatley, a friend of mine who was a correspondent on the show. I called Dixie and asked if she wanted to interview Morris Day. She just about flipped out and told me they had been trying to find Morris for a while and didn't know how to get in touch with him. I told her I was in LA with Morris, and we could come by anytime she wanted us.

Morris was also in conversations about recording his first solo album. Even though the Time had disbanded, Morris was still under contract with Warner Bros., and since Morris already had the full support of Mo Ostin and others at the company, it made sense for him to stay with the label. As I understand it, Prince did make an overture to produce the album, but Morris insisted on his independence and that Prince would not be involved in any way. I could sense not only how excited Morris was at the prospect of doing his own thing, but how motivated he was to succeed. He was determined to shine free from the shadow of Prince, and I was committed to help him in every way. That included keeping him mentally and physically fit.

Morris's condo in Santa Monica was less than three blocks from Ocean Avenue and the Pacific Coast Highway. Every morning, Morris and I would walk down to the beach and jog back and forth between Wilshire Boulevard and the Santa Monica Pier. And even though we worked hard during the day, we were not averse to taking in the Hollywood nightlife. We hung out just about every night I was in Los Angeles, which included spending time with Vanity.

She had moved to California from Minneapolis more than a year earlier. It didn't take her long to establish her solo career, signing with Motown in early 1984. Vanity's first solo album, *Wild Animal*, was released that November and included the hit single "Mechanical Emotion," a duet with Morris. Although Vanity missed out on *Purple Rain*, she had spent the spring of 1984 in New York City filming Berry Gordy's *The Last Dragon*. She had appeared in a few low-budget films previously, but this was her first starring role in a major motion picture. *The Last Dragon* received mixed reviews. Personally, I liked it a lot, and as a New Yorker, I enjoyed the way the film featured the cityscapes of Harlem, lower and midtown Manhattan, and Queens. More than anything, I was happy that Vanity was able to venture out and establish a career on her own terms.

Toward the end of August, after Morris had done pretty much all the major media in Los Angeles, Sandy Gallin sent us to New York City, where he had booked Morris on *Late Night with David Letterman* and a few other media appearances. I remember sitting in the greenroom watching Dave interview Morris. The audience seemed to respond well to Morris, and he made them laugh on several occasions. Dave asked Morris about Prince a couple times, and Morris was generally magnanimous about all that had transpired over the last year or so. I am not sure if Dave had heard the rumors about Prince and Morris's falling out, or if he was just asking general questions. Morris noted that he and

Prince were still friends, but added that he didn't see the two of them working together again in the future. All in all, it was a fun night and quite an experience visiting 30 Rockefeller Plaza.

Sandy soon joined us in New York and invited us to a party at Calvin Klein's Manhattan apartment. As Morris and I arrived, we noticed a small number of well-known people, most notably Whoopi Goldberg, who was also a client of Sandy's. We spent most of the night talking to Whoopi and Calvin Klein, both of whom were quite friendly.

About twenty-five years later, my grandnephew Qaasim was on the television program *The View* with his bandmates in support of the Nickelodeon television series *The Naked Brothers Band*. Before Qaasim's segment, his grandmother Tina, my youngest sister, turned to Whoopi and said, "Pepé says hello." Whoopi turned and asked, "Are you talking about Pepé Willie?" When Tina relayed the story to me, I couldn't believe that Whoopi remembered me from a party nearly a quarter century earlier. I was impressed and touched that she even knew who I was.

After we were finished in New York, Morris returned to LA to begin work on his album and I flew back to Minneapolis. I continued working for him, but after a while I sensed that Morris had no intention of compensating me for my consulting services. I spent the better part of that summer with him, and we made an agreement that I would be paid for my services. After all, I needed to make a living as well. I sent him an invoice, which was standard. I was not asking for a lot of money, just what we had agreed upon. Morris didn't respond to the bill and wouldn't take my calls either. I didn't want it to come to this, but after waiting and waiting, I contacted Mark Cristini of Cristini and Hartnett, my attorney at the time. Mark served Morris with a summons, and Morris still didn't pay. Unfortunately, our feud played out in the "Random Notes" section of *Rolling Stone*, where I suggested that Morris had a drug problem. He responded by saying, "Pepé has a brain problem."

Ultimately, I decided it wasn't worth pursuing the matter, and I let it drop. I didn't want to hurt Morris, and I quickly regretted the drug comment. After all, I was still dealing with drug issues of my own. The disagreement pretty much ended our friendship, which had been strong for the better part of a decade. Still, I always hoped the best for him as he charted the course of his solo career.

21

MINNEAPOLIS GENIUS

BY EARLY 1985, Prince was just about the biggest rock star on the planet. The soundtrack to *Purple Rain*, which won multiple Grammy and American Music Awards, stayed number one on the Billboard album chart for nearly half a year before falling to number two in January 1985. The film also hit number one at the box office following its release and garnered Prince an Academy Award for best original score. The *Purple Rain* tour sold out nationwide, including five- to seven-night stands in cities such as Detroit, Chicago, St. Paul, Atlanta, Los Angeles, San Francisco, and New York. The Time, Sheila E., and Vanity all had hit albums, and both Morris Day and Jesse Johnson would soon follow with successful solo debuts of their own. André released his third solo effort, *A.C.*, in 1985, and the album yielded his biggest single, "The Dance Electric." Written by Prince, "The Dance Electric" earned top ten status on the Billboard dance and R&B charts.

A lot of huge records were released around that time, from Madonna to Bruce Springsteen, Duran Duran to U2, Tina Turner to the Jacksons. Still, from mid-1984 through the end of 1985, there was nothing bigger than the Minneapolis Sound. Not only did Prince and his associates dominate the charts, airwaves, and ticket booths, but other acts began to bite Prince's style, both visually and musically.

It was an amazing time in pop culture and music, and I was elated at the success Prince had achieved. Yet, as great as it was to have had some part in that phenomenon, I still yearned to build my own career. At this point, I had spent nearly twenty-five years in the music industry, in one way or another. Music was what I loved and lived for the most. It was in my DNA.

Of course, it wasn't as if I had stopped working—PMI was still operating—but I knew I had to make a move soon. I needed some capital to keep PMI going and began to consider the assets I had available to me. By far, the most valuable thing I owned were the master recordings of what we were calling the Cookhouse Five. These sessions, which included recordings of "If We Don't," "I'll Always Love You," "Games," "Better Than You Think," and "If You See Me," were the first five songs that 94 East recorded with Prince back in December 1975.

I visited a friend named Jeffrey Pink to get his advice about selling the rights to the Cookhouse Five. Jeffrey, who owned Hot Pink Records in Minneapolis, stopped me before I could even finish my sentence. He said, "Pepé, you don't want to do that. I have a better idea." Jeffrey suggested that we release the songs as a 94 East album. I was hesitant at first, but after some coaxing, I agreed. Jeffrey started to raise some money so we could overdub, remaster, and release the songs on the Hot Pink label.

As Jeffrey became more familiar with 94 East's other recordings that featured Prince, he recommended some tweaking to the track list to include only one song from the Cookhouse Five, which was "Games." He asked me to consider using "Lovin' Cup," "Dance to the Music of the World," and "Just Another Sucker" from our Sound 80 sessions. To round out the album, we picked "If You Feel Like Dancing" from the Palace Sound sessions in New York and "One Man Jam," which we had recorded in New York at the Music Farm.

I wanted Tony Silvester to be involved with the project, too, and I gave him a call. I explained what I was doing and that I would like him to coproduce the album with me. Without hesitation, Tony said he was on board and proposed that we begin work at Eddy Grant's Blue Wave Studios in Barbados. Eddy, who got his start in the 1960s in London's interracial rock band the Equals, was a close friend of Tony's. Perhaps the best way to describe Eddy is as a musician's musician, whose lyrics conveyed strong social and political messages. Although he was long respected and admired by critics and peers, it took nearly fifteen years for him to gain mainstream success in America. When Tony and I went to Blue Wave, Eddy was not far removed from three of his biggest solo hits, "I Don't Wanna Dance," "Electric Avenue," and the title track to the 1984 motion picture *Romancing the Stone*. After relocating from the UK to St. Philip, Barbados, a few years earlier, Eddy was generating a lot of interest in his recording studio, which was literally nestled on an island paradise. In addition to Eddy's own work, the likes of Mick Jagger, Sting, and Branford Marsalis were making good use of Blue Wave.

Our plan was to work on two of the album's six songs at Blue Wave, "Games" and "One Man Jam." Cowritten by Tony, Ike Paige, and myself, "One Man Jam" was originally recorded as a twelve-inch single by the Imperials under the title "Fast Freddy the Roller Disco King." Tony and I reconceived the song as an instrumental and added some overdubs. Prince played guitar, synthesizers, keyboards, and clavinet on the original recording, which is how we came up with the title "One Man Jam."

We also retained Prince's original guitar track for the rerecording of "Games," and we brought in some more heavy hitters to contribute their talents, including Mark Sullivan, who added a keyboard part, and Alvin Moody, who played bass, guitar, and keys on the song. Moody was just a youngster at the time but had already worked with Stephanie Mills and would go on to record with a range of notable soul and R&B artists. On drums, we brought in Jerome "Bigfoot" Brailey, a veteran of Parliament and Funkadelic as well as several P-Funk side projects, including his own band Mutiny. And finally, we had renowned producer Ralph Moss, whose credits include Wilbert Harrison, Tommy James, Roberta Flack, Eric Clapton, Lou Reed, Gil Scott-Heron, and Gladys Knight & the Pips. For some reason, only Alvin Moody received credit for his work on the recording, but Mark, Jerome, and Ralph all contributed.

Eddy took great care of us during our ten-day stay in Barbados. He had an efficient staff that met our every need. When we woke up in the morning, breakfast was waiting for us. We would go in the studio and then break for lunch, which would be fully prepared and waiting for us. Then it was back in the studio until we received the same treatment at dinnertime. These weren't run-of-the-mill meals either. It was like living at a first-class resort. I'm not sure if I've ever been as pampered as I was at Blue Wave. For his part, Eddy stayed out of our way and allowed us to work, but from time to time he would check in and make sure we had what we needed. He was a great host and a true gentleman.

Tony and I returned to New York to finish the other four songs for the album. We recruited Alvin to record an additional guitar part for "Just Another Sucker" and kept all of Prince's and André's contributions as they were. I added a few overdubs, mostly synthesizer and percussion parts, and by the late summer of 1985, we were nearing completion of the album.

As Tony and I were wrapping up the editing, I received a call from Jesse Johnson. His first solo effort, *Jesse Johnson's Revue*, had placed high on the Billboard 200 and R&B charts. He was now looking to record his follow-up and wanted to ask me a question. "Pepé," he asked, "can I have permission to use one of your songs on my next record?" "Sure," I replied. "Which one do you want?" Jesse said, "'Do Yourself a Favor.'" I told him it was fine with me, as it didn't appear that Prince was ever going to follow through with using it.

Jesse had a real laid-back, cool persona, but when he was excited about something, you could hear it in his voice. He seemed genuinely pleased that I gave him permission to use the song. I was pretty excited myself, if a little surprised. I wasn't aware that Jesse was even familiar with the song. I never asked, but I am sure Prince shared his recording with him, since Jesse referred to the song as "Do Yourself a Favor" instead of "If You See Me." Either way, it meant a lot to me that Jesse wanted to do the song.

I now realized I had to make a phone call of my own. With the 94 East album basically done, it needed a title, and it didn't require too much thought to come up with one. In deference to Prince's otherworldly talent, even as a teenager, I decided to call it *Minneapolis Genius*.

I didn't have a direct line to Prince anymore, so I called

Bob Cavallo and told him what I was doing. I think Prince was in France working on his next film, *Under the Cherry Moon*, but I was hoping Bob or someone else from Prince's management team could get word to him about *Minneapolis Genius*. I was also hoping to get Prince's blessing on the project.

Bob said he didn't think it was a good time to tell Prince. I asked him why. He didn't elaborate but simply reiterated that it wasn't a good idea. I said okay and let him know I intended to release the album regardless of whether he consulted Prince. He told me he understood, and that was the end of our conversation. I still felt I needed to notify Prince in some fashion, so I reached out to him the only way I knew how at the time, which was through the mail.

PMI was in the process of amending Prince's original contracts from the Cookhouse and Sound 80 sessions from demo contracts to an actual album contract. This required us to pay him union scale wages for his work, and we forwarded that to him along with a letter describing *Minneapolis Genius*. Not long after we sent payment to him, we received the canceled checks, so it seemed he must have known about everything. The fact that I hadn't heard from him left me hopeful that he was all right with what I was doing, which was very important to me.

Despite what some people have suggested, it was never my intention to exploit or misuse my relationship with Prince. Prince was family, and I never took a dime from him. It wasn't even my idea to create this record. I was just trying to sell the rights to my music so that I could keep PMI operational. Aside from "Just Another Sucker," which I cowrote with Prince, these were my songs. I put so much of my life, my joy, and my pain into this music. And, as any songwriter or musician would, I wanted people to hear it. Sure, I realized Prince's contribution is what would initially attract most people, but I believed the songs that composed *Minneapolis Genius* were worthy of attention, and I took the opportunity to release my music to the world.

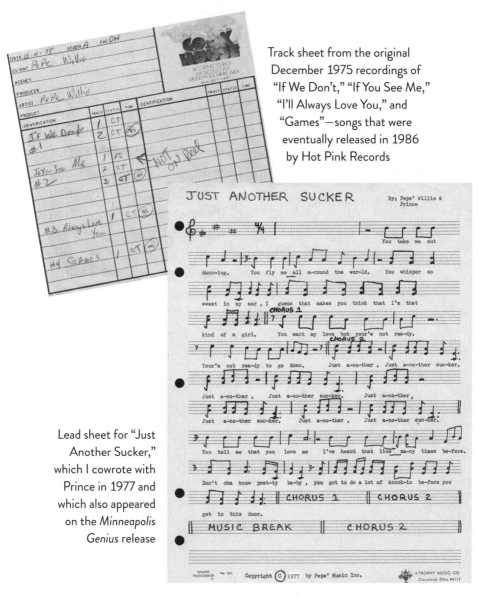

Track sheet from the original December 1975 recordings of "If We Don't," "If You See Me," "I'll Always Love You," and "Games"—songs that were eventually released in 1986 by Hot Pink Records

Lead sheet for "Just Another Sucker," which I cowrote with Prince in 1977 and which also appeared on the *Minneapolis Genius* release

22

DO YOURSELF A FAVOR

FIRST AVENUE was my favorite nightspot in the Twin Cities. I've heard people say that some buildings have a soul, and, having spent time at historic venues like Madison Square Garden, the Brooklyn Fox Theatre, and the Copacabana, I must concur. First Avenue is without question one such building with a soul. Although Prince officially performed there only nine times (plus four impromptu appearances at someone else's gigs), he contributed a lot to First Avenue's soul. The former Greyhound Bus Depot was first established as a club in 1970, when it was known as the Depot, and by the time it became First Avenue in 1981, it was one of the hottest music venues in America. The filming of *Purple Rain* there and the subsequent release of the movie in 1984 helped to elevate First Avenue to another level. I saw every show Prince played there during the 1980s, as well as performances by countless other artists. Even on nights when there was no live music, First Avenue was the place to be. I would run into Jimmy Jam and Terry Lewis quite often, and Prince loved to hang out there too.

One night when I was hanging out at First Avenue in the mid-eighties, I ran into someone I had met in the same spot almost two years before: Wendy Pridgen, a local woman who had been a fellow extra in *Purple Rain*. As we talked, she mentioned that she was hoping to get into a studio to do some recording and asked if I could help. I told her I would be happy to record her anytime, and we arranged a date to start. I sensed that Wendy had talent, but I was floored when I heard her sing. We worked on several songs at PMI. And although my studio had pretty much everything you needed to produce a quality demo, I thought Wendy would benefit from a larger production space. So I took her to New York.

We met up with Tony Silvester at Power Play Studios in Queens and started to rework a few of the songs we had demoed in Minneapolis, along with a couple of new ones. One track that stood out to me was called "Tender Love," which happened to also be the title of a current Force MD's single written and produced by Jam and Lewis. After we cut the basic track for "Tender Love," Tony had Tony Moran and Albert Cabrera mix it. Known collectively as the Latin Rascals, Tony and Albert were fast becoming one of the hottest mixing teams around, and they went on to a prestigious career working with major pop artists and playing a huge role in the freestyle explosion out of New York.

The work they did for Wendy was fabulous. While I tried to temper my hopes, I started to believe that Wendy had the potential to be really big. I know that Tony Silvester and the Latin Rascals agreed. And then, just like that, it was over. We had invested a lot of money in Wendy, and shortly before we began to shop her around to the labels, she called me with startling news. "Pepé," she said, "I truly appreciate everything you've done for me, but I can't do this anymore." My heart dropped as she explained that she had been exploring her faith and was dedicating her life to God.

I don't remember if she became "born again" or joined some sort of cult. I would never interfere with someone's spiritual beliefs, so I respected her wishes. I assured her that there were no hard feelings and let her know that I hoped she found what she was looking for. I thought about Gayle and Dez and the circumstances that caused them to leave Prince's camp, but this was a little different. While Gayle and Dez struggled with Prince's explicit subject matter, they never turned their backs on music, be it secular or religious. Wendy, on the other hand, couldn't reconcile her newfound faith with any aspects of the pop-culture world. Years later I experienced the same with Colonel Abrams, who had recorded brilliant vocals on several PMI tracks, including Hank Cosby's "Fortune Teller." I desperately wanted to put out some of his material, but by then he had become a Jehovah's Witness and didn't want any of the songs released.

Although disappointed that Wendy no longer wanted to pursue a music career, I still had things I was looking forward to. *Minneapolis Genius* would soon be released, as would Jesse's version of "Do Yourself a Favor" on his upcoming *Shockadelica* album. And it would be another encounter at First Avenue, one that in retrospect I regret, where Prince and I discussed these matters in person for the first time.

One cold winter night in early 1986, I was hanging out at First Avenue with a friend. There was no concert that night, just one of the club's popular dance nights. It was early in the evening when I saw Prince and his date walking toward our table. I was excited to talk to him, since it had been a few months since we crossed paths. Everyone in the club shifted their eyes in his direction. Before I could even greet him, Prince snapped, "Pepé, what's up with this album you're doing? Why didn't I hear about it?" I told him I had called Bob to tell him all about it months earlier. "Those are your people," I continued, "and they should have told you then." I added that we also sent him a note, revised his contract, and paid him. The fact that the checks had been cashed led me to assume he was cool with it.

Then he wanted to know about "Do Yourself a Favor." As the tension in our conversation escalated, people formed a circle around us, like schoolkids gathering for a fight. "I heard you're letting Jesse do that song," shouted Prince. "You know that I was going to put it on one of my records." To which I responded, "When? 1999?"

Everyone around us laughed, which didn't thrill Prince, of course. He glared at me, then he turned around and walked away. On the outside I tried to play it off like it was no big deal, but in my heart, I didn't feel good about what had transpired. Prince and I had had a few moments of disagreement in the past, but never like this. I am sure he thought I was trying to embarrass him, and the laughter of those around us didn't help. But I certainly didn't mean to mock him, particularly in front of a bunch of people.

I thought about our exchange for days and debated whether to reach out to him. Maybe I could explain my position better without the distraction of a crowd. Perhaps I could show a little more grace and listen to what he had to say. After sleeping on it for a couple of nights, I decided to let it go. I figured he didn't want to talk about it either.

A few weeks later I was invited to a party at Bobby Z.'s house. I hoped this would be my chance to mend fences with Prince. Not long after I arrived, I spotted him in the corner by himself. As I walked up, Prince made eye contact and smiled, which put me at ease. I said, "Hey, are we cool?" Prince responded, "Yeah, man. We're cool." That made my day, maybe even my year. The last thing I could bear is for Prince to think I didn't have his back.

We spoke for another five or ten minutes. He was very cordial and seemed to be in a good mood. "Kiss," his new single from the *Parade* album, would soon hit number one on just about every US chart and at least in the top five everywhere else. Prince's second major motion picture, *Under the Cherry Moon*, also was nearly released.

As we parted ways at Bobby's party, I told him to keep up the good work and that I was proud of him. He smiled graciously and said, "Thank you, Pepé." I didn't know it at the time, but that would be one of the last times I visited with Prince and connected with him in a meaningful way.

Minneapolis Genius was released in February 1986. I never entertained the idea that it would sell hundreds of thousands of units. That said, the album sold pretty well. I was more concerned with how it would be received critically, and although there weren't a lot of reviews, those that were written were generally favorable. Of *Minneapolis Genius*, Snapper Music later wrote: "Pepé Willie's 94 East will always be remembered as the band that gave the young Prince Rogers Nelson his first studio experience—let's face it, a good enough reason to be remembered. What's often overlooked is the skill and talent of Willie's ensemble and the influence it had on the developing 'Minneapolis Sound'—not to mention the influence it had on the developing Prince." Even at seventeen, Prince was a budding genius and the one who would draw ears to the *Minneapolis Genius* project. Still, it was great to see mention of how talented the rest of the group was.

Jesse Johnson's *Shockadelica* album hit the stores just a few months after *Minneapolis Genius*. It was Jesse's most successful album, achieving platinum status and charting three hit singles. One song featured a duet with Sly Stone. Jesse's band, the Revue, included Sonny Thompson on guitar and keys; William Doughty, of Grand Central fame, on percussion; and Gerry Hubbard, another close friend, on bass. Although not released as a single from *Shockadelica*, "Do Yourself a Favor" was the B side to "Lovestruck," the lead single from Jesse's 1988 album, *Every Shade of Love*. I told Jesse I appreciated that gesture and was eternally grateful that he recorded the song in the first place.

Prince never mentioned the song again to me or, to my knowledge, to Jesse. But in typically cunning Prince fashion, he managed to have the last word. Prince's 1987 single "If I Was Your Girlfriend" featured a blazing, guitar-heavy B side titled "Shockadelica." I imagined this was just a friendly jab at Jesse. Prince did say later that a great album title deserved a song of the same name, which Jesse's album did not have. Prince was always adept at sending messages to let you know that he knew what you were up to at any given time. It was part of his charm, I suppose.

23

HALL OF FAME

IN JULY 1987, just days before my thirty-ninth birthday, my life changed forever when my one and only child, Danielle, was born. For most of my adult life, I never considered having kids; it was just not a focus for me. My life revolved around music. I figured that if children were ever to be a part of my life, they would have to wait.

I met Danielle's mother, Michele Anderson, in early 1986, and we clicked right away. When I found out that she was pregnant, a new sense of purpose washed over me. I was going to be a father, and I knew that nothing I did for the rest of my life could compare. As happy as I was, I also struggled with feelings of anxiety that were deeper than anything I experienced before. I knew Michele would be a terrific mother; I just hoped I could be a good father. I wanted Danielle to have everything. I didn't want her to experience the kind of pain and suffering that I had as a child. There were so many times growing up when I didn't think I'd even make it to my sixteenth birthday. Now, I felt so fortunate to have made it this far while experiencing all that I had. But nothing meant more than being a father.

After Danielle was born and I held her in my arms for the first time, I realized instantly that I needed to make some changes in my life. I had used drugs regularly since I was a teenager, and cocaine remained the one addiction I hadn't overcome. I was almost forty years old and a new father, and I knew I couldn't do it anymore.

So I made a visit to the Veterans Affairs hospital in south Minneapolis. The outpatient treatment was a success, and I never used cocaine again.

Now that I was clean and thinking ahead to what Danielle's future might hold, I spent a lot of time reflecting on my own life, as well as on all that was happening in the music world, especially with the Minneapolis Sound that Prince helped to spawn. Morris had two top ten R&B albums and was appearing on television and film. Vanity's career was also burgeoning in similar ways. Jesse was killing it, preparing to release his third solo record while also producing other acts. Sheila had made a name for herself as a solo artist and as the new drummer in Prince's band. Wendy and Lisa were embarking on a successful music partnership of their own. Prince's Paisley Park label was producing new talent like Mazarati, the Family, Jill Jones, Taja Sevelle, and the jazz collective Madhouse, which included former 94 East drummer Dale Alexander. Then there were Jimmy Jam and Terry Lewis. Getting fired from the Time by Prince may have been the best thing to happen to them. Their Flyte Tyme Productions helped to lift up established and emerging artists alike, made Janet Jackson one of the biggest stars of the decade, and revived the career of New Edition. Today, Jam and Lewis hold the distinction of writing and producing more number-one hits than any duo in popular music history. And of course, there's André. In addition to three solo albums and contributions to motion picture soundtracks, André was producing hits for the likes of Jermaine Stewart, James Ingram, Evelyn "Champagne" King, Pebbles, and the Minneapolis-based trio the Girls. His partnership with former Shalamar singer Jody Watley, whom he later married, garnered her the 1987 Grammy Award for Best New Artist. All told, André would produce four hit albums for Jody.

When I reflected on the collective achievements of all the artists who had worked with Prince or come out of his camp, I found it amazing to think about all they had accomplished. Minneapolis had more than its fair share of talent, to be sure, but a lot of talented people don't make it in this business. I realized how lucky I was to be around this amazing collection of musicians and was honored to have been a part of it. Still, I wondered if anyone else had noticed. I hoped at least Danielle would be proud of me.

In the early 1980s, multimedia entrepreneurs Pete and Kimberly Rhodes established the Minnesota Black Music Association to help showcase the great African American talent coming out of the Twin Cities. They also hosted an annual awards show that recognized artists across musical genres, including rock, gospel, blues, jazz, R&B, classical, and world music. The annual Minnesota Black Music Awards became one of the biggest parties in Minneapolis, and it didn't take long for it to gain national attention. The event seemed to get bigger every year, as it bounced to different Twin Cities venues, such as the Prom Center in St. Paul's Midway neighborhood and the Carlton Celebrity Room in Bloomington. Over the years, notable honorees and performers comprised a "who's who" of local talent: André Cymone, Morris Day, Dez Dickerson, Jesse Johnson, Cynthia Johnson, Rockie Robbins, the Lewis Connection, Sue Ann Carwell, Nettie Sherman, the Steeles, Sounds of

Blackness, Alexander O'Neal, Cherrelle, Morris Wilson, Enterprise, Sonny Thompson, David Eiland, the Girls, Brownmark, Mazarati, the Jets, Mint Condition, and more. Owen Husney also received special recognition for his contributions to the local scene.

Of course, Prince and the Time were frequently honored. During the 1986 ceremony, both the Time and Flyte Tyme Productions were inducted into the Minnesota Black Music Hall of Fame. The next year, the awards show was relocated to Roy Wilkins Auditorium in downtown St. Paul. The move was made in order to accommodate what might have been the second-most memorable Minnesota event of 1987 (that is, after the Minnesota Twins' World Series victory): a reunion performance by the Time.

Sometime the following summer, I received notice of what would be one of the biggest moments of my career. On October 1, 1988, I was to be inducted into the Minnesota Black Music Hall of Fame. At that point it occurred to me that someone had indeed noticed my contributions to the Minneapolis Sound.

That year's event was held at Orchestra Hall in Minneapolis and featured performances by Jesse Johnson and his side project dáKrash, Sue Ann Carwell, Alexander O'Neal, Sounds of Blackness, and Prince's sister Tyka, who had recently released her first solo album. I held out hope that Prince might attend. A few weeks prior to the awards ceremony, he kicked off the North American leg of his *Lovesexy* tour at Met Center. Just a few days before the Minnesota Black Music Awards, I was told he had been hanging out at the Fine Line club downtown during a brief break in the tour schedule. I thought, if he was still in town, maybe he would make his way to the ceremony. Alas, Prince had a sold-out two-night stand coming up at Madison Square Garden and was due back east.

While I was disappointed he wasn't there to see me be honored, it wasn't lost on me that he was back in my old stomping grounds in New York. And as I stood in his hometown about to receive one of the greatest honors in my life, two things occurred to me. The first was that my induction into the Black Music Hall of Fame was confirmation that I had some part in the journey Prince had taken from north Minneapolis to perhaps the most famous stage in the world, Madison Square Garden. And second, that Prince's supernatural talent, vision, and determination are what enabled me to be standing onstage in Orchestra Hall.

For that journey, I could never thank him enough.

EPILOGUE

LOVE AND LOSS

TOWARD THE END OF 1991, I was producing a few tracks for Anthony Gourdine at Metro Studios in Minneapolis's Warehouse District. It had been a crazy last few months to the year. The Minnesota Twins won their second World Series and the entire state was overcome with jubilation. Less than a week later, the Halloween blizzard of 1991 effectively shut down the Twin Cities for days. Fortunately, Anthony arrived after we dug ourselves out of several feet of snow.

During the recording sessions, Anthony and I reminisced about the glory years of Little Anthony and the Imperials. Then, sometime after the New Year, to my considerable excitement, the Imperials were invited to perform at an "oldies" show at Madison Square Garden. The group's lineup would include Anthony, Clarence, Sammy, and Ernest. It didn't take long for everyone to get on board, and Little Anthony and the Imperials were reunited, at least for one night. When they took the stage that winter evening in 1992, the Imperials brought the house down—just like they used to at the Brooklyn Fox or the Copacabana or just about any venue they ever played. It was like old times. The performance was so well received that the group was booked for another concert, the fortieth-anniversary celebration of Dick Clark's *American Bandstand*, which was broadcast on national television. After a short deliberation, the band decided to make the reunion permanent and planned a tour.

I joined them on the tour for as many dates as I could, reprising my role as valet. On more than one occasion, I also provided direction to the lighting technician. I didn't really have much experience in this realm, but Anthony asked me to assist since no one outside of the group knew the songs or changes better than I did. It was rather simple once Anthony told me what he wanted.

During this busy first half of 1992, I also participated in a documentary produced by local filmmaker Bill Pohlad called *Prince: Unauthorized*. The film featured interviews with many of us who were around in the early years, including myself, Morris, Dez, Prince's cousin Chazz, Owen, Chris Moon, Steve Greenberg, local music writer Steve Perry, and the general manager of First Avenue, Steve McClellan. Although a small independent production, *Prince: Unauthorized* was well received and widely distributed on videotape. Pohlad, the son of local businessman and long-time Minnesota Twins owner Carl Pohlad, has since made his name in Hollywood as an A-list producer. Among his production credits are *Brokeback Mountain*, *Into the Wild*, *Chicago 10*, *Food, Inc.*, *The Runaways*, *Love & Mercy*, *Wild*, *The Tree of Life*, and *12 Years a Slave*. The documentary's director, Scott McCullough, has also established himself as an award-winning director, photographer, and editor. In addition to short films and commercials, McCullough has directed RIAA Gold Certified music videos, including some for Prince and other Paisley Park artists.

With PMI, another project I undertook in 1992 was *Common Sense Music*, an industry publication similar to *The Music Outlet* that we published in the early 1980s. When I went on the road with the Imperials, I had to leave behind a lot of the responsibility with PMI for a few months. Fortunately, Kristie and Marcy picked up the slack while still performing their other duties.

The time I spent on the road with the Imperials felt like a rebirth. It helped provide me with a new sense of purpose. I imagine it seemed like that for the guys in the group as well, as there were no plans to call it quits after the tour. Little Anthony and the Imperials were back for the long haul. As they proceeded, a litany of honors came their way, some of which were long overdue. In 1993, Little Anthony and the Imperials received the Rhythm and Blues Foundation Pioneer Award. It was the first time I'd been back to the Palace Theatre in Hollywood since Prince held his after-party there following the *Purple Rain* premiere in 1984. In addition to the Imperials, Wilson Pickett and Martha and the Vandellas were honored and James Brown was there to receive the Ray Charles Lifetime Achievement Award. As the Imperials made their way to the stage to receive their award, Ernest Wright told me to follow them up so that they could hand their awards to me before they addressed the audience. Walking by the first row, I noticed James Brown, and I blurted out, "Hey, James." He shouted back, "What's up, brother?" and motioned for me to sit next to him. He didn't know me, so I wasn't sure why he wanted to talk to me. Even though I could barely understand a word he said, all I could think about was that I was sitting next to James Brown. I looked up and noticed that the members of Boyz II Men were already presenting the Imperials with their awards. I said, "Oh shit, Mr. Brown, I gotta go," and I joined the guys onstage.

That night, I also ran into Shelia E., who was performing with one of the bands. It had been years since I first met her in Minneapolis, but I don't think I had formally introduced myself to her at the time. So I went up to her and said, "Hi, Sheila. I'm Pepé." She responded, "I know who you are." I wasn't sure if she had remembered our first encounter, or if perhaps Prince had mentioned something about me. I suppose it didn't matter. She and I talked for a few minutes. She was very sweet and not nearly as shy as she had been years before.

The Imperials followed this honor with induction into several other halls of fame, including the Vocal Group Hall of Fame, the Long Island Music Hall of Fame, and the Hit Parade Hall of Fame. In addition to a rigorous tour schedule over the next decade and a half, the Imperials made the rounds on television, including on NBC's *The Today Show*, multiple rock and roll specials, and a return to the Ed Sullivan Theater for an appearance on *Late Show with David Letterman*. They even went back to recording and released their first live record, as well as an a cappella album.

Inspired by all that the Imperials were doing, I refocused on my own songwriting and the future of PMI. As I plotted our next move, I received an unexpected phone call. It was from a recording engineer known as Chopper, who worked at the former Cookhouse Studios, now known as Creation Audio. Chopper said, "I found this tape in our archives marked, 'Pepé Willie, DO NOT USE.'" My mind started spinning; I knew what it had to be. He asked, "Do you want it?" I nonchalantly said, "Sure," and then drove the twenty miles from Maple Grove to Nicollet Avenue South like I was trying to qualify for the Indianapolis 500.

I got the tape home and showed it to Kristie and Marcy. Indeed, it was the original two-inch master recording of the Cookhouse Five. A decade earlier, I had been looking to sell the rights to these songs, but when Jeffrey Pink suggested the *Minneapolis Genius* project, I put those thoughts aside. The only song from the Cookhouse Five that made the cut on that album was "Games," which we rerecorded.

The tape had been sitting on a shelf for nineteen years and was not in good shape. Some of the edges had started to shred. The first thing I needed to do was "bake" the tape. I called on Eddie Ciletti, who is a master of recording technology and a pioneer in the process of baking, a procedure designed to temporarily restore the audio quality of a tape so it can be safely transferred to another format. Next, I needed to make a safety copy on two-inch tape. Locally, the most logical place to do that was Paisley Park, so I called and made an appointment. The safety copy of the Cookhouse Five recordings was made in Studio A at Paisley in September 1994. I don't remember who engineered the session, but at the time, Tommy Tucker Sr. was the principal engineer at Paisley Park. Tommy, who passed away in 2012, was a legend in the Twin Cities music scene. In addition to his successful tenure with Prince, he cofounded Metro Studios and Master Mix Studios and established both the IPR College of Creative Arts and the Minneapolis Media Institute. Moreover, he was just a wonderful guy. During the summers, he would take us on his boat on Lake Minnetonka. He was gracious, thoughtful, and generous.

The final step in preserving the Cookhouse Five recording

was to transfer the safety copy to a digital audio format known as ADAT, which was relatively new technology. I called Tommy's son, Tommy Tucker Jr., and scheduled a session at Terrarium Studios on Central Avenue in Minneapolis. Like his father, Tommy had an impressive résumé that included work with Prince, a multitude of Minneapolis artists, and national acts like George Benson, Paul Shaffer, Deon Estus, and Nu Shooz.

Not long after we had restored the original Cookhouse Five recordings, I received a call from Glenn Larusso, whom I knew through Tony Silvester. A longtime producer and manager at Salsoul Records and its subsidiary Double J Records, Glenn said that he heard I was in possession of some lost 94 East tracks that featured Prince. He added, "If you're interested, I can find you a deal to license or sell those tracks."

I wasn't going to sell them, but I told him I would be interested in a licensing agreement. Glenn came back to us with Charly Groove, a label based in the United Kingdom. The label had recently reissued albums by Funkadelic, James Brown, Curtis Mayfield, and Ohio Players, so Charly Groove seemed like a good fit, and we reached an agreement. The result was 94 East featuring Prince: *Symbolic Beginning*. Released in 1995, the two-CD set included the *Minneapolis Genius* album, the original Cookhouse Five sessions, two songs recorded at Prince's home studio on France Avenue South, a rehearsal track, and instrumental versions of "If You See Me," "Games," and "Better Than You Think."

I wanted to talk to Prince about the release and thought I might get the chance to do so that summer. For a few months, Prince had been throwing late-night parties at Paisley Park, known collectively as "Love4OneAnother."

Admission was usually nominal, sometimes even free, and the parties almost always featured a live performance by Prince and the New Power Generation. One night, Prince's cousin Chazz and I decided to go to one of these parties. We weren't there long before Prince's brother Duane, who was working security for Prince at the time, escorted us out of the building. He said plainly, "You guys gotta go. You gotta go." We couldn't figure out why, but Prince must have told him to kick us out. I wasn't sure if maybe he was upset about *Symbolic Beginning* or what, but it didn't make sense to me.

The next day I was still upset, and I called Bobby Z. to tell him what happened. Before I could finish, Bobby said, "Pepé, don't worry about it. It had nothing to do with you." I didn't know exactly what to make of that, but it made me feel a little better. I wondered if something was going on between Prince and Chazz, or perhaps Duane and Chazz. Whatever it may have been, I decided to let it be.

In the years to come, I went back to Paisley Park for a number of shows, one of his Celebration events, even a fundraiser for Minneapolis mayor Sharon Sayles Belton. Although I never talked to Prince, I was always greeted by his staff and treated well.

In 2002, I established a new label under the PMI umbrella called Reo Deo. The label's first release was scheduled to be a new 94 East album composed of ten brand-new songs along with "10:15" and Hank Cosby's "Fortune Teller," featuring Prince on guitar. One day, I answered the phone and heard the low, monotone voice on the other end say, "Hi, Pepé. This is Prince." My first thought was, this has to be a prank, one of my friends messing with me. I replied, "Really. Who is this?" The voice repeated, "This is Prince." I still didn't believe it, so I waited for him to say something else to help me recognize the voice. But there was nothing but silence. Exasperated, I asked one more time, "Come on now. Who am I really talking to?" "Pepé," the voice said, "this is Prince." And I finally recognized that it was indeed Prince. I tried to be cool but I couldn't contain my excitement. "Prince," I said. "How you doin,' man?" In typical fashion, he responded, "Fine." Then I said, "What's up? What's goin' on? Man, I am so happy to hear from you."

I couldn't imagine why he was calling me after so many years. After a few moments of small talk, Prince got to the point. Having fulfilled his publishing deal with Warner Bros. in the spring of 2000, he was now in the process of trademarking "Prince" and was concerned that his name was being used illegally. He told me it had come to his attention that several 94 East records overseas featured his name and likeness.

That was true. For years, in both Europe and Japan, various labels had reissued unauthorized versions of songs that had been recorded for the *Minneapolis Genius* and *Symbolic Beginning* releases. Whenever we found them, we sent cease-and-desist notices and took additional legal action as necessary. I assured him we had nothing to do with any of those records and were attempting to stop them at every turn. Many of the unauthorized releases are still out there today, but it is exceedingly difficult to litigate in other countries.

Nevertheless, Prince wanted to protect his copyright and said, "I don't know, Pepé. That's my name." I retorted that there were illegal releases of my music that used his name and image yet failed to mention my name or 94 East. Then I brought up his version of my song "If You See Me," which has been widely bootlegged as "Do Yourself a Favor" since the mid-1980s. His tone quickly changed. "Pepé," he said, "they stole it right out of my house." I heard the vulnerability in his voice, reminding me of the Prince I always knew. He seemed contrite and genuinely troubled by what had happened with the song, and I sensed that this was his way of apologizing. He said, "Pepé, we played on a lot of songs together, and you have the right to make a living." With this turn of the conversation acknowledging our past, I said, "You know, we should get together and have lunch, shoot some hoops, hang out." I'll never forget his response, which left me dumbstruck. Prince replied, "I don't talk to people." And that quickly, Prince reverted back to the guy I didn't know, the one I'd heard about from others.

I couldn't understand what he was talking about. I thought to myself, *What the fuck does that mean? You don't talk to people? I know that you talk to people!* But at that moment, I didn't have a reply. I was speechless. Not wanting the conversation to end like that, I thought maybe I could reach him by bringing up his family. I started by mentioning his cousin Chazz, who had three young daughters whom Prince had never met. He said, "Who?" I couldn't believe he said that, so I repeated, "Your cousin, Chazz!" All he said was, "Oh." His response bothered me to no end. He quickly changed the subject back to business and let me know that his attorneys would get in touch with me. Not knowing what more to say, I replied, "Oh. Okay." And that was the end of our conversation.

A week or so later, Prince's representatives contacted us. We provided them with information on all the 94 East bootlegs that we were aware of throughout Europe and elsewhere. After examining the PMI website, Prince's attorneys informed us that Prince's name appeared a few times more than mine. They wanted us to adjust this discrepancy and make sure that my name appeared on the site more than his. Kristie and Marcy took care of this right away, along with a handful of other requests. We complied with everything they asked of us. Then, we received another call during which they suggested that the symbol on the cover of 94 East's *Symbolic Beginning* record too closely resembled Prince's "Love Symbol." To my mind, this was a ridiculous assertion. The two symbols looked nothing alike. I said to Kristie and Marcy, "We're done. We are not changing anything more."

That said, I was still hoping to get a dialogue going with Prince and wanted to offer him the rights to the Cookhouse Five. I tried to get in touch with L. Londell McMillan, who at the time was Prince's lead attorney. McMillan, a fellow Bed-Stuy native, has also represented Michael Jackson, Stevie Wonder, and Chaka Khan, among others. At first, we couldn't even get his office to return our calls.

When Kristie finally made contact with an attorney in McMillan's Manhattan office, the person on the other end refused to reveal her name. Dumbfounded, Kristie said, "This is a business call. You are a lawyer. We are discussing a legal matter and you won't even tell me your name?" The woman's response remained, "No." And, with that, we decided to move on. Meanwhile, our legal representatives at Faegre & Benson continued talking to Prince's attorneys to work out a deal that would allow us to use Prince's name. This was particularly important, as we were preparing to release 94 East's latest album featuring "10:15" and "Fortune Teller."

In February 2003, we received a certified letter from Faegre & Benson indicating that we had been granted the right to use Prince's name on our new record and subsequent recordings, as long as his name didn't appear in larger type than 94 East's name. Even though Prince and I had drifted apart and hadn't had much contact in the preceding fifteen years or so, it meant a lot to me that he agreed to this one-of-a-kind deal.

Some sad news came later that year, however, when on October 7, 2003, Bernadette Anderson passed away at the age of seventy-one. André later told a sweet story about how Prince had visited her in the hospital. As difficult as it was for André and his siblings to lose their mother, it must have been very difficult for Prince, too, who had also lost his own parents in the previous two years.

About a month and a half after Bernadette's passing, I received more heartbreaking news. Teddy Randazzo died in his Florida home. He was just sixty-eight years old. Less than two years before, Hank Cosby had died at age seventy-three. Hank and Teddy were posthumously inducted into the Songwriters Hall of Fame in 2006 and 2007, respectively. I wish they could have been there to experience that incredible honor. In November 2006, Tony Silvester passed away at age sixty-five. I was no stranger to losing loved ones, including many well before their time, but this was getting to be too much and difficult to bear. Still, I found solace in remembering all that these people had meant to me and all the other lives they touched. I realized that the best way to honor them was to continue paying forward all the knowledge, kindness, spirit, and love they shared. That helped me to cope, and I carry their memories with me each day.

My spirits would be bolstered by some forthcoming milestones of success and recognition for Prince. In the spring of 2004, he was inducted into the Rock and Roll Hall of Fame in his first year of eligibility—a no-brainer. He followed that with a wildly successful tour in support of his album *Musi-cology*. The year also marked the twentieth anniversary of *Purple Rain*, which garnered a lot of attention. Warner Bros. released a deluxe edition of the film with extras. My phone rang quite a bit that summer with calls from media outlets wanting interviews. It was the same for Owen, Chazz, Chris Moon, members of the Revolution, and so many others who had been a part of Prince's past.

Although 94 East never got the chance to perform pub-licly after our Polydor contract was canceled, I started to get the bug. Since we had recently released a new album, I asked Kristie and Marcy if they would be interested in putting a stage show together. And the three of us, with a little help from Reo Deo recording artist Eric "E-Klass" Waltower, got our first taste of performing together when we appeared in the 2005 independent film *Siren*, with a cast that included Michele Fiore-Kaime, Erin Gray, Gary Gra-ham, and Anthony Gourdine.

Then, just as things were picking up with 94 East and I was feeling good about the future, tragedy struck my family. My sister Carol's son Rashaad, her only child, was murdered in Baltimore. He had just turned twenty-one and had a son of his own. Rashaad was a talented kid and could have done anything or been anything he wanted to be. But as can so often happen, he got in with the wrong crowd. His mom did her best to keep him on the right path, and when Rashaad's son was born, we were hopeful he would refocus his life. One night, however, Rashaad found himself in the wrong place at the wrong time and was shot to death. I immedi-ately flew to Washington, DC, to be with my sister. It was the most miserable flight I'd ever taken. I couldn't believe I was on my way to bury my nephew. I was so heartbroken for Carol. Rashaad's funeral was very hard on my sister, and now, like too many small children, my grandnephew would grow up without his father. Our family was devastated.

I thought back to my days running with the Stonekillers and the Warren Street Gang in Brooklyn. Those were some heady times. You were always aware that you were one wrong move from prison or death. Today, it seems to me, too many young boys in American cities, as soon as they reach adolescence, they start counting the days until their death. They expect it. It wasn't quite like that when I was coming up. How did we get here? I was feeling as depressed and hopeless as I had in a long, long time.

As the years rolled on, I was spending a lot of time in Las Vegas, where my uncle Clarence had been living for a while. It was always great to spend time with him. Not to mention I loved the area's ample golf courses. In 2007, my nephew Keith "Wild Child" Middleton relocated to Las Vegas as well. A star of the award-winning Broadway show *STOMP*, Keith was preparing for its run at the Planet Hollywood Resort and Casino. Around that same time, Keith's oldest son and my grandnephew, eleven-year-old Qaasim, got his start in the business with an appearance in the HBO documentary *The Music in Me*. Shortly thereafter, he was featured on the Nickelodeon show *The Naked Brothers Band* as the group's lead guitarist.

After graduating from the LaGuardia High School of Music & Art and Performing Arts in New York, Qaasim performed on the fourteenth season of *American Idol*, finishing in the final eight. More recently, Qaasim and his younger brother Khalil appeared as two-thirds of "The Notorious Three" in the Netflix series *The Get Down*, which explored the early days of hip-hop music and culture in the late 1970s

South Bronx. I always expected great things from Qaasim and Khalil. After all, their parents Keith and Toni are exceptionally talented. Even as young boys, Qaasim and Khalil seemed poised to take that mantle and run with it.

Someone else important to me was spending a lot of time in Las Vegas back then, in early 2007. Prince was about four months into his six-month residency at the Rio All-Suite Hotel and Casino. Billed as Club 3121, Prince's nightly after-hours gig was about the biggest thing happening on or near the strip at that time. One afternoon, after eating lunch at the Rio, I was walking to my car, and I could hear the muffled sound of music coming from the building. At that time of day, I knew it had to be a sound check, and I figured there was a good chance it was Prince.

As I walked toward the backstage door and the music got louder, I knew it was him. I took out my cell phone and called Chazz, who originally was supposed to have accompanied me on the trip to Vegas but had to cancel due to another commitment. That first call went straight to voicemail. I waited a few minutes and tried again, but still no answer. I decided to leave a message and said, "Hey, Chazz. This is Pepé. I am outside the backstage door at the Rio and I can hear your cousin's sound check." I held the phone up to the door in hopes he could hear at least some of Prince's sound check on his voicemail.

Then, a security guard came running across the parking lot toward me. He started apologizing, stating, "I am so sorry. I was taking care of something across the street. You are probably trying to get in, aren't you?" I smiled, but before I could respond he punched in a code and I followed him through the door. I thanked him and walked toward the music. Before I knew it, I was backstage looking at Prince.

It was magnificent to see him onstage, completely in his element. I wanted him to see me, so I walked around to the front of the stage. As I made eye contact with Prince, I noticed a couple of security guards looking in my direction. I gave Prince a nod and he immediately nodded back. The security guards relaxed, realizing that we knew each other. I walked toward the back of the venue and found a place to sit. I watched as Prince and his band ran through a few songs until the bassist broke a string. At that moment Prince came down from the stage and began walking along the far right wall toward the upper seating area. Still holding his guitar, he made his way to the very top of the venue and turned left. He then walked all the way along the back to the other side. I wondered, *What in the world is he doing?* When he reached the side I was on, Prince headed down the stairs toward me. I started to smile, still wondering what was with the meandering walk around the perimeter of Club Rio. Nevertheless, I was elated that I was about to have my first face-to-face conversation with Prince in several years.

As he got closer I excitedly said, "Prince! How are you?" Prince smiled, said "Hi," and walked right past me on his way back to the stage. Inside, I started to laugh. I thought, *This is some weird, funny shit.* Just then, one of the security guards approached me and said, "Sir, I am going to have to ask you to leave." I said, "Wait a second. We're family." I explained that I had known Prince since he was twelve and I was his first producer. The man said, "Sorry, if he didn't stop to talk to you, you've got to go."

I couldn't believe it, or perhaps I just didn't want to. I tried not to take it personally. Although my last few contacts with Prince weren't exactly like the good old days, we'd known each other for nearly forty years. We had been through so much together. I suppose I would have expected him at least to say more than "Hi" before showing me the door. This wasn't the first time I'd walked in on one of his rehearsals. His previous reaction had been decidedly friendlier than this one. As it turned out, this would be the last time I had any face-to-face contact with Prince.

A couple of months later, in the spring of 2007, I had another opportunity to relive a moment from my past. The Brooklyn Paramount Theatre, which had been converted into a basketball arena for LIU-Brooklyn in the early 1960s, was opening its doors one more time for rock and roll shows. The concerts were hosted by legendary radio personality Bruce Morrow, known as "Cousin Brucie," and featured Little Anthony and the Imperials, the Drifters, the Penguins, and others. Speaking to the *New York Daily News* in advance of the performances, Morrow said: "Most of us who are considered to be rock and roll mavens consider this the birthplace of the rock and roll shows, and the first place where there was an interracial audience. . . . It was a great mixture for all kinds of acts. It was a melting pot. It taught people how to get along."

The days leading up to the Paramount shows were tremendously exciting for me. I spent a lot of time reminiscing about the days of my youth. I thought about all the ways that Brooklyn and the area around Flatbush Avenue had changed over the years. And all the ways it had not.

I was hanging out backstage with the Imperials at rehearsals a day or two before the shows, and I noticed the theater's famous Wurlitzer organ, which had been built specifically for the Brooklyn Paramount when it opened in 1928. I couldn't believe it was still there. It turns out,

LIU-Brooklyn continued to use it at basketball games and other events. The organ, which was known as the Publix 4 model, was the first of only two such organs ever built by Wurlitzer and the only one still in existence. I walked over, sat down, and began to play. I let my mind drift back to the early days of rock and roll and all the amazing artists I'd witnessed during my teens. Then I went back even farther, and thought about the vaudeville days, legendary singers like Bing Crosby and Ethel Merman, and all the jazz icons who played the Brooklyn Paramount, like Duke Ellington, Charlie Parker, Ella Fitzgerald, Dizzy Gillespie, and Miles Davis, to name a few. I marveled at the fact that this organ had been here for all of that.

The concerts were great, and as usual, the Imperials stole the show. LIU-Brooklyn built a new basketball arena, and there is talk that the Brooklyn Paramount will be renovated into a state-of-the-art performance venue. That would be nice. Of course, I don't think any replacement could top the charm and character of the original Brooklyn Paramount or, for that matter, the Brooklyn Fox.

Later that summer, there was great excitement in Minneapolis when Prince announced three concerts to be held on July 7 at three separate venues, all within blocks of one another: an afternoon gig at Macy's department store on Nicollet Avenue, an evening concert at Target Center, and an after-show across the street at First Avenue. It was his first appearance in twenty years at the club he helped to make famous. Downtown Minneapolis was a mob scene that day. Thousands waited outside in the heat for hours to try to get tickets to the First Avenue show.

I was interviewed by Jason DeRusha of the local CBS television affiliate, WCCO. I just wanted to talk about how great

Prince was and how proud I was of him. Prince continued the momentum of that year by launching a twenty-one-night stand at London's O2 arena. As he neared his fiftieth birthday, Prince was on top of the music world once again.

Of all the eventful happenings in 2007, nothing was bigger for me than the birth of my first granddaughter, Jamiah. For most of my twenties and thirties, I never thought about having children. Then, when my daughter Danielle was born, my universe was changed forever. And, when she gave birth to Miah, as we call her, it was as if heaven had completely washed over me for the second time.

Another landmark moment came in early 2009. A little more than fifty years since forming on the streets of Brooklyn, Little Anthony and the Imperials got word that they were to be inducted into the Rock and Roll Hall of Fame. The induction ceremony was normally held at New York's Waldorf Astoria hotel—which is where Prince had been inducted five years earlier—and it would have been cool for the Imperials to be honored in their hometown. But for the first time ever, in 2009 the induction ceremony was held at Cleveland's Public Auditorium—which made sense considering that the hall of fame is based in Cleveland, the city where Alan Freed coined the phrase "rock and roll." It turned out to be a fabulous location. The ceremony on April 4 was also the first time the event was open to the public. In addition to Little Anthony and the Imperials, the others welcomed into the class of 2009 were Bobby Womack, Jeff Beck, Metallica, and Run-D.M.C.

Five members of the Imperials were there to be inducted by Smokey Robinson: Clarence Collins, Anthony Gourdine, Sammy Strain, Ernest Wright, and Nathaniel Rogers. Original member Tracy Lord, who had passed away, was represented by his sons. A lot of people felt the group's inclusion in the hall was long overdue. And Smokey intimated as much during his induction speech when he invited the Imperials to the stage to receive their trophies and take their "well-deserved" place in rock and roll history.

It was a special night all around. As cool as the Imperials were, I know that inside they were overjoyed. They had dedicated nearly their whole lives to this craft. It was clear they were adored by the fans every time they took the stage. But still, to hear your name called as you are inducted into the Rock and Roll Hall of Fame—what a feeling that must be. I was so happy for those guys.

Later that year, Little Anthony and the Imperials were invited back to the Madison Square Garden stage, seventeen years after they had reunited. The occasion was the Rock and Roll Hall of Fame's twenty-fifth anniversary concert, held on October 29, 2009. The Imperials, along with B. B. King, Jerry Lee Lewis, Darlene Love, Buddy Guy, Aretha Franklin, and Smokey Robinson, were there to represent the "old guard" of artists who emerged prior to the 1960s. Among the other performers at this historic two-night event were Stevie Wonder, Crosby, Stills & Nash, Bruce Springsteen, Mick Jagger, Lou Reed, Patti Smith, Simon & Garfunkel, John Fogerty, James Taylor, Ozzy Osbourne, Metallica, and U2.

More accolades would follow for the Imperials, including induction into the *Goldmine* Hall of Fame in 2014 and, four years later, the National Rhythm and Blues Hall of Fame. I don't think there are too many more honors out there for the Imperials to receive. Their impact on music has been deep, as evidenced by the dozens of artists across genres who have covered their material. The influence of the Imperials can be seen in other soul music havens, from Philadelphia to Chicago, Motown to Memphis. And while too many rock and roll heroes died young and tragically, there was Uncle Clarence, fifty-one years in the business and approaching seventy years of age. I was so happy that he was still here. From the moment he first pulled me through the backstage door at the Brooklyn Paramount Theatre, he changed the course of my life forever, and probably saved it too.

I received more great news from the Rock and Roll Hall of Fame in late 2010 when its representatives asked to house the original master recordings of the Cookhouse Five in its library and archives in Cleveland. That was an incredible honor for me and 94 East, to be sure.

Beginning around 2009 was when 94 East started to perform regularly onstage as well. Our first big gig was at the Third Annual Prince Family Reunion Concert, where alumni from the local scene gathered to pay tribute to Prince at the Cabooze, another prominent Minneapolis venue. The concert showcased a host of Minneapolis all-stars representing just about every slice of the Prince catalog: Dez Dickerson, Matt Fink, Bobby Z., Eric Leeds, Michael Bland, Jellybean Johnson, St. Paul Peterson, Susannah Melvoin, Margie Cox, Mike Scott, Stokley Williams, and Prince's sister Tyka, among many others. What made the night particularly special to many fans were the reunions of two of the first acts signed to Paisley Park Records: Mazarati and the Family.

94 East opened the show, backed up by Mint Condition's Homer O'Dell on guitar, Jerry Hubbard on bass, Donnie La Marca on keyboards, and Kirk Johnson on drums. As we took the stage, the emcee announced to the crowd, "Ladies and Gentlemen, the Godfather of the Minneapolis Sound: Pepé Willie and 94 East."

After the performance, I thought about the introduction and said to myself, *Hey, I like that.* But then I wrestled with the description a bit. Although it was great to hear, I hadn't thought about my contributions to the Minneapolis Sound in such a grand fashion—or at least I hadn't since I was younger, as I was reminded by a friend, who pointed out I had made similar boastful comments about myself in a 1986 interview with the *Los Angeles Times.* Whatever the case, I am without question so proud to have been a part of the lives and careers of Prince and so many others. I am awestruck when I reflect on all the talent that came out of this area: André, Morris, Dez, Matt, Bobby, Sue Ann, Mark, Jimmy and Terry, Jellybean, Monte, Michael, Sonny, Ricky and Paul Peterson, and on and on. The list is too long to name everyone. Although I can't take credit for the success of Prince and all these artists, had I not been around in those early days, the path might have looked a little different.

Later in 2009, 94 East performed at the Second Annual Benefit Concert for the Rock and Roll Hall of Fame at the Koka Booth Amphitheatre in Raleigh, North Carolina, in September. We were asked to play this event by Rick French, whom we had met at the Rock and Roll Hall of Fame induction ceremony the previous April. Rick, a trustee of the Rock Hall, was also the chairman and CEO of French | West | Vaughan, a nationally renowned public relations agency. Among 94 East's other performances during this period were benefit, television, and club gigs in Chicago, Cleveland, Orlando, and the Twin Cities. Our band frequently included Matt Fink on keyboards and Marshall Charloff on lead guitar. Marshall would go on to front the popular Prince tribute band the Purple Xperience, which he established with Matt in 2011.

Perhaps the most sentimental concert 94 East played was in August 2011 at the corner of Plymouth and Penn Avenues in north Minneapolis. Earlier that spring a tornado ripped through the neighborhood, killing one, injuring dozens, and destroying or damaging hundreds of homes and businesses. As part of its annual Family Day Celebration, the Minneapolis Urban League put on a special benefit concert called "Arms Around the Northside." Founded in 1926, the Minneapolis Urban League was one of the central gathering places in the neighborhood. André's mother Bernadette Anderson was associated with the organization for years, including as its president. Her daughters Sylvia, who handmade a lot of Prince's earliest outfits, and Linda, an original member of Grand Central, also worked at the Urban League. It made perfect sense that their brother and north side native son André Cymone was tapped to headline the concert. PMI worked with the Urban League to organize and promote the show. I asked an old friend, Marshall Thompson of the Chi-Lites, to perform as well. Marshall had recently recorded the song "Hold on to Your Dreams," which President Barack Obama adopted for his reelection campaign.

Just a few minutes into 94 East's performance at the benefit, the power went out and things were delayed for about a half hour. We were able to continue our set, but we had to cut it short. Then our band—which included Matt Fink on keyboards, Marshall Charloff on guitar, Ace Mack on bass, and Kristie, Marcy, and me on vocals—backed up André's set. André also brought along his protégé, Malo Adams, to play guitar. Malo grew up under the tutelage of both André and Prince and founded the acclaimed Twin Cities–based funk/rock trio known as Tribe of Millions.

I believe this was André's first public performance in

Minneapolis in more than two decades. It took me all the way back to 1975, too, as Prince's cousin Chazz sat in on drums for a few songs. Later in the set, André called up Bobby Z., who did the same. Bobby was performing for the first time since his heart surgery the year before.

Bobby often talks about how fortunate he was to survive. I know it helped that Prince was there to support Bobby and his family throughout the ordeal. Bobby was inspired to help others by partnering with the American Heart Association and establishing the nonprofit organization My Purple Heart. In February 2012, Bobby organized the first of what would be three annual concerts known as the "Benefit to Celebrate Life" at First Avenue. The first concert was historic for bringing the Revolution back together for the first time in more than a quarter of a century. Prince gave his blessing to the reunion, and there was hope that he might show up to play with his former bandmates. About an hour before the show, I noticed Prince's longtime guitar tech, Takumi, milling about near the stage with the famous Hohner telecaster and the iconic white cloud guitar from *Purple Rain*. I thought, *This is going to be amazing.* Alas, Prince didn't appear. I later learned that he arrived at the club but never got out of the car and eventually left.

It was still a great night, as were the next two benefits in 2013 and 2014. The second annual concert heavily featured both André and Dez. I am not sure if being back onstage in his hometown served as the inspiration, but in 2014 André returned strong with *The Stone*, his first album in twenty-nine years. Since then, he has released an EP and another album, *1969*.

It seemed as if things were starting to come full circle and that the Minneapolis Sound was going through a renaissance of sorts. Although Prince had been touring and recording with his new band, 3rdeyegirl, for a few years, there were whispers that he planned to put the Revolution back together. André was back at it, the Family reformed as fDeluxe, and Bobby was reuniting veterans of the local music scene for his benefit concerts. Then, the Numero Group, a Chicago-based archival record label, released the Grammy-nominated *Purple Snow: Forecasting the Minneapolis Sound*. This thirty-three-track compilation featured songs from the 1970s by the likes of André Cymone, the Girls, Flyte Tyme, Sue Ann Carwell, Alexander O'Neal, Mind & Matter, Rockie Robbins, the Lewis Connection, and 94 East, among others. The label also released "If You See Me" as a single and a limited-edition vinyl version of *The Cookhouse Five*.

At Reo Deo, we released several new 94 East singles, including "Dial My Number," which won "Best Pop / Soul Song" at the 2015 Akademia Music Awards in Los Angeles. Reo Deo artists Monaye Love and Micailah Lockhart also took home awards for "Best Pop / Ballad Music Video" and "Best R&B / Ambient Song," respectively. Life was good.

And for me it would only get better. In 2015, my daughter gave birth to her second child, my grandson Cameron. For all the dreams and aspirations I've had throughout my life, I've learned there is nothing more rewarding than being a father or, for that matter, a grandfather—or "GP," as I prefer to be called.

Of course, even as we blissfully welcome little ones into the world, it is always difficult to say goodbye to the ones who leave. Near the end of 2015 and into 2016, two deaths had a profound impact on everyone who had been associated with Prince and the Minneapolis Sound. First was the passing of Kim Upsher, who died in November 2015. Then, in February, we lost Denise Matthews, better known as Vanity. There's no doubt that Prince took both of these losses especially hard.

I often worried about how lonely Prince must have been. At that point, it had been nearly twenty years since he and his wife, Mayté Garcia, lost their son less than a week after he was born and then lost another child to miscarriage the following year. I can't help but wonder how different things would have been if Prince had had a child in his life. He also lost his parents within a few months of each other in 2001–02, and he didn't seem to have much contact with his family at that point. With only a few exceptions, most of us who had been around him in the early days were no longer part of his world. There was a time when we called Prince "the lonely guy." How I wished he didn't have to be. I always looked at that as his choice. He didn't have to be lonely. He had plenty of people who loved him and would do anything for him.

Thursday, April 21, 2016, was a typically chilly and wet spring day in the Twin Cities. I had a doctor's appointment later in the day, but other than that there wasn't much on my schedule. Shortly after ten o'clock in the morning, the phone rang. It was my daughter, Danielle. As soon as I said hello, she asked, "Dad, is Prince dead?" It took me a second to process what she said and then I replied rather confidently, "No, he just has the flu." She went on to tell me that a friend of hers who worked at Paisley Park told her that Prince had died, and it would be on the news shortly. I thought, *No way. That can't be.*

Kristie, who overheard the conversation from the other room, shouted, "It's gotta be a hoax!" I got off the phone with Danielle and turned on the television. The local CBS affiliate WCCO was reporting that a body was found at Paisley Park, but there was no word on who it was. TMZ was already reporting that it was Prince, but the local and national network news had not confirmed. Kristie continued to say, "It's a hoax. It's a hoax."

Then the phone rang again. This time it was Owen Husney calling from Los Angeles. Before I could utter a word, he said, "Did you hear?" I thought, *Oh, no.* At that moment I knew Prince was gone. My mind, body, and spirit went completely numb. It was a feeling unlike anything I'd experienced in my entire life. I just could not believe it was true.

Shortly after I hung up with Owen, confirmation came from the television screen: Prince had passed away at the age of fifty-seven. The phone started to ring off the hook with family, friends, and associates calling to commiserate. The whole thing was surreal.

It was difficult to pull myself away from the television, yet I also couldn't bear to watch. The only thing that gave me any solace that day was the love, respect, and admiration being directed toward Minneapolis from all corners of the globe. It was amazing. The monuments of the world were awash in purple lights.

Prince dominated the twenty-four-hour news cycle that weekend. It was an affirmation not only of his talent but of the joy, emotion, and inspiration he elicited in so many. As devastated as I was, that gave me something to hold on to. That and all the memories I shared with him over the years. It is a pretty remarkable thing to witness a teenager with a singular purpose chart a course to conquer the music world and succeed.

The phone continued to ring for days with calls from

people who asked me to talk about Prince. Calls came in from *Rolling Stone, Billboard,* CNN, the BBC, ITV in London, local media outlets, and others. I tried to compose myself the best I could, but talking about this brother brought me to tears every time.

About a week after Prince's death I was driving on Interstate 494 when I noticed an electronic billboard with a photo of Prince and the caption, "Prince: 1958–2016." I let out a visceral scream at the top of my lungs, "Priiiiiiince!" The tears started to flow so much I could barely see. I pulled onto the shoulder to compose myself.

Things like that still happen to me, usually out of the blue, sometimes in the middle of the night. I still cannot accept that he is gone. I think about all he meant to me and, for that matter, to the world. The adulation from the music community was endless and universal. I hope he knew how much he was loved not only by his fans but by so many of his fellow musicians as well. A quote from Bono of U2 stands out to me. He posted on Twitter the lyrics to Prince's 1987 song "The Cross" and wrote: "I never met Mozart. I never met Duke Ellington or Charlie Parker. I never met Elvis. But I met Prince." What praise.

The world will never forget Prince Rogers Nelson. I will always love and remember Prince as my family and as my friend. His music will live forever.

AFTERWORD

KRISTIE LAZENBERRY
AND MARCY INGVOLDSTAD

FREQUENTLY CALLED "the girls" and also affectionately referred to as the "Wilson sisters" (a name Pepé came up with because he thought it "sounded soulful"), we are Marcy Ingvoldstad and Kristie Lazenberry—the other two-thirds of 94 East. You know the saying "behind every great man is a great woman"? Well, behind Pepé Willie, there are two great women—us.

We are forever linked as best friends, songwriters, and vocalists—Kristie on the high notes and Marcy on the low ones. We've been friends since college, and our friendship and music partnership seemed like destiny. We spent many a night in college harmonizing and dancing along with the latest R&B songs as if we were our own group. We called ourselves "Salt & Pepper" (nearly two decades before hip-hop royalty Salt-N-Pepa arrived on the scene). Little did we know that we were on our way to fulfilling an improbable dream.

Pepé met us not long after he moved to Minnesota in the mid-1970s. Once he discovered that we could sing, he knew he had the background singers he was looking for to create his band. This is where the strength of our friendship really came in, strength we needed, as Pepé was not always the easiest person to work with. He demanded the best of us in everything, including something we had never done before—studio recording. Sometimes we would come up short of expectations, and we'd get frustrated and occasionally be reduced to tears.

The three of us officially became bandmates when 94 East formed in 1975. The following March, we established Pepé Music Inc. (PMI) and became full-time business partners and shareholders. We believed in this man, his music, his vision, and his music business knowledge. Pepé's generosity and the faith he demonstrated in our abilities has meant the world to us. Since the Minnesota chapter of Pepé's story began, the two of us have been present, either out front as part of 94 East or behind the scenes tending to the business side of things. We have witnessed, participated in, or learned firsthand about everything that transpired in the creation of the Minneapolis Sound. To have been right there to see Prince progress from a teenager just starting out to an international icon on top of the music world was among the most magnificent experiences of our lives.

Even if our roles are not always acknowledged by those who rode Prince's career and the development of the Minneapolis Sound, we are here to bear witness. It has been an extraordinary journey, one that has enabled us to write music and record music, perform onstage, work with legendary artists and producers, and learn the ins and outs of a crazy, demanding, and exhilarating business. We would not trade any of it for the world.

With that in mind, we would like to share some of our own personal reflections.

——————————— MARCY INGVOLDSTAD ———————————

In the basement at 3809 Upton Avenue South, Kristie, Pepé, and I often jammed with Prince before the rest of the band arrived for rehearsals, and sometimes after they left. It would be Kristie on her mother's xylophone, me on keyboards, Pepé on rhythm guitar, and, of course, Prince on lead guitar. During these jam sessions, we would look to one another for cues and affirmations. Although Pepé and Prince were world-class musicians in our eyes, they treated Kristie and me as equals and alleviated any anxiety or fear we may have felt. It was such a pleasure to play with those guys.

One day, Pepé and Prince presented Kristie and me with a song they wrote, "Just Another Sucker," with the intention of having us sing lead. We were like, *What? Really?* We rehearsed the song over and over again. To be honest, I was somewhat taken aback by the lyrics, which I thought were mean-spirited, and it made me uncomfortable. So I had to turn it around in my mind; make it fun, flirty, and innocent. That was the only way I could sing it.

The best part was when Kristie and I split off into our harmonies, I would notice Pepé and Prince looking at each other, smiling and nodding as though we had nailed it. That acknowledgment had such an impact on Kristie and me. It gave us confidence that we could not only do the song, but also make it in the world of music.

Another great memory is rehearsing "Dance to the Music of the World" the day before we were going to Sound 80 to record the song, along with "Lovin' Cup" and "Just Another Sucker." As usual, it was Prince on lead guitar, Pepé on rhythm guitar, and Kristie and me supporting Prince on background vocals. Prince—the consummate jokester—started to ad-lib some funny lines and crack a joke or two. He was so funny, and he left us in stitches. As the band leader, Pepé was continually trying to rein the three of us in. Whenever we started goofing off, Pepé would tighten the screws. He was a taskmaster, and although he allowed us to have some fun, Pepé always got us to focus on the job at hand. And, the next day, our studio session went off without a hitch.

KRISTIE LAZENBERRY

Among my most vivid memories from those early days is accompanying Pepé up to Morris Day's attic, where Grand Central rehearsed. As I was relatively new to the world of music, it was fascinating to watch Pepé work with Prince and the rest of the band, which at that time included André, Morris, Linda Anderson, and William Doughty. I remember all the afros, big and round. They were all so young, so talented, and so naïve. They weren't yet aware of how this all was supposed to work. They didn't know what they didn't know. The five of them would joke around like the kids they were.

The attic had a huge chalkboard, just like the ones our teachers used back in the day, and Pepé would write on it to illustrate the basic construction of a commercial song. They listened intently, like good students in class, absorbing everything Pepé was teaching them. How amazing it would be to be able to go back in time, knowing what I know now, and watch them through those eyes.

A few years later, after Prince signed with Warner Bros. and the band used our south Minneapolis home for their rehearsal space, Pepé, Marcy, and I were in the basement jamming on a rare off day for the band. Prince stopped by as we were playing "Just Another Sucker," a song Prince and Pepé had recently written. Pepé and Marcy were on guitar, and I switched between keyboards and my mother's old xylophone from when she played in bands in the fifties. At that particular moment I was playing the keyboard line that Prince had written. I had picked out the chords after listening to a demo of the song.

Prince heard what I was playing and walked over to investigate further. After a few moments he asked, "How do you know that?" I told him, "From listening to the track." He shot me this look that let me know he was impressed I could do that by ear. I never thought it was that big of a deal, but when I saw his reaction, I thought, *Wow, I actually impressed Prince.* Nearly forty years later, it means so much more to me now than it did then.

As much as Marcy and I admired Prince for his abilities, we adored Pepé. Not just for his musical vision and his ability to get more out of you than you thought possible, but for his bigger-than-life personality and his charm. One of the things I love about Pepé is his uncanny ability to talk his way through almost any door. In April 2009, Little Anthony and the Imperials were being inducted into the Rock and Roll Hall of Fame. Pepé and I traveled to Cleveland for the ceremony, which was one of the most exciting times in my life, as I am sure it was for Pepé. We had a wonderful time visiting the hall of fame museum and just hanging out in the hotel with the likes of Smokey Robinson and others. Pepé's uncle Clarence was able to secure limited-access passes for us to attend some other festivities as well.

To me, those credentials were fabulous, but it was unusual for Pepé, who almost always got an "all-access" pass when working with his uncle's group. Now, I have seen Pepé successfully make his way into many rooms, even when he wasn't on the guest list, but this time I was freaking out. After all, this was the Rock and Roll Hall of Fame.

We were walking toward a room in one of the event venues, and I sheepishly said, "Pepé, what are you doing? We don't have access to go in there." But he kept walking while I hung back a bit. Before I knew it, we were both through the door and in another part of the venue. Then it happened again at the next door. I was like, *Pepé, what in the world are you saying to these people? How are you getting us in?* But, like I said, he could talk his way into any room. He's just got it like that.

——————— MARCY INGVOLDSTAD ———————

I have always been a writer of words, someone who fills spiral notebooks with lamentations, dreams, and observations reflecting my profound love of life and all living things. I also often tooled around on the piano composing little pieces for my own pleasure, sometimes sharing them with friends.

In my deep reverence and love for God, I have always sensed a spiritual calling to continually create prose, music, and art. There go I, but for the grace of God. That motivation always provided me with substance, but it was through my collaboration with Pepé that I found form and function. And as a result, my greatest pleasure is in the writing of songs.

I don't believe I could have ever achieved this artistic expression without Pepé's mentorship. His own songwriting was, and is, an inspiration to me. He always took me to task, both demanding and expecting the best I had to give. My ability to craft songs only got better and better.

Pepé would say, "Only write hits! There are no album fillers." He'd say things like, "Write what you know," and "You have to believe what you're singing." I could go on and on about everything he has shared with me over these past four decades.

Mere words are insufficient to express my thanks for Pepé's inspiration, hard work, perseverance, and honesty. The presence of God, the unconditional love of my parents, the devotion and eternal sisterhood of Kristie, and the enduring influence and friendship of Pepé are the constants in my life. And for this I am forever grateful.

—————— KRISTIE LAZENBERRY ——————

I like to believe it was fate that I met Pepé Willie and started on a journey that ultimately made me a part of the Minneapolis Sound, one of the most significant chapters of music history. I learned so much from Pepé—far more than music alone. Yes, I learned to write, record, copyright, and license music, all critical facets of the industry. But more importantly, I learned to be confident, speak my own truth, and see myself as talented. These skills have been important to me and served me well in all areas of my life. So many of the things I have seen, the people I have met—including Bootsy Collins, David Letterman, and Paul Shaffer, among countless others—and the emotions I have felt, I owe to Pepé. He is insightful, honest, thoughtful, loving, passionate, and eternally devoted to his friends and his family.

Whether hanging onto his coattails as we made our way into places I never imagined I would be or watching him in the studio bring out the true potential in an artist time after time, Pepé Willie continues to amaze me.

We are both eternally grateful for the opportunities and experiences that Pepé opened up to us. Pepé is a remarkable human being, and his story is an inspiration to many. Overcoming a difficult childhood and turbulent teenage years on the streets of 1960s Brooklyn, he somehow came out on the other side even stronger, scarred but intact.

From Pepé's tutelage under his uncle Clarence and the rest of the Imperials, as well as the great Teddy Randazzo and so many other central figures in the history of rock and roll, he learned the importance of sharing the knowledge with the right people. Pepé put this wisdom into practice through the time, effort, determination, and dedication he gave to several young, talented musicians from Minneapolis, including perhaps the greatest of all time: Prince Rogers Nelson.

Pepé sought no reward other than the satisfaction of helping those he loved and cared for. We are here to bear witness to all of this. We were there.

Marcy, me, and Kristie, 1981

ACKNOWLEDGMENTS

———————————— PEPÉ WILLIE ————————————

I want to offer thanks and appreciation for the following people.

To my mother, Agnes Collins Leake: How I loved to hear you sing when I was growing up. I remember it like it was yesterday. I can't believe you are gone. I love you, Mom.

To my father, Linster Herbert Willie Sr.: Perhaps if you have lived, we would have developed the relationship I always wanted. And maybe I would have gotten that hug.

To my sisters Pearl, Dodie, Carol, and Lydia: I learned so much from you. You toughened me up, but also helped to make me sensitive. I love and admire all of you.

My love to the Collins family: Grandpa George Collins Sr. and Grandma Mary Jones Collins; my aunts Muriel, Dottie, Annette, Gussie, and Lorraine; uncles Charlie, Clinton, Curtis, Clarence, and George Jr.; and my cousins, nieces, nephews, great-nieces and -nephews.

My love to the Willie family: Grandpa Guy and Grandma Anna; Aunt Sarah and Uncle Edmund; Rosanna, Lamont, Frankie, and Uncle Jimmie; and my cousins, nieces, nephews, great-nieces, and great-nephews on the Willie side.

To Mattie: You were like a mother to me. I could never thank you enough for all the history, culture, and art you exposed me to. It made such a difference in my life. My love to you and my sister Gloria.

To Carol, Renee, Matthew, and Leroy Anderson; Rodney, Little Tina, Carl Sr., and Carl Jr. Albright; Junior and Paul Brown; and the Fares family, the Middleton family, the McMaster family, and the Bunch family: Thank you for your love and support. It means the world to me.

To Bubba, Angel, Russell, and Ike, my best friends from Brooklyn: You all had such an impact on my life. I'm so lucky to have found you guys. Angel, how I wish you were still here.

A special thanks to my nephew Keith "Wild Child" Middleton. I am proud of all you have accomplished in this business. You are a true artist, as are my great-nephews Qassim, Khalil, and Makai. My love to Toni Seawright. Thanks to your father, Kenny Middleton. And, of course, to your partners in the group Hydra; your brother Rodney and Graeme Sibirsky. My love to you all.

To my nephew Rashaad, who had so much to give yet whose life was so senselessly cut short: You were your mother Carol's pride and joy. You are missed.

To all the wonderful musicians, songwriters, and producers I have had the great fortune to work with in my lifetime: There are far too many to mention, but I must acknowledge Tony Silvester, Hank Cosby, Colonel Abrams, Ben Obi, and Jerome "Bigfoot" Brailey.

To the legendary musicians, singers, industry professionals, and other wonderful people who were front and center in the early days of the Minneapolis Sound: You all made my decision to stay in Minneapolis quite simple. Friends like André Cymone, Morris Day, Dez Dickerson, Sue Ann Carwell, Wendell Thomas, Pierre Lewis, Andre Lewis, Dale Alexander, Bobby Z. and Vicki Rivkin, LaVonne Daughtery, William "Hollywood" Doughty, Owen Husney, Cliff Segal, Lauren Segal, David Z., Matt and Andra Fink, Charles and Victoria Smith, Mark Brown, Jill Jones, Lisa Coleman, Wendy Melvoin, Sheila E., Cynthia Johnson, Jesse Johnson, Jimmy Jam, Terry Lewis, Denise Matthews, Terry Jackson, Kim Upsher, Wendy Pridgen, Mark Sullivan, Sammy Sylvester, Jerry Hubbard Jr., Jacqui Thompson, Rockie Robbins, Paul Peterson, Ricky Peterson, Jason DeLaire, Roger Dodger, Tommy Tucker Sr., Tommy Tucker Jr., Al Beaulieu, and Jon Bream. And of course, Cookhouse Studios, Sound 80, Terrarium, and Creation Studios. Dik Hedlund, Chopper, Minnesota Black Music Awards, Kim and Pete Rhodes, Shampayne, and Grand Central.

To the Manderville family, including Shauntel, Frank Collier, Edna Mae, and my golf buddy, Eddie: What a journey it has been. Your love and support mean the world to me. You will always be my family.

To DeRonda "Kalua" Corbin: Thanks for your friendship and making all this a reality.

To Sylvia, Linda, Fred Jr., Edward, Patricia, and, of course, Bernadette Anderson: Your love and support for your own children, Prince, and so many other young people were vital in the making of the Minneapolis Sound. You are indeed the Queen of the North Side.

Our friends from Brooklyn to Minneapolis who have supported us over the years: Ronald Grant, Barbara Taylor, Mark Cristini, Alex Hartnett, Ann Dunn Wessberg, Sandy Jackson, and Parell Caplan.

To my close friends and collaborators Jeffrey Pink and

James Heuer of Hot Pink Records and Eric Paulson of the Navarre Corporation: I appreciate all you've done for me.

To Mike and Mark McDermott: For your friendship and introducing me to my second favorite pastime, golf.

To my other golf buddies and my friends at Tobacco Grove in Maple Grove, Minnesota: You make every day a good day.

To the artists on the Reo Deo label, Eric "E-Klass" Waltower, Monaye Love, Micailah Lockhart, and F.A.I.T.H.: You are all so talented and a pleasure to work with. Thanks to you and your families for their love and support.

To historian and archaeologist Kristen Zschomler: Your dedication to the Minnesota Landmark project and the preservation of historic sites related to Prince and the Minneapolis Sound has been something to behold. Thank you so much.

To Arlene Burke Gant and Dakota Gant of the Upbeat Dancer: You are making a difference in kids' lives.

To Stephen Easley of AllMojo Management and SXSW: Your introduction to this business was similar in many ways to my own. So happy that you're in my corner now.

To Rick French of French | West | Vaughan and the Rock and Roll Hall of Fame: I don't know what else to say; you are the man.

To everyone at Minnesota Historical Society Press, especially director Josh Leventhal, managing editor Shannon Pennefeather, design and production manager Dan Leary; publicity and promotions manager Alison Aten, and freelance copyeditor Adam Wahlberg: I am eternally grateful for your collective faith, hard work, remarkable talent, and enduring dedication to this project.

To Michele Anderson: You are a wonderful mother and

grandmother. My love to you and your family. We miss you.

To Chris Jenkins and Eric Jackson: Thank you as well.

To Marshall "Barely White" Charloff: You are too funky. It is a privilege to continue working with you all these years. Always appreciated your respect.—"Barely Gordy"

To Tony Kiene: I am still waiting to see you on the court. You can't stop the hook. And, by the way, thank you. Our collaboration continues. We got more books to write!

To LeRoy Francis Lazenberry and "Momma" Marcella Ingvoldstad: You believed in 94 East from the start. Your love, inspiration, and unwavering support have carried us for more than forty years. You are loved and missed.

To Little Anthony and the Imperials: Anthony Gourdine, Ernest Wright, Nathaniel Rogers, Sammy Strain, Harold Jenkins, George Kerr, Bobby Wade, and the late Tracy Lord.

To my uncle, mentor, and founder of the Imperials, the one and only Clarence Collins: I can never repay you for all you have done for me. Just know I am forever grateful and you have my respect, admiration, and love for all time.

To my other musical mentor, the renowned songwriter and my dear friend Teddy Randazzo: Your patience, wisdom, faith, and love made a lasting impact on my life. You are loved and dearly missed. I will never forget you and all that you did for me.

To Prince Rogers Nelson: What could I possibly say to adequately describe the imprint you made on my life and, for that matter, on the entire world? Your passing tore a gaping hole in the universe. But the otherworldly talent, music, and love you left behind has put it back together again. There will never be another like you. I love you.

To Kristie Lazenberry and Marcy Ingvoldstad: My musical collaborators, my pillars of support, and my best friends.

Words are insufficient to say just how much you mean to me. My undying love to you and your families.

And finally, to my daughter, Danielle: I never knew how much love I had to give until you came into this world. You are my pride and joy and nothing I ever do in this life will compare to being your father and the grandfather to Jamiah and Cameron. I love you so much.

TONY KIENE

Eternal thanks to my late father, Francis Anthony Kiene Jr., and my mother, Karen Ann Kiene: You gave me the freedom to chart my own course in life. Although I may have taken detours you didn't understand, you remained with me every step of the way. Your unconditional love, trust, and encouragement mean the world to me. I love you more than words could ever say.

To my sister, Bronwyn Ann: Perhaps the most accurate appraisal of a parent is measured by the grace, kindness, and integrity exhibited by their adult children. You are the living embodiment of this sentiment (much more so than I), as is Katie, whom I'm proud to call both my niece and my goddaughter. Love you both (Adam and Jake too). And love to all members of the Kiene, Hughes, Downard, Booth, White, Wagner, McDonald, and McKnight families.

To my wife's family, Bobby and Darlene Macon: I'm so proud that you call me your son. My love to Kelli, Ron, Azianara, ZiZi, Tré, and Little Bobby. To Aunt Jean: You helped guide me through one of the most difficult stretches of my life, which means the world to me. And my love to everyone in the Macon, Moss, Meeks, Birdo, Fox, Cobb, Bradley, and Anderson families.

To my mentors: the late Antonio Zamora, pioneer, jazzman, and a second father. You will be dearly missed by so many who call the BCC home. My love to Betty; the late Anthony J. Lemelle Jr., for your spirit, genius, and generosity; the late Frederick "Dennis" Greene, for your artistry, insight, and inspiration; and last but not least, Floyd W. Hayes III, for your patience, intellect, partnership, and helping me to meet your expectations while exceeding my own. None of this would have been possible without you. My love to Charlene, Kia, and MyTy.

To Jeff Anderson: Where would I be without your friendship? It means so much to me. A very special thank-you to the Coco Boys, John Carlson and John Rafalski: So much knowledge, so much to share, such great friends. You two are the best.

To Eric Phillips: Your loyalty, generosity, and dependability are unmatched. I'm indebted to you for life, a debt that extends to your family as well. My love to you all.

My deepest gratitude to some of the biggest Prince fans I know, and more importantly, three of the best friends ever: Mark Raines: No one has ever made me laugh harder than you. My love to you, Lisa, Brooklyn, and Briana; Antonio Garfias: Our paisley journeys together are some of my best memories ever. Love to you, Stephanie, Simon, and Milo; and to my "brother from another mother," Peter Okeafor: Our love of Prince made us friends. Your wisdom, honesty, and loyalty made me a better person. Love you, man.

To Paige Elliott, Jerry Freeman, and Tracey Williams-Dillard of the *Minnesota Spokesman-Recorder*: Thank you for believing in me. To Neil Cossar, Alison Howells DiMascio, and Sue Houghton: Thanks for including me. And many thanks to the Rev. Dr. Clarence Hightower for your loyalty and trust.

To the extraordinary Jacqui Thompson: Thank you for your vision, leadership, and the opportunity of a lifetime. And to Robin Stevens, incomparable project manager and copy editor extraordinaire: I could have never imagined a better teammate than you.

A heartfelt thanks to all my other friends from the PRN Alumni Foundation: St. Paul Peterson, Kimberly Arland, Jerry Hubbard Jr., Jeff Munson, Karen Lee, Sam Jennings, Lisa Chamblee, Shane T. Keller, Scott McCullough, Kat Dyson, Cassandra O'Neal, Stacia Lang, Craig Rice, Hans-Martin Buff, Peggy McCreary, and Susan Rogers.

A special acknowledgment to Judson L. Jeffries and Shannon M. Cochran, for helping to pioneer the comprehensive study of Prince and the Minneapolis Sound in the academy. And to Dr. Jeffries, thank you so much for your advice, acceptance, time, and tutelage.

To Josh Leventhal, Shannon Pennefeather, Dan Leary, Alison Aten, Adam Wahlberg, and the entire staff of MNHS Press: Thank you so much for making all of this happen. It means more than you could ever know.

Thanks to the many others who have supported and inspired me along this journey: Sylvia Amos, Linda Anderson, Va-Lesha Davis, Kathy Gagnon, Laurie Carlos, Lou Bellamy, T. Mychael Rambo, Austene Van, Malo Adams, Miquel Purvis, Robyne Robinson, Jon Bream, Walter Banks, Pete Rhodes, Dwight Hobbes, Anjanette DeCoudreaux, Marlene Cooper, Angela LeBlanc-Ernest, Patricia Weaver, Pamela Ayo Yetunde, John Lee, Duane Tudahl, Kristen Zschomler, Emma Balázs, Arun Saldanha, Bryan Schmidt, Sandie Albarella, Theresa Lumpkins, Mozell Jefferson, Valley

Hintzen, Tasha Byers, Erin Koegel, Maiya Yang, Cassidy Titcomb, Madeline Ramirez, Marvin Gonzalez, Barry Reimnitz, Damon Drake, C. Leigh McInnis, Wallace McLaughlin, Charles Pace, Vernon Williams, Lewis Gordon, Leonard Harris, Carl Briscoe, Winston Napier, Harry Targ, Renee Thomas, Leonard Neufeldt, Nancy Gabin, Robert Lamb, Nathan Rosseau, Chuck Hunt, Vikas Gumbhir, Lee Jones, Jenny Case, Sam Stahlman, Lorraine Lassig, Kathy Traylor-Holzer, Deb Harvey, Molly Reinhoudt, Ingrid St. John, Lia McWhorter, Yasmeen Peer, Andre Hollingsworth, Rich Benson, the crazy amazing Laura Tiebert, and my purple pen-pal from the Pacific Northwest, Carolyn Sayre.

To Michelle Louise Streitz: I'm grateful for our cosmic purple connection. You've done St. Cloud proud. Love God, Love Life, Lovesexy! And to the one and only Neal Karlen: I'm so fortunate to know you. A sheynem dank!

To the original funkmaster himself, Father Fred Shaheen: I never ceased to be amazed by you. So happy that our paths crossed. Thanks for your time, your words, and your faith.

To Chazz: What can I say? You are the man. But you might want to add some more range to that jump shot (35 feet?). My best to the family.

To the one and only Clarence "Wahoo" Collins: There is no question as to where your nephew got his "cool" from. Thanks for teaching him so much about the business.

To Marcy and Kristie: I could never repay your kindness, faith, and love. You are more than just friends; you are my big sisters, and I love you so much.

To Pepé: I still can't believe that, in an out-of-character moment, I blurted out your name and subsequently found one of my best and most loyal friends in the world. Next to Prince, you are the coolest man I've ever met. Thanks a million. All my love to you and your family.

To Prince: Words could never measure the influence you have had on my mind, my heart, and my soul. To me, you were, and always will be, the best ever.

To Bobbie Jo: My wife, my best friend, the love of my life, and my soulmate. I treasure every moment of our lives together, and I know I am nothing without you. You make everything in my life right. You are my rock; you are my dream. I truly adore and love you, always and forever.

Finally, to my daughter, Kiara Darlene: My princess, my pride and joy, my angel, and my heart. I'm awestruck by your intelligence, strength, talent, and perseverance. You are so beautiful and, without question, the best thing that ever happened to your mother and me. Remember what Mom always says: "You do you!" Rock out, Kiko. I love you more than you'll ever know. And Machiko loves you too.

All thanks and praise to God.

INDEX

 IF YOU SEE ME

was designed and set in type by Judy Gilats
in St. Paul, Minnesota. The text face is Garvis Pro
and the display face is Brandon Grotesque.